JERUSALEM
RISING

JERUSALEM RISING

Countdown to Armageddon

DAVID HEAD

VINEDRESSER

Published by Vinedresser Publishing

JERUSALEM RISING: Countdown to Armageddon
Copyright © 2018 by David Head

All rights reserved. No portion of this book may be reproduced in any form—mechanically, electronically, or by any other means, including photocopying, recording, or by any information storage and retrieval system—without permission in writing from the author, except as permitted by the United States of America copyright law.

ISBN (13): 978-0-692-10471-2

All Scripture quotations are from the King James Version of the Holy Bible. All emphases in bold and/or italics is solely the author's doing.

Cover design by Cris Wanzer
www.ManuscriptsToGo.com

First edition 2018

Printed in the United States of America

Vinedresser logo by Jason Mays

Contact the author: headdavid2020@gmail.com

"When the Lord shall build up Zion, he shall appear in his glory."
— Psalm 102:16

Acknowledgments

My deepest and sincerest gratitude goes out to the following: Jesus Christ, for giving me the gifts, insight and understanding for this project. Pastor Mike Rollins of Living Stones Ministries for his many contributions to this endeavor, and for connecting me with LSM secretary, Beverley Clark, who did a great job with my many edits and revisions over a period of five years. My designer, Cris Wanzer, for her outstanding work bringing to life my vision for the cover and interior designs. My grandparents, Ray and Evelyn Sterne, for their prayers and teaching me about Christ when I was a child. My parents, Pat and David Head, for not giving up on me through my dark years. My brother, Barry Head, and family, and stepmother, Brenda "Mom B" Head, for their continued love and support. My aunt Paulette Sterne and Peggy "Mom Peggy" Hughes for their help. And a special thanks to Brother Terry Hess for his generous contribution to this project. I'm forever grateful and indebted to you all.

In Loving Memory of Ray & Evelyn Sterne
and Pat & David Head

Contents

Acknowledgments vi
Prologue viii

■ ■ ■

1 IN THE LION'S BELLY 1
2 THE FRIENDLY BEAR 15
3 THE FOUR-HEADED LEOPARD 25
4 SATAN'S SEAT 35
5 JERUSALEM RISING 51
6 GOG AND COMPANY 67
7 THE MAN OF SIN 81
8 DOWN TO EARTH 99
9 THE FIRST RESURRECTION 121
10 BABYLON THE GREAT 147
11 THE HOUR OF TEMPTATION 165
12 WHEN THE LIGHTS GO OUT 179
13 THY HOLY MOUNTAIN 195
14 THE SECOND RESURRECTION 207
15 THE NEW JERUSALEM 217

■ ■ ■

Epilogue 221
About the Author 225
Endnotes 226

Prologue

Jerusalem was established as the capital of Israel by King David 3,000 years ago (2 Sam. 5:3-7). David's son and successor, Solomon, built the first Jewish Temple on Temple Mount in Jerusalem (2 Chron. 3:1). After many years of disobedience and idol worship, God allowed the Babylonians to destroy the Temple and take many Jews captive back to Babylon in 606-586 B.C. (2 Chron. 36:18-20). Following the conquest of the Medes and Persians over the Babylonians, the Jews were allowed to return to Jerusalem to build a second Temple (Ezra 1:2-3).

About 40 years after the time of Christ, the Romans destroyed the second Temple in 70 A.D. and the Jews were scattered throughout the world just as Christ had warned (Luke 21:20-24); with the exception of a remnant of both Jewish and Christian communities remaining. The Romans then later renamed the land of Judea (Israel) to Palestine in an attempt to erase the land of its Jewish heritage.

Following the founding of Islam in 622 by Mohammad, Arab Muslims controlled Palestine between 640-1099. Between 688-91 they built the Dome of the Rock on Temple Mount where, they claim, Mohammed allegedly ascended into heaven. A more truthful story told is that they built the Dome to overshadow Christian churches which were attracting Arab converts. The Arab Muslims living in Palestine would later become known as the Palestinians.

Around 1880, Jews from around the world began migrating back to their ancient roots in the land of Israel just as many biblical prophecies foretold would occur in the last-days (Isa. 11:11-12). On May 14, 1948, the Jews declared the rebirth of the nation of Israel. On June 7, 1967, they recaptured back full control of Jerusalem during the Arab-Israeli Six-Day War. Since then there has been more wars and uprisings by Muslims who contest with

Prologue

lies, propaganda and murderous terrorist attacks that Jerusalem has always belonged to them.

Jerusalem is the most contested and controversial piece of real estate on the planet which, unbeknown to most, is itself a fulfillment of Bible prophecy. Through the Prophet Zechariah the Lord foretold that in the last-days "Behold, I will make Jerusalem a cup of trembling unto all people round about, when they shall be in the siege both against Judah and against Jerusalem. And in that day will I make Jerusalem a burdensome stone for all people: all that burden themselves with it shall be cut in pieces, though all the people of the earth be gathered together against it" (Zech. 12:2-3).

According to the book of Daniel, there are still seven years left of unfulfilled Bible prophecy that has Jerusalem at the epicenter (Dan. 9:24-27). The countdown will begin on the seven years with a decree issued by a future world leader known among Christians as the Antichrist (Dan. 9:27). The decree will confirm the Jews' right to rebuild their third Temple on Temple Mount which they will do right next to the Dome of the Rock (Rev. 11:1-2). The decree will also create the temporary illusion of "Peace and safety" for Israel and most other nations throughout the first half of the seven years (1 Thes. 5:3).

The prophetic Scriptures repeatedly emphasize, however, that the second half of the seven years will be the most horrific time period in the history of mankind (Dan. 12:1). The Prophet Jeremiah referred to it as the "Time of Jacob's (Israel's) Trouble" (Jer. 30:7). The Minor Prophets called it "The Day of the Lord" (Zeph. 1:1-18). Jesus said it will be the "Great Tribulation" (Matt. 24:21), and the Apostle John wrote of it as the "Hour of Temptation" (Rev. 3:10). It will culminate with a globally devastating outpouring of God's wrath and the Battle of Armageddon (Rev. 16).

1

IN THE LION'S BELLY

"Surely the Lord God will do nothing, but he (first) revealeth his secret unto his servants the prophets."
— Amos 3:7

The Prophet Daniel was in his teens when he was carried away as a captive by the Babylonians in 606 B.C. As a member of the royal seed of Judah, the Babylonians took him and others to be servants in the palace of the king of Babylon (Dan. 1:1-6). Early into the captivity, the Babylonian King Nebuchadnezzar had a dream one night, after an evening of pondering over the future of his empire. The dream had so greatly disturbed him that he called for his wise men to not only interpret the dream, but to also tell him what the dream was about. After they failed to meet the king's humanly impossible demands, the king then ordered that they all be put to death (Dan. 2:1-13).

When Daniel heard of the decree, he asked to be allowed to see the king. When he was brought before the king, Daniel asked him to delay his decree and to give him time to answer the king's request, believing that God could give him the answer. That night, the Lord revealed the king's dream and its interpretation to Daniel in a dream of his own. Upon rising the next day, he gave thanks to the God of his fathers for granting his petition (Dan. 2:14-25).

When Daniel was brought back before the king, he first acknowledged that there was not a man on earth who could meet the king's demand, but there was a God in Heaven, in whom he believed, that could, who gave him the answer to the king's request. Daniel began by telling the king that his dream came as a result of his concern over the future of his empire. The dream, Daniel explained, was that of a huge image of a man that had a head of gold, its breast and arms of silver, its belly and thighs of brass, its legs were of iron and its feet were part iron and part clay. Then, Daniel continued, the king had seen a stone cut out of a mountain without the use of man's hands, which was thrust down upon the image upon its feet, shattering it to tiny pieces that were carried away by the wind. The stone then became a great mountain itself and grew until it covered the entire earth (Dan. 2:26-36).

Daniel went on to explain to the king that the head of gold represented the then Babylonian Empire. The breast and arms of silver, the belly and thighs of brass, and the legs of iron, with its feet part iron and part clay, all depicted three more empires that were to succeed in succession, one after another, following the Babylonian era. As Daniel explained, the stone that was cut out of a mountain without hands, which broke the image to pieces and grew to cover the whole earth, represented a Kingdom that God would establish that was to succeed all these earthly kingdoms and abide forever (Dan. 2:37-45).

Looking back in history, we know that the Babylonian Empire was succeeded by the Medo-Persian era; afterwards followed the Grecian, then Roman Empires. The Roman Empire was depicted by the legs of iron, which had feet of part iron and part clay. Daniel explained that the clay depicted a weakness in that empire, the same as if iron were to be mixed with clay, which doesn't mix (Dan. 2:41-43).

The "potter's clay," as it is referred in Daniel 2:41, depicted the Jews within the Roman Empire (Isa. 64:8). Through a series of treaties, the Jews of the Roman era were granted special privileges by the Romans unlike any other group of people. In the treaties, the Jews were exempt from mandatory Roman civic oblations, such as Caesar worship, which violated their belief in the One True God. During the Roman era, the Jews were numerous throughout the empire and were very influential in their communities. Therefore, their presence was both a problem and weakness to the then mighty Roman Empire.

The Stone that was carved out of a mountain, without hands, depicted Jesus Christ, who is often referred to in the Scriptures as a "Stone" (Matt. 21:42-44; 1 Peter 2:4-8). The mention of the Stone being cut out of the mountain "without hands" implies that it was an act of God and not man. The "mountain" from which the Stone was cut out of represented the Kingdom of Heaven from which Christ came; for in the Scriptures, the word "*mountain*" is used in reference to depict earthly kingdoms, the Kingdom of Heaven, and the Kingdom of God on earth that is to follow all earthly kingdoms (Ezek. 28:14; Jer. 51:24-25; Isa. 65:25).

The Stone is depicted in Nebuchadnezzar's dream smashing into the feet of the image and not its head, because it was during the time of the Roman Empire when Christ came "down from heaven" (John 6:38). The life, death, and resurrection of Jesus Christ fulfilled the ceremonial Jewish law of the Old Covenant and established the New Covenant, thereby making the Old like dust in the wind (Matt. 21:41-45). Also, with the spread of Christianity throughout the pagan world, many turned to the faith, which virtually dissolved the false religion of paganism, which had been preserved down through time in the aforementioned empires, making it like dust in the wind as well (Acts 17:6-7).

■ ■ ■

Several decades after Nebuchadnezzar's dream, Daniel had a dream of his own which depicted the first three empires of Nebuchadnezzar's dream, but skipped over the Roman Empire to the end-times empire of a world dictator, referred to among Christians as the "Antichrist." In Daniel's dream, the Babylonian Empire was depicted as a lion, the Medo-Persian as a bear, and the Grecian as a leopard with four heads. The Antichrist's empire was described only as being "dreadful and terrible, and strong exceedingly; and it had great iron teeth: it devoured and brake in pieces, and stamped the residue with the feet of it: and it was diverse from all other beasts that were before it; and it had ten horns...and, behold, there came up among them another little horn, before whom there were three of the first horns plucked up by the roots: and, behold, in this horn were eyes like the eyes of man, and a mouth speaking great things" (Dan. 7:1-8).

Baffled by his dream, Daniel approached the angel in the vision and asked for the interpretation. The angel explained to Daniel that the four beasts represented four kingdoms. Daniel then got more specific and requests to "know the truth of the fourth beast, which was diverse from all the others, exceedingly dreadful, whose teeth were of iron, and his nails of brass; which devoured, brake in pieces, and stamped the residue with his feet" (Dan. 7:17, 19).

The angel then proceeded in response to Daniel's curiosity and said, "The fourth beast shall be the fourth kingdom upon earth, which shall be diverse from all kingdoms, and shall devour the whole earth, and shall tread it down, and break it in pieces. And the ten horns out of this kingdom are ten kings that shall arise: and another (little horn) shall arise after them; and he shall be diverse from the first (ten), and he shall subdue (overthrow) three kings (nations). And he (little horn/Antichrist) shall speak great words against the most High (God), and shall wear out the saints of the most High, and think to change times and laws: and they (Great Tribulation saints) shall be given into his hand, until a time (one year) and times (two years) and the dividing of time (half a year). But the judgment shall sit, and they (Christ and His saints) shall take away his (Antichrist's) dominion (at Christ's Second Coming), to consume and to destroy it unto the end. And the kingdom and dominion, and the greatness of the kingdom under the whole heaven, shall be given to the people of the saints of the most High, whose kingdom is an everlasting kingdom, and all dominions shall serve and obey him" (Dan. 7:23-27).

This fourth beast is said to have teeth of iron and nails of brass. As you may recall, the image in Nebuchadnezzar's dream used brass and iron to depict the Grecian and Roman Empires. What this clue signifies is that the empire of the Antichrist will arise from the foundation that was laid by the Grecian and Roman Empires, and it is this foundation that today's Western democracies of Europe and America are built upon. From within this structure, perhaps Western Europe, the Antichrist will rise to have control, of sorts, over seven powerful nations. He will then overthrow three more nations, perhaps in the Middle East, that were all once part of the Grecian and Roman Empires.

> *Note: The angel explained to Daniel that the "ten horns" represent "ten kings," or rather ten nations. Most prophecy scholars say that the ten toes on the image of Nebuchadnezzar's dream represent the same "ten kings" as the "ten horns"; however, this is not true. Nowhere in the Scriptures do toes or fingers in prophetic visions allude to seats of authority; only horns upon beasts do the honor. See Daniel 8:20-21 and Revelation 17:12. The only relation that Nebuchadnezzar's dream has to Daniel's vision of the fourth beast is what I just explained above concerning the brass and iron.*

Continuing, the angel explained that the Antichrist is going to "speak great words against the most High," which he will do when he makes his claim to be the Jews' Messiah, i.e., Christ. He will then go on to change times, which will probably include the Western calendar, which dates back to the birth of Jesus Christ. He will also change laws that will be in contrast to God's laws. He will then persecute the Great Tribulation saints who will be given into his hands for a period of three and a half years (Rev. 13:5-8). Following the Great Tribulation, Christ will then return to rule the world with His saints, whose Kingdom shall endure for a thousand years on this earth, then continue forever in the new heaven and the new earth (Matt. 24:29-31; Rev. 19-20:6; 21:1).

■ ■ ■

In 536 B.C., the combined forces of the Medes and Persians overthrew the Babylonian Empire just as the prophetic dreams foretold. Darius the Mede was then appointed by the Persian King Cyrus to sit on the throne previously occupied by the Babylonian kings. Babylon was then a province of the empire of the Medes and Persians (Dan. 9:1; 2 Chron. 36:23). In that same year, Daniel, now perhaps in his eighties, remembered the Prophet Jeremiah's prophecy stating that the Jews' captivity in Babylon would only last for seventy years (Dan. 9:2). Now that the seventy-year timeframe had run its course, Daniel petitioned the Lord on behalf of his people, the Jews, and their beloved city Jerusalem (Dan. 9:3-20).

As Daniel prayed, the angel Gabriel appeared to him and said, "O Daniel, I am now come forth to give thee skill and understanding. At the beginning of thy supplications, the commandment came forth, and I am now come to shew thee; for thou art greatly beloved: therefore understand the matter, and consider the vision" (Dan. 9:22-23).

The Vision

Daniel 9:24-27 tells us:

[24] *Seventy weeks (seventy sevens/490 years) are determined upon thy people (the Jews) and upon thy holy city (Jerusalem), to finish the transgression, and to make an end of sins, and to make reconciliation for iniquity (Christ's death), and to bring in everlasting righteousness (God's Eternal Kingdom), and to seal up the vision and prophecy (Daniel's prophecies), and to anoint the*

most Holy (Kingship of Christ).

²⁵ *Know therefore and understand, that from the going forth of the commandment to restore and to build Jerusalem unto the Messiah (Christ) the Prince, shall be seven weeks, and threescore and two weeks (483 years): the street shall be built again, and the wall (around Jerusalem), even in troublous times.*

²⁶ *And after threescore and two weeks (at the end of the 483 years) shall Messiah be cut off (death of Christ), but not for himself (die for the sins of man): and the people of the prince (Caesar/Satan) that shall come shall destroy the city (Jerusalem 70 A.D.) and the sanctuary (second Temple 70 A.D.); and the end thereof shall be with a flood (of Roman soldiers), and unto the end of the war (between Jews and Rome 66-70 A.D.) desolations are determined (for the Jews, Jerusalem and the Temple).*

²⁷ *And he (Antichrist/Satan) shall confirm the covenant (Old Covenant) with many (the end-times Jews and their foes) for one week (seven years): and in the midst of the week (midpoint of the seven years) he (Antichrist) shall cause the sacrifice and the oblations to cease (in the third Temple to be built in the end-times), and for the overspreading of abominations (offensive acts toward God) he (Antichrist) shall make it (third Temple) desolate, even until the consummation, and that determined shall be poured upon the desolate (predetermined judgments of God to be unleashed upon the wicked during the Great Tribulation; Rev. 14:10).*

The Prophet Jeremiah foretold of a Babylonian captivity that was to last for seventy years. In response to Daniel's inquiry following the completion of the seventy years, the Lord then pronounced another period of time upon the Jews, Jerusalem, and the Temple of seventy times seven years, equaling 490 years. The prophecy included a timetable to the appearing of their Messiah (Jesus), the destruction of their second Temple (which at the time had not been built yet), the coming of the Antichrist, the third Temple to be built in the end-times, and the judgments to be poured out upon the wicked during the Great Tribulation.

The countdown on the 490 years was to begin when a certain decree would be issued by someone in power to restore the wall around Jerusalem that had been destroyed by the Babylonians in 586 B.C. The rebuilding of the wall, we are told, is to occur during a troublesome time for the Jews. From history, we know that this decree was given by the Persian King Artaxerxes exactly 483 years before the death of Christ occurred around 30-33 A.D. (Neh. 2:1-20). With the death of Christ, the remaining seven years of the prophecy were put on hold until the time of the end, which will be the final seven years of human history, before Christ returns to establish the Kingdom of God on earth at His Second Coming.

Following the crucifixion of Christ, God gave the Jews a period of about forty years to accept Jesus as their Messiah through the ministries of the Apostles of Christ. Afterwards, God lifted His protection and allowed Satan the real (though invisible) "prince" of the Roman Empire, to destroy Jerusalem and the Temple in 70 A.D.

The words *"prince"* and *"king"* are used interchangeably throughout the Scriptures in reference to both spiritual and human agents. For example, in Daniel chapter ten we see where fallen angels are referred to by using the word *"prince."* In the same chapter, the word is also used to depict good angels, such as the case involving "Michael, one of the chief princes," who is the archangel over God's heavenly host of angels and who is the chief prince over the nation of Israel (Dan. 10:13-21). In Daniel 10:20, one of the fallen angels is referred to as the "prince of Persia" and another, the "prince of Grecia." As Michael is the prince over the affairs of Israel, these two fallen angels are over the nations of Persia and Greece.

In the book of Isaiah, chapter fourteen, the Prophet begins in verse four by addressing what appears to be the "king of Babylon." As we continue to read, however, one comes to realize that

In the Lion's Belly

the reference is directed at Lucifer (Satan), who is the real (though invisible) "king of Babylon" (Isa. 14:4-15). We see a similar example of this in the book of Ezekiel, where the "prince of Tyrus" claims that "I am a God, I sit in the seat of God." In this passage, the word "prince" alludes to the human king of Tyrus (Ezek. 28:2-6). As Ezekiel continues, he then shifts the attention from the human prince to invest Satan, the spiritual prince of Tyrus, by referring to him as the "king of Tyrus" who was behind the human king's folly in claiming to be God (Ezek. 28:11-17).

Armed with this knowledge, we can now better understand who the "*prince*" is in Daniel 9:26 and who the "*he*" is in verse 27. In verse 26, the word "*prince*" alludes to both Caesar and Satan, but it is Satan who is the primary subject; for in verse 27, which jumps ahead two thousand years to the time of the Antichrist, the word "*he*" is a continuation of the last person mentioned in verse 26, who was Caesar/Satan. Therefore, in verse 27, the "*he*" is a reference to both the Antichrist and Satan. In Second Thessalonians, the Apostle Paul referred to the Antichrist as he "whose coming is after the working of Satan" (2 Thes. 2:3, 9). The Apostle John wrote that it will be Satan who will give the Antichrist "his power, and his seat, and great authority" (Rev. 13:2).

In Daniel 9:27, we read how the Antichrist is going to "confirm the covenant with many for one week (seven years)." Notice that it states "the covenant" and not "a covenant" as some mistranslations have it. Daniel was only familiar with "the covenant," which God had made with Israel through his forefathers Abraham, Moses, and David. In this covenant, God had Abraham build an altar, Moses a tent (or rather, Tabernacle), and finally, the Lord influenced David to have his son Solomon build the first Temple (to replace the Tabernacle) upon the same mount Abraham had built the altar.

In "the covenant" there is a place of worship which is the

Temple, which also is a huge part of Daniel's vision of the 490 years. In the final "week," or rather the final seven years of the prophecy, the Antichrist is going to "confirm the covenant" by being instrumental in providing the necessary means for the Jews to build the third Temple on Temple Mount in Jerusalem, where the Temple has before twice stood. On the very day this decree is given, the countdown will begin on the final seven years, just as the countdown began on the previous 483 years with the Persian king's decree for the wall to be rebuilt around Jerusalem.

Once the Jews build their third Temple, they will begin the "oblations" according to the law of the Old Covenant. In the middle of the final seven years, the Antichrist will suddenly put a stop to the daily oblations at the Temple. In the process, he will speak "great words against the most High" when he claims to be the Jews' long anticipated Messiah, whose arrival the Jews of today (who do not believe in Jesus) still await. He will then go on to demand to be worshipped and to make war with all who oppose him for the remaining three and a half years. During that time, referred to as the "Great Tribulation," the judgments that have been predetermined by God will be unleashed upon the wicked (Rev. 8-19).

■ ■ ■

The book of Daniel is second to none in comparison to other Old Testament books when it comes to considering their content of end-times prophecy. Some of Daniel's prophecies greatly baffled him, especially the ones pertaining to the last-days; however, many of his prophecies recorded in chapters seven through eleven pertained to the rise and fall of the aforementioned empires and some of their exploits. We will be looking into some of those exploits in the following chapters of this book.

Most of Daniel chapter seven, the last verse of chapter nine, and the last ten verses of chapter eleven on through to all of chapter twelve, all pertain to the exploits of the Antichrist and his empire in the last-days. As Daniel's prophecies were coming to a close in chapter twelve, the angel told him to "shut up the words, and seal the book, even to the time of the end: many shall run to and fro, and knowledge shall be increased" (Dan. 12:4). In other words, what the angel is saying here is that Daniel's prophecies concerning the end-times would not be able to be fully understood until the time of the end, and that the time of the end would be characterized by an increase in travel and knowledge.

At no time in history has there been such an increase in travel and knowledge as what we saw develop in the twentieth century. Not only that, but we also witnessed the rebirth of the nation of Israel in May of 1948, which itself was the fulfillment of Bible prophecy in major proportion. And, on top of that, the Jews regained full control over the city of Jerusalem in 1967 — and in order for them to build the third Temple, they must control Jerusalem. We will be looking more in-depth into these events in the latter chapters of this book.

As the angel continued in chapter twelve to give more details of the end-times, Daniel was compelled to reply saying, "And I heard, but I understood not: then said I, O my Lord, what shall be the end of these things? And he said, Go thy way Daniel: for the words are closed up and sealed till the time of the end" (Dan. 12:8-9). Here we are again informed that Daniel's end-times prophecies were "sealed," or rather "closed up" by God, inhibiting our ability to comprehend them in full until the time of the end. Throughout the twentieth century, many books were written on the end-times. As each decade passed, God unsealed more and more of the end-times Scriptures to His saints, and as a result, more and more books were written. As time goes on, this will continue unto the end. Even this book you are now reading is part of this ongoing process.

In conclusion to Daniel chapter twelve, the angel stated, "And from the time the daily sacrifice shall be taken away, and the abomination that maketh desolate set up, there shall be a thousand two hundred and ninety days. Blessed is he that waiteth, and cometh to the thousand three hundred and five and thirty days. But go thy way till the end be: for thou shalt rest, and stand in thy lot at the end of the days" (Dan. 12:11-13).

Here the angel informs us that there will be a period of 1,290 days from the time the Antichrist stops the daily sacrifice in the third, yet unbuilt, Temple. This coincides with Daniel 9:27, but with added detail. This added detail lets us know that the Antichrist is going to stop the daily sacrifice exactly 30 days before the official time begins on the Great Tribulation, which is set to last for three and a half years, or rather 1,260 days. We will later be looking at pieces of the prophetic puzzle that may just reveal exactly when, even the day, the Antichrist will stop the daily sacrifice.

The angel also mentioned an added 45 days to the total 1,290, making a total of 1,335 days. This added period of 45 days tacked on to the end of the Great Tribulation is not to be ignored, for it will be during that 45-day period that Christ will destroy the wicked with a fiery judgment; revamp the earth for the Kingdom Age; establish a Millennial Temple; and assign Israel and the Church their allotted inheritance in the Kingdom. Once the 45-day period concludes then the official countdown will commence on the thousand-year reign of Christ. We will be taking a closer look at these events in the latter chapters of this book.

And last, the angel told Daniel to just go on about his daily business and to not be concerned about the vision of the end-times; that he would soon "rest," or rather die, then be resurrected to stand in his allotted inheritance in the Kingdom of God at the "end of the days," or rather once the prophetic 1,335-day time period had run its course in the last-days.

The Prophet Ezekiel, who also has a book in the Bible that bears his name, was a captive, along with Daniel, in the belly of the lion (Ezek. 1:2-3). Like Daniel, he, too, penned many prophetic Scriptures. His prophecies, however, primarily concerned the nation of Israel, their presence among the family of nations in the last-days, and their everlasting endurance in the Kingdom of their Messiah. We will be looking at his prophecies later.

Both Daniel and Ezekiel lived long, productive lives in the land of their exile. Their ministries and prophecies encouraged hope in the hearts of their captive Jewish counterparts concerning their future. Their end-times prophecies are invaluable to the piecing-together of the very complex end-times puzzle. According to tradition, both Daniel and Ezekiel died in Babylon far from their beloved homeland of Israel, but ever so close to their even more beloved God.

2

THE FRIENDLY BEAR

Daniel was a high-ranking government official in Babylon when it was overthrown by the Medes and Persians. The Persian kings were more humane than the Babylonians. Their policy was to allow conquered people to return to their homeland if they so desired. With that being so, we can clearly see the hand of Providence in the victory of the Medes and Persians over the Babylonians occurring at the same time the Jews' seventy years of exile had run its course.

It is believed by some that Daniel may have shown the Persian King Cyrus the prophecy in the book of Isaiah, which called King Cyrus by name well over one hundred years before he was born (Isa. 44:28-45:6). The prophecy foretold that Cyrus would be a great conqueror who would favor God's people, the Jews. The prophecy was written to demonstrate that the God of the Jews is the One and only True God, who alone has the ability to foretell the future with such accuracy as to call Cyrus by name.

Cyrus was so impressed by the God of the Jews that it led him to send out a proclamation throughout his empire stating, "The Lord God of heaven hath given me all the kingdoms of the earth; and hath charged me to build him a house at Jerusalem, which is in Judah (Israel). Who is there among you of all his people? His God be with him, and let him go up to Jerusalem, which is in Judah, and build the house of the Lord God of Israel, (he is the God), which is in Jerusalem" (Ezra 1:2-3).

Before the Babylonian captivity, the Temple in Jerusalem was the center of religious fervor for the Jews who worshipped the Lord. Like Daniel, many of them were led away as captives throughout the vast Babylonian Empire. Along with the captives went their knowledge of the truth of the One and only True God. At first, the exiles gathered together at someone's home on the Sabbath day to worship the Lord. This, in turn, led to the idea of building a place to worship, called the synagogue (assembly). Over time, the God-fearing Jews of the Diaspora multiplied and spread, building synagogues everywhere they settled. They also had to learn the language of the land of their exile, while at the same time teaching their children their native tongue of Hebrew. In the midst of chastising His people, the Lord took opportunity to set up lighthouses of truth about Himself among the heathen nations. After all, it was God's intention from the start to reveal Himself to the world through His elect nation of Israel.

As a result of Cyrus' proclamation, 50,000 Jews throughout the empire came together to make the journey to Judah. Not long after their arrival, they all gathered in Jerusalem to keep the Feast of Tabernacles in the seventh month of Tishri. Although the city and the Temple still lay in ruins, it was still a time of great feasting and joy over their return. After the celebration, preparations were then put into motion to rebuild the Temple (Ezra 2:1-3:7).

In the second year of their return, in the second month of Iyar, they laid the foundation for the second Temple (Ezra 3:8-11). Being a cause for celebration, the noise of the festive occasion grabbed the attention of the nearby Samaritans, who had been closely watching the returnees since their arrival. Professing to believe in the Jews' God, the Samaritans approached the elders of Judah and asked if they could help with the building of the Temple. The elders ignored their false profession and denied their request. This angered the Samaritans, who then set out to thwart the Temple project, which they successfully managed to do for nearly fifteen years. However, as usual, it was Satan who was the real culprit working through the Samaritans to hinder the building project (Ezra 4:1-24).

During the fifteen years that the Temple project lay unattended, the Jews focused on building their homes and businesses. After about fifteen years had passed, the Lord raised up the Prophets Haggai and Zechariah to stir up the people to resume the work on the Temple. Again, the Devil tried to stop them, but this time to no avail. After five years of steady building, the Temple was finally finished. At the dedication ceremony, twelve goats were offered up in sacrifice for a sin offering for all the twelve tribes of Israel. Shortly thereafter, they kept the Feast of Passover in the first month of Nisan (Ezra 5-6).

> *Note: The Jews' captivity in Babylon began in 606 B.C. and ended in 536 B.C. The Temple, however, was not destroyed until 586 B.C. Some scholars believe that God intentionally allowed Satan to thwart the Temple project so that it, too, lay desolate for seventy years. For it was in 516 B.C. that the Jews finished the Temple as stated above.*

Although thousands of Jews migrated back to their homeland, many opted to remain where they were. Among those who decided to stay was a beautiful young lady by the name of Hadassah (Esther; her Persian name), who had been raised by her older cousin, Mordecai. They lived in the city of Shushan, the capital of the Persian Empire, where the Persian King Ahasuerus resided, and where Mordecai worked as a keeper of the gate to the king's palace.

After Queen Vashti infringed upon the king's authority one day, he was compelled by his advisors to depose her. Following this, a search was made for candidates to replace the queen, and Esther was chosen. Esther's beauty caught the attention of all and it was no surprise when the king chose her to be his new first lady (Esther 2:8-17).

As a keeper of the king's gate, Mordecai was able to keep a close eye on his cousin, as well as other matters of interest. Shortly following Esther's crowning, Mordecai overheard two of the king's chamberlains plotting to assassinate the king. After he informed Esther of the plot, an investigation ensued. When the thing was found to be true, the men were put to death and the entire matter was written in the king's book of records, including Mordecai's involvement (Esther 2:21-23).

In the following years, the king appointed a man by the name Haman to be his new prime minister. Haman was a descendant of King Agag of the Amalekites, who were long-time enemies of the Jews dating back hundreds of years (1 Sam. 15:8). It was customary for the king's servants to bow to the heads of state when passing, but Mordecai, being a Jew, preferred death rather than to bow to an Amalekite. The other servants tried daily to persuade him to bow each time Haman passed, yet to no avail. Finally, Mordecai told them that he was a Jew and the reason for his defiance. Up to this point, Haman had decided that Mordecai had to be put to death. When he found out that Mordecai was a Jew, however, Haman then hatched a plot to have all the Jews throughout the empire killed as well (Esther 3:1-6).

Haman went to the king one day and informed him that there were certain people in all the provinces of his kingdom who were a diverse people, adhering to their own laws and customs and not the king's. Haman then recommended to the king that he have the people put to death, in which the king agreed and approved that a decree be written. Unknowingly to the king, however, he had just approved the death warrant of his queen and Mordecai, who had earlier saved his life (Mordecai had told Esther not to reveal her Jewish identity back when she was chosen as a candidate for the queenship; Esther 2:10).

The Persians used a system of throwing dice to decide an important matter, which in the Bible is referred to as casting "Pur" (Esther 3:7). In the matter concerning Haman's plot, the dice were cast on Nisan 13th and fell on the number twelve. It was then determined that the murderous plot was to be carried out on the 13th day of the twelfth month known as Adar. Letters were then written and sent out to all the provinces in the empire announcing the deadly decree. Beginning in Shushan, there was great mourning and perplexity among the Jews as the news spread throughout the empire (Esther 3:12-4:3).

When Mordecai and Esther heard of the decree, they agreed that Esther had no choice but to unlawfully approach the king, for which, under Persian law, she could be put to death (Esther 4:4-17). Esther then proclaimed a fast among the Jews in her city. On the third day of the fast, she went to stand before the king, and to the tune of her relief, the king held out his golden scepter, which granted her approval to approach him. To her delight, the king highly approved of her presence and offered her up to half of his kingdom if she so desired. She then told the king that her request was for the king and Haman to join her for some wine. At the gathering, the king again enquired to know of the real reason for Esther's approaching him. She then told the king that if he and Haman would join her again the next day, that she would then disclose her petition (Esther 5:1-8).

Haman left the palace feeling joyful that he had been honored by the queen, but when he saw Mordecai at the gate, his joy turned to anger. When he arrived home, he told his wife and friends of his good day at the office. However, he then told them that "Yet all of this availeth me nothing, so long as I see Mordecai the Jew sitting at the king's gate." His wife and friends then suggested he build a gallows, then seek the king's approval to hang Mordecai before his next meeting with Esther and the king the following day (Esther 5:9-14).

That night, the king had trouble sleeping, so he ordered his servant to bring in the book of records to be read to him. After the king was reminded by the records how Mordecai had saved his life, he learned that Mordecai had not yet been honored for such. The next morning, Haman arrived early to seek the king's approval to hang Mordecai. Before he could speak, however, the king first asked him, "What shall be done unto the man whom the king delighteth to honor?" Supposing it was he whom the king wanted to honor, Haman suggested the king have one of his noble princes to parade the man around the city in the king's royal apparel, riding upon the king's horse. Approving, the king then ordered for Haman to take Mordecai and do unto him as he had just suggested. After completing the king's wishes, Haman went home in shame. Not long after he arrived home, the king's servants came to escort him to his meeting with the king and queen (Esther 6:1-14).

At the meeting, the king wasted no time in getting to Esther's petition. Without delay, she informed the king that her life, and the lives of her people, had been sold to be destroyed, and asked the king to spare their lives. The king then replied, "Who is he, and where he is, that durst presume in his heart to do so?" Esther replied, "The adversary and enemy is this wicked Haman." Suddenly, Haman was struck with fear and began to plead for his life. One of the king's servants then came forward and told the king of the gallows that Haman had built to hang Mordecai. The king then ordered for Haman to be taken immediately and hanged thereon instead (Esther 7:1-10).

After these things, Esther revealed her relation to Mordecai to the king, who in turn appointed her cousin to be the new prime minister. Esther then pleaded for the lives of her people, asking the king to reverse the decree, but according to Persian law that could not be done. Instead, the king gave Mordecai approval to write up a new decree to counter Haman's decree. In the new order, the Jews were granted permission to arm themselves and fight their enemies on the 13th of Adar. As the news reached the provinces, there was great celebration among the Jews. As a result of the new decree, many non-Jews converted to the religion of the Jews out of fear of their God (Esther 8:1-17).

Meanwhile, Mordecai's fame spread throughout the empire, and all the king's rulers, lieutenants, deputies, and officers began to favor the Jews out of fear of the new prime minister. And when the 13th of Adar arrived, they joined with the Jews to help them kill their enemies. At the end of the day, the king asked Esther if she had any more requests. She then asked the king to grant the Jews living in Shushan permission to kill their enemies on the 14th as well, and for Haman's ten sons to be hanged on the same gallows as he (Esther 9:1-18).

Following these things, Mordecai instituted a new holiday for the Jews to observe annually on the 14th of Adar in commemoration of their deliverance from Haman's murderous plot. Letters were sent out to all the Jews in all provinces informing them of the new holiday and that they were to keep it yearly, at which time they were to give gifts one to another and to the poor among them. And being that Haman used the "Pur," or rather the "Lot," to determine the day on which to execute his plot, they named the holiday "Purim" meaning that his plot fell upon his own head (Esther 9:19-32).

■ ■ ■

In the years after the era of Esther and Mordecai, the Jews were highly respected throughout the empire. Around the year 450 B.C., there was a Jew by the name of Nehemiah who served the Persian King Artaxerxes as his cupbearer. One day his brother, Hanani, and other Jews arrived from the province of Judah to visit him and to report on the welfare of his people. They informed him that the Jews in Judah were not doing so well and that the wall around Jerusalem still lay in ruins. Up to that time, the Jews who had returned to Judah had only built the Temple and the city's infrastructure, but the wall still remained in ruins since the day the Babylonians had destroyed it in 586 B.C. After hearing this, Nehemiah fasted and prayed for God to grant him favor with the king to go to Jerusalem to rebuild the wall (Neh. 1:1-11).

After several months had passed, there was still no answer

from the Lord in regard to his prayer, and it was unlawful for him to just approach the king on his own. One day, however, in the first month of Nisan, the king noticed Nehemiah's sad countenance and asked him what the matter was. Nehemiah, realizing his prayer was now being answered, informed the king the plight of his people and their beloved city. The king then asked him if he had any requests, so he asked the king for permission to go to Jerusalem to rebuild the wall. The king then wrote out a decree granting him safe passage for his journey and for all the supplies he would need for the mission (Neh. 2:1-9).

> *Note: This decree to "restore and to build Jerusalem" was the fulfillment of Daniel's prophecy that began the countdown on the 483 years to the death of Christ. The prophecy states that the "street shall be built again, and the wall, even in troublous times" (Dan. 9:25). And it was no wonder that the Lord waited several months to answer Nehemiah's prayer; for it would be in the month of Nisan during Passover that Christ would be crucified 483 years after the decree was issued as foretold by Daniel (Dan. 9:26a).*

Three days after Nehemiah arrived in Jerusalem, he went out one evening alone to view the wall he had come to repair. Afterwards, he met with the elders and told them the reason for his coming and of his support from the king. When word reached the Samaritans, who lived nearby, they accused him of wanting to fortify the city in a plot to rebel against the king. Knowing that their false accusations would not hold, Nehemiah told his accusers that God was with him to prosper the work of his hands and that they had no "...portion, nor right, nor memorial, in Jerusalem" (Neh. 2:10-20).

Under the leadership of Nehemiah, the Jews banded together to rebuild the wall, which also included the repairing of the streets (Neh. 3:1-21). When the Samaritans saw this, they conspired to attack them in an attempt to stop the Jews from securing the city (Neh. 4:1-8). The Jews, however, got word of their plot and armed themselves in the event of an attack. Half of them worked while the other half stood guard. Seeing this, the Samaritans became discouraged and watched from a distance the fulfillment of Daniel's prophecy, unknowingly that they were a part of the fulfillment themselves (Neh. 4:10-23). Despite the constant threat of attack, the Jews finished the wall during a "troublous time" in the sixth month known as Elul (Neh. 6:15).

■ ■ ■

From ensnaring the children of Israel into idolatry, to thwarting building projects, and plots of genocide, the Devil strives in vain to hinder God's plans for Israel. Satan is the sole driving force behind all of Israel's opposition, which is clearly indicated in the Scriptures (Zech. 3:1). Up to this point, the Devil understood the special relationship God has with Israel and that they were to somehow be involved in the redemption of mankind from their sin. What Satan did not know, however, was that his opposing schemes against the Jews would soon prove to be his demise, and that he himself would be instrumental in the redemptive process that was to take place one day upon an old, rugged Roman cross.

3

THE FOUR-HEADED LEOPARD

In Daniel chapter seven, the Prophet recorded his vision of four beasts, one of which was a leopard with four heads that depicted the Grecian Empire, which was to succeed the Medo-Persian Empire. Leopards are known for their speed, which was depicted for the quick conquest the Grecians would have under the leadership of Alexander the Great. When Alexander died in his prime at the age of 33, his four generals divided the empire into four smaller kingdoms. These four kingdoms were depicted by the four heads.

Two years after his vision of the four beasts of chapter seven, Daniel had another vision depicting a ram with two horns and a goat with one horn (Dan. 8:1-5). In the vision, an angel informed Daniel that the ram with two horns represented the combined forces of the Medes and Persians, each horn representing their individual seat of authority (Dan. 8:20). The goat, the angel explained, depicted the Grecians; and the "great horn between his eyes" their "first king," who we know was Alexander (Dan. 8:21).

In his vision, Daniel saw the goat charge toward the ram (Medo-Persia) from the west (Greece) and violently attack the ram, breaking its two horns, signifying Alexander's victory over the Medes and Persians (Dan. 8:5-7). Continuing, the angel said that the "goat waxed very great: and when he was strong (in his prime), the great horn (Alexander) was broken (his death); and for it (in his place) came up four notable ones (four generals) toward the four winds of heaven....Now that being broken, whereas four stood up for it, four kingdoms shall stand up out of the nation" (Dan. 8:8, 22).

The four smaller kingdoms of the fragmented Grecian Empire roughly consisted of the regions of Greece, Asia Minor, Syria, and Egypt. Syria, the largest of the four, stretched across from the Mediterranean Sea north of Israel, all the way to Persia. This kingdom is commonly referred to by historians as the Seleucid Empire, named after General Seleucus I Nictor. Egypt, the second largest of the four, was known as the Ptolemaic Empire, named after General Ptolemy I Soter. Along with Egypt, the boundaries of the Ptolemies included all of North Africa and Israel.

Some of the exploits of these two empires were foretold by the angel, which are recorded in Daniel 11:4-35. In this particular section of Scripture, the Prophet refers to these two empires as the "king of the north" and the "king of the south" in respect to their geographical location to Israel. During the era of these two kingdoms, they periodically engaged in war with one another, with the nation of Israel caught in the middle and falling under the domain of the victor.

Under the Ptolemies, the Jews lived in fairly peaceful conditions. They built synagogues in the city of Alexandria, which developed into a very influential center for Judaism, the religion of the Jews, as they worshipped God under the Old Covenant. At the request of Ptolemy II, seventy Jewish elders skillful in the Hebrew and Greek languages were summoned from Jerusalem to translate the Hebrew Old Testament into Greek. This translation became known as the Septuagint, which proved to be invaluable to the many Greek-speaking Jews and Gentiles around the Mediterranean for many years. Judea (Israel) remained under the control of the Ptolemies from about 323-198 B.C., at which time the Seleucid ruler, Antiochus III, gained supremacy over the region.

■ ■ ■

Returning back now to where we left off in Daniel chapter

eight, we read that out of one of the four Grecian kingdoms, there "came forth a little horn, which waxed exceedingly great, toward the south, and toward the east, and toward the pleasant land (Israel). And it waxed great, even to the host (Jewish priesthood) of heaven; and it cast down some of the host of the stars to the ground, and stamped upon them. Yea, he (little horn) magnified himself even to the prince (high priest) of the host, and by him the daily sacrifice was taken away, and the place of his (position of high priest) sanctuary was cast down. And an host (apostate Jews) was given him (little horn) against the daily sacrifice by reason of transgression, and it cast down the truth to the ground; and it (false religion of little horn) practiced and prospered. Then I heard one saint speaking, and another saint said unto that certain saint which spoke, How long shall be the vision concerning the daily sacrifice, and the transgression of desolation, to give both the sanctuary (Temple) and the host to be trodden under foot? And he said unto me, Unto two thousand and three hundred days; then shall the sanctuary be cleansed" (Dan. 8:9-14).

History recorded this "little horn" to be a Seleucid king, who went by the name Antiochus IV Epiphanes, whose exploits were also foretold in Daniel 11:21-32. In giving himself the name "Epiphanes," which means "glorious one," Antiochus made his claim to divinity. With the help of the king of Pergamene, Antiochus had gained the throne of the Seleucid Empire "by flatteries" and "treachery" (Dan. 11:21).[1] The Pergamene kings were influenced by the religion of Babylon as a result of the Babylonian priesthood fleeing to Pergamum after the invasion of the Medes and Persians.[2] Within time, Pergamum developed into a mini Babylon, of sorts. It may have been what Antiochus saw in Pergamum that influenced his own claim to be divine, as did the Babylonian and Pergamene kings.

In 171 B.C., Antiochus, in fulfillment of Daniel's prophecy, removed the Jewish priests from their office and replaced them with apostate Jews (Dan. 11:21-24). This event marked the beginning of the countdown on the prophetic 2,300 days of the truth being cast down and the defilement of the Temple. Around 167 B.C., he led a military campaign against the king of the south (Ptolemaic king); however, unbeknown to Antiochus, the Ptolemaic king had made a league with the Romans, who around this time had begun to exercise their muscle in the region, causing Antiochus to retreat. Upon his return to his home base in Syria, Antiochus stopped at Jerusalem to vent his anger on the Jews, who he viewed as a rebellious people in his kingdom. In desecrating the Temple even further than he had already, Antiochus ordered for a swine to be sacrificed on the altar, which was an atrocity even to the apostate Jews who worked for him. He also placed an image of the Greek god, Zeus, in the Temple and demanded that all Jews worship him and his god or be killed (Dan. 11:29-31).[3]

In response to Antiochus' madness, some of the good Jews came together to form a militia to fight against him (Dan. 11:32-35). After several years of bloodshed, the good Jews emerged as victors, gaining back control of Jerusalem and the Temple. On the 25th day of the ninth month, known as Chisleu, they dedicated a new altar to replace the one Antiochus had desecrated. The Temple was then ceremonially cleansed and re-dedicated unto the Lord. This event would afterwards be commemorated each year, which they referred to as the "Feast of Dedication" (John 10:22). Today, it is known as Hanukkah (Hebrew "Dedication").

The latter part of Daniel, chapter eleven, abruptly shifts from the exploits of Antiochus to the Antichrist, which is very common in the complex makeup of the end-times prophecies (Dan. 11:36-45; we'll review these later). The same is also the case in Daniel chapter eight, as chapter eleven. And we must keep in mind here that Satan is the main character behind Antiochus' exploits, and it will be Satan who will be the one working through the Antichrist. Even though the things that Antiochus has already done are strikingly similar to what the Antichrist is going to do, the emphasis of the latter part of Daniel chapter eight is on the Antichrist. We saw this also in Daniel chapter nine, where the prophecy jumped from the Caesar of Rome to the Antichrist of the end-times in just one short verse (which we reviewed in chapter one). And, just as Caesar (Roman), and Antiochus (Grecian), were both European, these clues may reveal that the Antichrist, too, will rise out of Europe.

Beginning in Daniel 8:23, it states: "And in the latter time of their (Gentiles') kingdom, when the transgressors are come to the full (end-times), a king (Antichrist) of fierce countenance, and understanding dark sentences, shall stand up. And his power shall be mighty, but not by his own power (Satan's power): and he shall destroy wonderfully, and shall prosper, and practice, and shall destroy the mighty and the holy people. And through his policy also he shall cause craft to prosper in his hand; and he shall magnify himself in his heart, and by peace shall destroy many: he shall also stand up against the Prince (Jesus Christ) of princes; but he shall be broken without hand (by God)...wherefore shut thou up the vision; for it shall be for many days" (Dan. 8:23-26). We'll cover these events in the latter chapters of this book.

■ ■ ■

The resistance that was organized against Antiochus developed into what historians refer to as the "Hasmonean Dynasty." Named after their forefather, Hasmon, the Hasmonean domain, which began in Judea, eventually spread to include the regions of Samaria and Galilee to the north, and Idumea in the south. The name "Idumea" is the Greek rendition of "Edom," which was the name of the region before the Grecian era.

The Edomites were the descendants of Jacob's twin brother, Esau, making them cousins of the Israelites (Gen. 36:1, 9). Jacob

(Israel) had obtained the birthright from the elder Esau, which later resulted in bad blood between the siblings that carried on through their descendants. The conquest of the Hasmoneans, who were Israelites, resulted in a forced conversion, of sorts, of many Edomites to Judaism. The Jews, however, regarded them with deep suspicion and prejudice, calling them "half Jews."

Over time, the Hasmonean Dynasty began to deteriorate over power struggles that resulted in civil war. This, in turn, brought Rome into the region, and thus into Jewish politics. In 63 B.C., the Roman General Pompey entered the city of Jerusalem as conqueror, turning the territory of the Hasmoneans into a Roman province.[4] In 47 B.C., Julius Caesar appointed an Idumean by the name of Antipater to be procurator for the Romans over the regions of Judea, Samaria, and Galilee. After Antipater's death, his son Herod was then recognized by Rome as his father's successor. Later, the Romans conferred on him the title "King of the Jews." The Jews detested having an Edomite rule over them, and even worse that he had been given the title of being their king.

Although King Herod the Great, as he became known, professed to believe in the God of the Jews, he was a heathen in practice and a monster in character. One of his good traits, however, was his passion for architecture. His best effort to try and win over the Jews' acceptance of him was his commitment to renovate the Temple to a magnificent splendor. The Jews welcomed the renovation, but it still didn't change their opinion of Herod, who, in their eyes, had no right to be called "King of the Jews."

■ ■ ■

The Old Testament is primarily the story of God's establishment of, and special relationship to, the nation of Israel. Over a period of about 1,500 years, the Jewish Prophets and writers penned, as they were inspired by God, the Old Testament part of the Bible. During part of the course of that time, God dispersed the Israelites among the other nations as a result of having to chastise them for their many sins. Along with them, however, went the truth of the One and only True God.

The Grecians united the continents of Asia, Europe, and Africa by establishing a universal language. The Romans later built roads, providing a quicker and safer way of travel around the Mediterranean. The world was now ready for the coming of the Messiah, who, as was foretold by the Jewish Prophets, would come to establish the eternal Kingdom of God.

By 4 B.C., nearly 450 years had passed on Daniel's prophetic 490 years since the decree had been issued to rebuild the wall around Jerusalem. This decree began the countdown to the appearing of the Messiah and His death at the expiration of 483 years (Dan. 9:24-26a). The decree, as you may recall, was issued by the Persian King Artaxerxes in the first month of Nisan (Neh. 2:1). It would be in that same month of the Jewish calendar that Christ would be crucified, during the Feast of Passover, exactly 483 years from the decree in fulfillment of the prophecy, and in fulfillment of what the feast had symbolized for 1,500 years.

Just days before Jesus was to be crucified, He warned His disciples of a near future destruction of Jerusalem (Luke 19:43-44). Jesus later went on to tell them: "And when ye shall see Jerusalem compassed with armies, then know that the desolation thereof is nigh...for there shall be great distress in the land, and wrath upon this people (Jews). And they shall fall by the edge of the sword, and shall be led away captive into all nations: and Jerusalem shall be trodden down of the Gentiles (non-Jews), until the times of the Gentiles be fulfilled" (Luke 21:20-24).

Around the year 66 A.D. a false Jewish Messiah had stirred up Messianic fervor among the non-believing Jews giving impetus to an insurrection against Rome's control over Jerusalem. This led to a series of battles between Rome and the Jews which lasted between the years 66-70. Near the end, the Romans had besieged Jerusalem cutting off all food and water supplies causing untold thousands of deaths. In the end the Romans broke down the massive gates of the city using battering rams. Thousands more were then slaughtered and the second Temple was destroyed just as Jesus had foretold. This event was the fulfillment of Daniel 9:26b which we first reviewed in chapter one.

Early in the Jewish revolt of 66, it is commonly believed that the Apostle John and other believers fled Jerusalem as they remembered the Words and warnings of Jesus. It is held that John settled in the Asia Minor (modern Turkey) city of Ephesus where there was already a thriving Christian community due to the missionary efforts of the Apostle Paul. Not far from Ephesus the cities of Smyrna, Pergamum, Thyatira, Sardis, Philadelphia and Laodicea had thriving churches of their own. It is said that John served as bishop over these churches for over 30 years.

During those years the Church greatly multiplied as many Gentiles turned to faith in Christ and renounced the pagan religion of Rome. The Christians' repeated rejection of Roman customs brought them into frequent conflicts with hostile crowds and Roman authorities. As a result, a severe persecution broke out upon the saints around the year 95 A.D. During that time the Apostle John was apprehended and taken to the Isle of Patmos which the Romans used to banish certain prisoners from society. While there the Lord appeared to John in a vision and told him to write what he was about to be shown and send it to the seven churches in Asia Minor (Rev. 1:9-11).

In chapters two and three of the book of Revelation we find what is referred to by Christians as "The seven letters to the seven churches." In the letters the Lord addresses each church on various issues which included warnings, encouragements and admonishments. Included in the Lord's address to the church in Pergamum He said "I know thy works, and where thou dwellest, even where Satan's seat is: and thou holdest fast my name, and hast not denied my faith, even in those days wherein Antipas was my faithful martyr, who was slain among you, where Satan dwelleth" (Rev. 2:13).

The reference to Satan's seat here is to be taken literally and not figuratively. Satan's abode is upon the earth from where he oversees his objectives in deceiving mankind and gratifies his desire to be worshipped. Jesus saw fit to point out where Satan's seat was then for good reason. How long had it been there and why will be examined in the next chapter. And, if Satan's seat was in Pergamum in the first century, then where is it today in the twenty-first century? Also, does Bible prophecy reveal that Satan's seat may even one day be in Jerusalem? We'll be looking into these things plus much, much more throughout the remainder of this book.

4

SATAN'S SEAT

Beginning at the Tower of Babel, the religion of Babylon grew into a bureaucracy of priests who ministered the ceremonial rites of a religion that worshipped their kings as gods. The Scriptures reveal this in Daniel 3:1-7, where the Babylonian King Nebuchadnezzar had a golden image made of himself and decreed for all to bow to it or be put to death. There is also evidence in the Scriptures that shows us how the religion of Babylon influenced other nearby cultures, as in the case involving the king of Tyrus (Ezek. 28:1-9). However, the Scriptures are also very clear that it is Satan who is the real (though invisible) culprit behind the follies of these human kings (Ezek. 28:12-19). For it is Satan who desires to be worshipped as God and he gratifies that desire through men (Matt. 4:9).

When the Medes and Persians overthrew the Babylonians, the priesthood of the Babylonian religion fled to far away Pergamum in western Asia Minor. As a result, a mini-Babylonish kingdom developed, which became known as the Pergamene kingdom, with the city of Pergamum as its capital. The kingdom was governed by a dynasty of self-deified kings known as the "Attalids," who occupied their throne in the spirit of Babylon.[1]

Gradually, the religion of Babylon spread deep into the nearby Greek and Roman cultures. In 175 B.C., it was the king of Pergamene who helped the evil Antiochus IV Epiphanes usurp the throne of the Seleucid Empire by treachery (being greatly influenced, perhaps by the religion of Pergamene, Antiochus later added the title "Epiphanes" which means "glorious one," implying divinity).[2]

In 133 B.C., the king of Pergamene, Attalus III, bequeathed

his kingdom in his will to Rome. By this time, Rome was being recognized as an emerging superpower by the surrounding nations, who began to fear them. The bequeathal, nevertheless, was a cleverly devised scheme by Satan in his quest to be worshipped on a bigger and grander scale, and to build a new and bigger Babylon.[3]

Midway into the first century B.C., the Roman General Pompey had secured all of Asia Minor, Syria, and Judea, turning them into provinces of the Roman Republic. Julius Caesar secured the region of Gaul, and then later fought with Pompey in a civil war over the dictatorship until his assassination in 44 B.C. by his own senate. Subsequently, more civil war ensued with Julius' son and heir, Octavious (Augustus), emerging as victor.

Throughout the Roman world, Augustus was highly praised for the peace and prosperity of the Republic. The Roman Republic was vast, with many races and languages, and was in need of a strong, unifying principle. By this time, the Babylonian religion had virtually saturated most of the Republic and Augustus began to be worshipped as a god. In 29 B.C., the Roman senate proclaimed Augustus Caesar "Lord of the Roman world," conferring on him the title "Pontifix Maximus," high priest, king, and god. Augustus then terminated the Republic and officially inaugurated the Roman Empire.[4]

The city of Pergamum was chosen by Rome to be the capital of the province of Asia Minor and seat of the Roman proconsul. In 29 B.C., Pergamum was the first to erect a temple to the worship of Caesar/Satan. Priests and priestesses were elected or appointed by the state to conduct the ceremonial rites of the religion. Within time, temples were erected in other leading cities where all Roman citizens were compelled to appear at the temple once a month to burn a pinch of incense and confess that "Caesar is Lord." Midway into the first century A.D., the spirit of Babylon was in full swing throughout the empire. By this time, Christianity had gained significant converts who were declaring that

"Jesus is Lord," which stirred up contention with the Roman citizens who worshipped Caesar (Acts 17:7).

By late in the first century, Christians had become even more numerous throughout the empire. For many years Rome had viewed Christianity as just another sect of Judaism that enjoyed religious freedom under a treaty with Rome. Once Christianity was recognized as a separate religion from Judaism, Rome declared it to be an illegal secret society, forbidden under Roman law. In 95 A.D., Rome decreed the death penalty for all violators of the state religion, primarily to go after the Christians. Thousands of the harmless sheep of Christ were then either murdered, imprisoned, and/or banished into exile. The brunt of the persecution was felt mostly in Rome and surrounding Italy.[5] Other than Rome, the Christians in Pergamum, where the Babylonian cult was first highly promoted, were greatly affected by the persecution as well. It was there that "Antipas," a disciple of Christ, was killed; and where Satan was still content to have his seat (Rev. 2:13), but shortly hereafter, obviously, have it in Rome.

This marked the beginning of Rome's persecution of the saints for their refusal to bow to Caesar/Satan. In the next two centuries, many more outbreaks of persecution would follow with periodic interruptions of calm. Nevertheless, the Church of Jesus Christ continued to greatly multiply, despite the numerous and sometimes extremely violent, horrifying efforts of Satan to destroy them. This, in turn, caused the Devil to resort to a more clever scheme against Christianity.

■ ■ ■

Early in the development of Christianity, the symbol of the cross began appearing in Christian circles as an emblem depicting their future hope, which rested upon the crucified, but risen Savior. This was also a constant reminder to the Devil of his defeat and future destiny in the Lake of Fire. Knowing the importance of the symbol to the saints, the Devil decided to use it as a means of deception to inaugurate his new scheme during the course of a civil war in the Roman Empire. Allegedly, the then Roman emperor, Constantine the Great (306-337), claimed that he saw a vision of a cross sitting above the sun, with the words "by this sign conquer" written above it.[6] That night, the emperor claimed that Christ appeared to him in a dream and instructed him to make the figuration of the cross to be carried at the frontline of battle, and he would win the war. Constantine did as he was told and won. He credited his victory to the God of the Christians, and allegedly became a believer himself.

Note: The Bible informs us that Satan can transform himself into an angel of light and that he is capable of performing "signs and wonders" to deceive; powers he used, I believe, to deceive Constantine (2 Cor. 11:14; 2 Thes. 2:9).

In the year 313, Constantine issued the "Edict of Toleration" granting freedom of religion to all, with Christianity being the primary benefactor. In 325, he issued a general exhortation to his aristocracy to embrace the God of the Christians; however, most refused. In response, Constantine moved his capital from Rome to Byzantium renaming it Constantinople, "The New Rome of the New Christian Empire."[7] Later in that same year, he called for a Church Council to be held in Nicea and summoned the then bishops of Rome, Alexandria, and Antioch. Constantine presided over the meeting in a self-imposed display of headship over the Church. At first, this all appeared to be a great victory for the true saints, but later would prove contrary to the notion. Also, at the Council of Nicea, Constantine began enacting a series of edicts against the Jews, who he considered to be an "evil perverse sect...and murderers of the Lord," which led to a long line of professing Christian leaders labeling the Jews "Christ killers."[8]

The Roman emperor, Theodorius (378-395), later made

Christianity the official state religion, making church membership compulsory (as it was with Caesar worship). The forced conversions to this false Christianity filled this false church with unrepentant, unregenerate souls who were not true followers of Christ. Gradually, the Babylonian religion of the empire would slowly drape itself with this new, satanic version of Christianity. The Apostle Paul would refer to it as "another Gospel" and "another Jesus" and not the Gospel nor the Jesus that he preached if he were around at that time (Gal. 1:6-12; 2 Cor. 11:1-4).

Note: At the close of the Apostolic Age, churches were independent of one another, with each being shepherded by a local pastor who served under a regional bishop. The Church was founded to be a witness-bearing institution of Christ, not an organization that forced the teachings of Jesus upon its subjects. Before Constantine's time, Christian worship services were simple assemblies. With the infiltration of Babylonianism, the new, devilish form of Christianity developed into elaborate, stately imposed ceremonies. Nevertheless, as always, God still had a faithful remnant of that era who kept the torch of truth burning.

In the year 395, the Roman Empire split, with Rome as the capital in the west and Constantinople the east. Despite the breakup, both continued in the practice of the new, false Christianity, with slight variations. Out of the ruins of the Western Empire developed what is known today as the Roman Catholic Church. Out of the East developed what we know today as the Eastern Orthodox Church, which is also the same as Greek and Russian Orthodox Christianity.

Some historians consider Leo I (440-461), bishop of Rome, to be the first official Pope. The title "Pope" derived from the Greek word "pappa" meaning "father." Leo proclaimed himself head of the whole Church, advocating universal Papacy. He also instituted celibacy upon the Roman priesthood, which created an atmosphere of sexual immorality that continues among the pretenders to our present time.[9] The Apostle Paul had warned in advance that "in the latter times some shall depart from the faith, giving heed to seducing spirits, and doctrines of devils...Forbidding to marry..." (1 Tim. 4:1-3). There is no doubt that God, who knows *the end from the beginning*, had the Babylonian Church in mind when He influenced Paul to pen the above passage.

In 476, the Western Empire collapsed under pressure from repeated attacks from the Germanic peoples known as the Barbarians. The Pope then became a more commanding figure, which was the intent of Satan in forming his false Christian church. What was once the territory of the Western Empire was now broken up into smaller Germanic kingdoms, furnishing the Pope the opportunity to make advantageous alliances.

Pope Zacharias (741-752) was instrumental in making Pepin, father of Charlemagne, king of the Franks, who were a Germanic people occupying western Germany. At the request of Pope Steven II (752-757), Pepin led his army into central Italy, overthrowing the Lombards and giving their land to the Pope. This was the beginning of what is known as the "Papal States," giving the Pope civil and spiritual primacy over his subjects. From Babylon to Pergamene to the Roman Caesars, the headship of the Babylonian religion (Pontifix Maximus, high priest, king, and god) had now been passed to the Pope, the self-proclaimed head of the Christian Church.

Charlemagne succeeded his father, Pepin, whose realm of authority included what is today Germany, France, Switzerland, Austria, Hungary, Belgium, and part of both Spain and Italy. Without delay, Charlemagne confirmed the civil and religious authority of the Pope. In return, Pope Leo III (795-816) recognized the king's authority, thus combining the two powers into what historians have dubbed the "Holy Roman Empire."

Pope Nicholas I (858-867) was the first to wear a crown. To promote his universal authority, Nicholas used, with great effect, the Pseudo-Isidorian Decretals, which had mysteriously appeared around 857.[10] These documents allegedly were written by Christian Councils of the second century, but were in fact deliberate forgeries made up by the pretenders. In the documents, the Papacy was made to appear to be a lineage that went all the way back to the Apostle Peter.

The Pope has now for many centuries proclaimed he is the successor to the Apostle Peter who the Roman Church claims was the first Pope. They base their claim on Matthew 16:18-19 where Jesus said to Peter "...thou art Peter, and upon this rock I will build my church..." (Matt. 16:18). The Greek word for "Peter" is *"petros"* (meaning a small stone), and the Greek word for "rock" is *"petra"* (meaning a huge stone). The "rock" foundation that Jesus was referring to building His Church on was not Peter himself, but Peter's earlier confession of Jesus that "Thou art the Christ, the Son of the living God" (Matt. 16:16). And contrary to the lie of the Babylonian Church, the Apostle Peter had a Divine foreboding toward those who would come after him who would "lord themselves over God's heritage" instead of "being examples to the flock" (1 Peter 5:3).

Pope Innocent III (1198-1216) conferred on himself the title "Vicar of Christ," supreme sovereign over the entire Church and the world. He ordered two Crusades (Rome's military campaigns against the Muslims for control of Jerusalem, 1095-1291) and took full control of the empire, resulting in much bloodshed. He later established the confessional booth, primarily for his subjects to inform on heretics (in this case true Christians) — and anyone, for that matter, who opposed his authority. He forbade the reading of the Bible by the lay folk, claiming that only his priests could relay the Scriptures and their meaning to the masses. Innocent also instituted what is known as the "Inquisition" for the extermination of Jews and true believers of Christ, whom the Babylonian Church claimed were not, and had them hunted down like wild game. The blood that was shed at the order of the

Popes rivaled the worst of persecutions ordered by the Caesars.[11] And no marvel, for there's no difference in Pope and Caesar, for they are in fact one and the same; just new clothes and new title, but same spirit of antichrist.

The Inquisition was called the "Holy Office," but there was nothing holy about it. It was Babylon's court for the detection and punishment of all who would not adhere to the Pope's religion. Anyone suspected was liable to torture, imprisonment, and/or to be burned alive at the stake. The victim's property and assets were then confiscated, making the Babylonian Church "filthy" rich. Hard for some to believe who live in the civilized world of the twenty-first century, but it is true, nevertheless. As a matter of fact, if given the opportunity, the Babylonian Church of today would not hesitate to reactivate the now dormant "Holy Office." In the not-so-distant future — according to the prophetic Scriptures — they will indeed get that chance and do it all over again, under the auspices of the Antichrist, whom the Scriptures declare to be the "man of sin" (2 Thes. 2:3).

Pope Boniface VIII (1294-1303), in his famous Papal decree *Unam Santam,* declared "That it is altogether necessary for salvation that every soul be subject to the Roman Pontiff."[12] Pope Sixtus IV (1471-1484) sanctioned the Spanish Inquisition, wherein thousands of Jews and true Christians were tortured and murdered in the name of the Babylonian Jesus. He also decreed that giving money to the church would free a loved one's soul from purgatory (a false teaching of the Roman Church that states that one's soul must pass through fire after they die to be purified before entering Heaven). But if someone were to donate a certain sum of money to the church on behalf of the departed, then the Pope would pray for the deceased and have their soul released from the flame into Heaven. Sixtus used the Papacy to enrich himself and his relatives, who rivaled the Caesars in pomp and wealth. Pope Innocent VIII (1484-1492) multiplied church offices and sold them to the highest bidder for vast sums of money.

He decreed the extermination of the true Christian folks known as the "Waldenesses." Many were burned alive at the stake in a public square and made the occasion for Babylonian festivities.[13]

■ ■ ■

Throughout the Dark Ages and beyond, Satan managed to keep the light of truth from the masses through the efforts of the Roman Church. Up to around the early sixteenth century, the Papacy had virtually gone unchallenged due to fear of torture, imprisonment, and/or death. That all changed, however, due to the courage of Martin Luther (1483-1546), a Roman Catholic monk. One day in 1508, while reading the book of Romans, a peace suddenly overtook him when he read: "The just shall live by faith" (Rom. 1:17). It dawned on Luther that salvation was by faith in Christ alone, and not the sacramental rites administered by the Roman Church as they claim.

In that same year, Luther took on a job as a teacher at the University of Wittenburg. In 1511, he went to Rome and was sickened by the corruption and vice of the Papal Court. Returning to Wittenburg, he began to preach sermons from the Bible, attracting large crowds from all over Germany. On October 31, 1517, Luther posted his famous *95 Theses* on the door of the Catholic Church in Wittenburg, nearly all of which attacked the authority of the Pope and Indulgences. Indulgences were another invention of the Roman Church to fill its treasury to support its huge appetite for wealth and pomp. They were sold for money, offering forgiveness of sins without one's confession or repentance. Others were offered Indulgences for joining Crusades or for hunting down heretics. Pope Sixtus IV was the first to sell Indulgences to have someone released from purgatory, which is still practiced by the Roman Church today.[14]

In 1517, the Pope sent John Tetzel throughout Germany selling certificates signed by the Pope, offering full pardon for sins.

This horrified the then 34-year-old Luther. By 1520, Luther was the most popular man in Germany. Copies of his *95 Theses* were eagerly sought all over the country, which ignited a blaze of light exposing the dark nature of the Papacy. In 1520, Pope Leo X issued a decree declaring that Luther retract his *95 Theses* within sixty days or be put to death. When Luther received the notice, he burned it publicly on December 10th. On that day, the people recognized that a new era had indeed begun.

In the early days of his ministry, Luther was sure the Jews would be delighted with his revised form of Christianity and join him in his endeavor against the Roman Church. He began to speak favorably of the Jews and their contribution to Christianity. However, after centuries of persecution from the Catholic Church, the Jews were suspicious of Luther's brand of Christianity as well. This, in turn, caused Luther to release vicious Jew-hating statements such as in his tract entitled *Concerning the Jews and Their Lies*. His publications, unfortunately, would later provide Adolf Hitler with many suitable texts in his twentieth century quest to rid Europe of all Jews.[15]

By 1540, all of northern Germany was protesting against the Babylonish Church. Although many had already been protesting against Rome's false Christianity for centuries, it is here where the name "Protestant" first began to appear. Pope Paul III (1534-1549) waged war against the Protestants in Germany by providing King Charles V with an army, which had been formed by the offering of Indulgences. The war lasted from 1546-55, ending with the Lutherans winning legal recognition of their own religion.

In the Netherlands, the Protestant action was second behind Germany, which was also under the domain of Charles V. Lutheran writings were ordered to be burned and religious gatherings, where the Bible was read, were prohibited. Charles decreed death by fire to all Anabaptists, who were a group of true Christians who had denounced their infant baptism by the Roman

Church and advocated the adult baptism of the Scriptures. Charles also prohibited the printing or possession of the Bible. His son and successor, Philip II, continued his father's edicts, and with Jesuit help, carried them out with great fury. Under Charles and Philip, over one hundred thousand Protestants were brutally massacred. They were thrown into dungeons, tortured, and then burned alive at the stake.

The Jesuits were a created office of the Roman Church to counter the Protestant Movement. Its resolve was to bring the masses into absolute obedience to the Pope. Their objective included the recovering of territory lost to the Protestants and to bring the whole world into subjection to Rome. In France, they were responsible for the St. Bartholomew's massacre, persecution of the Hugenots, revocation of the Toleration Edict of Nantes, and the French Revolution. In Spain, the Netherlands, south Germany, Bohemia, Austria, Poland, and elsewhere, they led in the slaughter of untold thousands of victims.[16] By their evil methods, they virtually halted the Protestant Movement and saved the Papacy from utter ruin.

Pope Urban VIII (1623-1644), with Jesuit aid, totally blotted out the Protestants in Bohemia. Pope Clement XI (1700-1721) declared that kings would reign only by his sanction and issued an edict against Bible reading. Pope Leo XII (1821-1829) condemned religious freedom, Bible Societies, and Bible translating. He declared that everyone separated from the Roman Church had no part in eternal life. Pope Gregory XVI (1831-1846) promoted Papal infallibility, which had developed over time with Papal assertion, claiming that the Pope was incapable of error, thus making himself equal to God. Pope Pius IX (1846-1878) upheld Papal infallibility and declared that every dogma of the Roman Catholic Church had been dictated by Christ to the Popes. He also declared that Protestantism was not Christianity. He decreed the "Immaculate Conception of Mary, Queen of Heaven, Blessed Virgin and Mother of God."[17]

Catholics are taught that Mary was miraculously conceived, as was Christ in her own womb, thus making her equal to Christ. They are also taught that Mary remained a virgin after giving birth to Jesus, which is a clear contradiction of Scriptures because Mary and Joseph did consummate their marriage after Jesus' birth, which resulted in children (Mark 6:3; Matt. 13:55-56). Catholics celebrate what is known as the "Feast of the Immaculate Conception" on December 8th each year, where the Pope lays a wreath at the Pedestal of the statue of Mary in the Piazza Di Spagna. They also celebrate what is known as the "Assumption of Mary" on August 15th when, they believe, Mary ascended into Heaven without dying, where she now serves as co-redeemer with Christ in the saving of souls.

The worship of Mary derived from the Romans' worship of Diana whose roots trace back to the Babylonian worship of Ishtar.[18] Each year, the Romans held a festival to this goddess, and silversmiths made much gain from selling small images of her (Acts 19:24-27). Likewise, today, the selling of small images of Mary brings in millions of dollars each year. The images are used by Catholics in the making of small shrines in their homes or cars, where incense is burned and prayers are lifted up to Mary, Queen of Heaven.

■ ■ ■

From the year 754, the Popes had been civil rulers over their kingdom, called the Papal States. Pope Pius IX guarded the Papal States with the help of ten thousand French soldiers. When war broke out between France and Germany, the soldiers were recalled in 1870. The then king of Italy took possession of Rome and added the territory of the Papal States to Italy. This humiliated the Pope, who had proclaimed Rome to be the "New Jerusalem" and who had decreed their total sovereignty over all the world.

In 1929, the Pope's power was somewhat restored by the Italian government in what is known as the "Lateran Treaty." In the treaty, the Pope was allotted 108.7 acres of land inside Rome, from where both Caesars and Popes ruled their empires as if in the seat of God over the world. The deep spiritual truth of the matter is that they indeed did, and do, sit in the seat of a god — *their* god, who is Satan; as it is in Rome where Satan established his seat long ago, and where he obviously is content to have it for the moment. This carved out piece of real-estate in the center of Rome that is owned by the Pope is known as "Vatican City." Totally surrounded by Italy, Vatican City is not part of the Italian government. It is an independent nation of its own right, just like Italy itself. And, just like other nations of the world, the Vatican exchanges ambassadors with virtually every other nation on earth and is very politically involved in worldly interests and affairs.

The Papacy arose from the ruins of the Roman Empire and in the name of "another Jesus" — not the Jesus of the Bible — they occupy their throne in the spirit of the ancient Babylonian kings and Roman Caesars. This was confirmed when they made their claim to infallibility, which they have not denounced and still hold to today. From Babylon to Pergamene to Rome, then on to the Pope, the head of the religion of Babylon is now cleverly dressed in a deceptive cloak of Christianity — a false Christianity, that is. From Pope infallibility, the worship of Mary, the veneration of images, purgatory, infant baptism, priests and nuns, and the confessional booth, to the claim of the Roman Church alone possessing the power on earth to forgive sins, and the like — all are what Jesus would refer to as "commandments and doctrines of men" (Mark 7:7).

By shrewd political alliance, deception, armed force, and bloodshed, the Papacy has maintained its power. Through the sale of offices, confiscation of wealth from its murdered victims, and the selling of Indulgences, the Papacy collected vast amounts of revenue, enabling it to maintain the most luxurious court in Europe. Over the years, however, the Papacy was forced to change along with the ever-changing world it is aligned with. Nevertheless, the Roman Catholic Church is still as evil and deceptive as ever. Only the tactics by which it survives have changed.

In 1962, Pope John XXIII launched what is known as the "Ecumenical Movement," which has gained impressive impetus since it began. The movement was devised by the Vatican in an attempt to gain the confidence of the Protestants, whom they refer to as the "Separated Brethren" and "Bible Believers," (the latter of which I take as a compliment). The Papacy still believes they are the only true church and that for salvation all must come under the authority of the Roman Pontiff.

Some of the Protestant groups that formed after the bloodshed of their forefathers are drifting farther and farther from the teachings of the Bible, and thereby are turning apostate. It is these groups who are making the ecumenical effort of the Vatican appear to be a success. These groups have now reached out to receive the Papacy with open arms as if they're a true Christian sect. Under the auspices of Rome and the World Council of Churches, the false Christian churches are all coming together under one umbrella of condemnation at a rapid pace to complete what the Bible refers to as "Babylon the Great" of the last-days (Rev. 17:5).

The majority of the world is oblivious to the history and evil nature of the Roman Church — primarily its own members. As the modern world developed, Satan was forced to change his tactics time and time again. In 1978, the Devil placed Pope John Paul II on the throne of Babylon to make the Papacy appear to be good to a world that was watching the Vatican more closely than ever. On May 13, 1981, Pope John Paul was shot during a celebration in honor to Mary, to whom he was deeply devoted. After surviving the assassination attempt, Pope John Paul credited

Mary for saving his life. When he died in 2005, a large "M" was tacked onto the top of his coffin in honor to his god.

On April 19, 2005, Cardinal Joseph Ratzinger was elected as the new Pope and chose the name Benedict XVI for his Pope name. Ratzinger, who is from Germany, attended Hitler's Nazi youth camp training during the pre-WWII era. His first day in office as the new Pope was April 20th, Hitler's birthday. On that same day, Pope Benedict stated in his speech during Mass that "The most important issue facing the church is the unity of all Christians and to reach out to other religions." Okay, let me translate that for you, because these guys have mastered the art of "beating around the *burning* bush," so to speak. What he means is that unless the Protestants return to Mother Rome, and other religions of the world convert to Catholicism, then they are doomed to Hell. In March of 2006, Pope Benedict dropped "Patriarch of the West" from the list of official titles for the Pope, because it implied a limited jurisdiction. In July of 2007, CBN reported that he publicly stated that the Roman Catholic Church is the only way of salvation.

On February 28, 2013, Pope Benedict abdicated from the Papacy stating that his frail health was preventing him from keeping pace with the rigorous demands of the Papal office. He was the first Pope to resign in 600 years. Many believe that his resignation was, in part, due to what became known as the "Vatileaks Scandal." Pope Benedict's butler, Paolo Gabriele, tired of "seeing evil and corruption everywhere in the church" leaked out sensitive documents to Italian reporter Gianluigi Nuzzi. In 2012, Nuzzi's blockbuster book *His Holiness: The Secret Papers of Pope Benedict XVI* was released exposing the corruption and scandal in the church.[19]

On March 13, 2013, Cardinal Jorge Bergoglio of Argentina (whose parents were Italian) was elected as Pope, and chose the name Francis. Argentina was a chief recipient of Nazi personnel and capital in the post-WWII era. Many Nazis ended up as active participants in the Argentine security, police, and military and helped to shape the development of these institutions. Argentine President Nestor Kirchner was the son of a Nazi.[20] Pope Francis was the first Jesuit, and the first South American elected to the coveted office. In his opening address to the enormous crowd waiting in St. Peter's Square, and those watching by television, Pope Francis proclaimed to his 1.2 billion followers that the first thing he was going to do later that evening was to "Pray to Mary for our (Catholics') protection."

The Papacy of the future will involve more changes that will be dictated by the changing world it seeks to dominate. The Vatican is being dressed by Satan in preparation to form a union with the coming Antichrist. For a brief period of time, this union will be a revival, of sorts, of the Holy Roman Empire where German kings and Popes ruled side by side exercising brutal force upon their subjects. During that time, a relentless campaign of death will be unleashed against the Jews, Great Tribulation Christians, and any and all who oppose the Antichrist's authority. For now, however, the Roman Catholic Church is just playing the role of a Sleeping Beauty as she waits for her Prince of Darkness to come and kiss her, to awaken her to reveal her true satanic nature for the entire world to behold for the last and final time. We will look more closely into these events in the latter chapters of this book.

5

JERUSALEM RISING

Several hundred years following the Tower of Babel dispersion, God called Abraham to leave his kinfolk and move his family into the land of Canaan, where, the Lord said, "I will make of thee a great nation (Israel), and I will bless thee, and make thy name great; and thou shalt be a blessing: And I will bless them that bless thee, and curse him that curseth thee: and in thee (Israel) shall all families of the earth be blessed (with God's Word, the Bible, and the living Word Jesus Christ)" (Gen. 12:1-5). As the story unfolded, the Lord promised Abraham to give his seed (Israel) the entire stretch of land along the Mediterranean coastline, from the Wadi el-Arish River in Egypt to the Euphrates River in Syria (Gen. 15:18). However, in all of the nation of Israel's history, they may have never actually possessed all of the promised real-estate. In part — a big part — would have been due to their failure to obey all the Lord's commands and heed His many warnings.

Through Moses, the Lord had warned the children of Israel from the start to be sure they observed all of God's laws and statutes. Failure to do so would result in them being uprooted out of their land and scattered among the other nations (Lev. 26:14-33). Nevertheless, the Lord promised that in the event this did occur, if they repented and turned to the Lord in the land of their exile, then the Lord would remember His covenant with them and restore them back to their land, even if this were to be the case in the "latter days," which God knew it would (Deut. 4:23-31).

Under the leadership of Moses' successor, Joshua, the Israelites conquered and divided the Promised Land among the twelve tribes of Israel. King David later extended the borders of Israel, and his son, Solomon, built up the kingdom of Israel from within, including the first Temple. During the reign of Solomon's son, Rehoboam, the kingdom split in two, resulting in the formation of the northern kingdom of Israel and the southern kingdom of Judah.

As a result of the divided kingdoms backsliding into idol worship, the Lord raised up Prophet after Prophet to warn both sides. After suffering long with His elect, the Lord allowed the Assyrians to conquer the northern kingdom of Israel, which resulted in them being scattered among the other nations as the Lord had said would happen. Not long afterwards, a similar fate fell upon Judah when the Babylonians invaded, destroyed the Temple, and took many captives back to Babylon.

After seventy years in Babylon, the Jews were allowed to return to their land by the decree of the Persian King Cyrus, following the Medo-Persian victory over the Babylonians. A mandate to their release and return was that they "build the house of the Lord" (Ezra 1:1-11). After returning to Jerusalem, the Jews laid the foundation for the second Temple around 535 B.C., in the second month of Iyar, just as Solomon had done with the first Temple centuries earlier (2 Chron. 3:2; Ezra 3:8). Centuries later, the Romans destroyed the second Temple in 70 A.D. and again the Jews were dispersed among the nations, but this time it was for their rejection of their Messiah, as Jesus had foretold and forewarned them (Luke 21:6, 20-24). Afterwards, the Romans renamed the land of Israel to Palestine in an attempt to rid the land of its identification with the Jewish people. Nevertheless, the Prophet Isaiah foretold that in the last-days the Lord would "set his hand again the second time" to restore Israel back in their land, and that it would be a "sign" to the nations of the validity of God's Word (Isa. 11:11-12).

■ ■ ■

For nearly two thousand years, the Jews had painfully yearned to return to their rightful God-given land. During those years, they encountered periodic outbreaks of persecution, most of which came at the hands of the Popes, who had dubbed the Jews "Christ killers."[1] Late in the nineteenth century, however, the hand of Providence ignited the hearts of His elect to return to their homeland beginning what is known as the "Zionist Endeavor."

Zionism was the movement for the national revival and independent statehood of the Jewish people in their biblical homeland of Israel. The name "Zionism" derived from the biblical word "Zion," which is a reference to the Holy Land, primarily Jerusalem (Zech. 8:3). A renowned Zionist, Moses Hess (1812-1875), in his book *Rome and Jerusalem* (1862), advocated the establishment of an independent Jewish state for the economic and social normalization of the Jewish people. Zionist Rabbi Hirsch Kalischer (1795-1874) taught that the Messiah would come only after the Jewish people were reassembled back inside biblical Israel. Rabbi Judah ben Solomon (1798-1878) preached the return to Zion for the Jews within the framework of traditional religious thought, but later developed elements held by the non-religious Jews who contributed greatly to the Zionist Movement. Yehuda Leib Pinsker (1821-1891) in his book *Auto Emancipation* (1882) argued that an emancipation granted by others could not solve the problem of the Jewish people, and that only territorial concentration and sovereignty could create normal circumstances.

The renowned Zionist, Dr. Theodor Herzl (1860-1904), after considering various solutions for the Jewish people, concluded that the Jews must leave the lands of their dispersion and become a state again of their own. In his famous book *The Jewish State* (1896), Herzl explained that the Jewish problem could not be solved by assimilation due to the strong existence of both anti-Semitism (hatred of Jews) and the Jewish will to survive. Herzl argued that Jews would never be accepted in foreign lands, and even if they were, they would still continue to yearn for Zion. The plight of the Jews, he stressed, could only be resolved by the establishment of an independent Jewish state with the consent of the greater powers. Herzl later described the state he envisioned in his book *Old-New Land* (1902).

Herzl was the first to translate into the political arena by establishing the "World Zionist Organization" (WZO). The WZO held its first congress in Basle, Switzerland, in 1897, carrying out diplomatic activities among the then more relevant powers of Germany and the Turkish Ottoman Empire who, at the time, occupied Palestine. Jewish settlement activities had already begun in Palestine around 1881, which heralded the start of practical Zionism. With the introduction of political Zionism, the combined approach of both practical and political Zionism greatly enhanced the Zionist Endeavor in Palestine. This combined approach was aided by the exploits of renowned Zionist, Professor Chaim Weizmann.

Throughout its history, the Zionist Movement had to decide among various options. These decisions were sometimes preceded by fierce debates. Some decisions, however, were coerced by events such as WWI or by the acts of individual leaders such as Weizmann. The Zionist leaders in Britain, most notably Weizmann, had started in 1915 to pursue a moderate pro-British orientation to gain Britain's support for the Zionist cause. By the end of WWI, the British had gained a prominent foothold in Palestine, which had been under the domain of the Turks for many years. Due to the efforts of Weizmann, the "Balfour Declaration" was signed by the British on November 2, 1917, on behalf of the Zionist Endeavor. While the declaration did not fulfill all the expectations of the Zionists, it did pave the way for extensive Jewish immigration and development in Palestine.[2]

By 1917, there were already about 70,000 Jews living in Palestine, which caught the attention of the then League of Nations. In 1920, the League of Nations issued a British mandate over Palestine, in part to oversee the Jews living there. British authorities recognized the WZO as the official agency to implement Zionist interests in Palestine, and it was statehood which topped the list of the WZO agenda. The 1920 mandate, however, had injected British authorities with the high hopes of a permanent rule over Palestine, and a Jewish state wasn't at the top of their list of things to do.

The large-scale immigration and Jewish settlement began to provoke violent Arab reactions, which caused the British to attempt to implement new immigration and land purchase policies. Due to vehement Jewish protests led by Weizmann, however, no new policies were enforced at that time. As a result of the Arab response, the Jews then began to recognize their need to arm themselves to protect their livelihood. The organization most credited for bringing in Jews to Israel was the Jewish Agency. Out of the various militias that developed early on, the Jewish Agency's Haganah (Defense) was the largest.[3]

Hitler's rise to power in Germany in 1933 gave new impetus to Jewish immigration to Palestine. In July of that same year, the then Vatican Secretary of State, Eugenio Pacelli, negotiated with the Nazi regime, securing an agreement to protect Vatican interest. Pacelli, who would later become Pope Pius XII, is believed to have received intelligence of Hitler's intentions for a Third Reich similar to Germany's First Reich of the days of the Holy Roman Empire (Germany's Second Reich [1871-1918] was known as the "Bismarck's Empire"). In the agreement struck between the Vatican and Hitler, the Roman Catholic Church was granted freedom to profess and practice their religion, the right for the Vatican to govern itself, assured recognition of its legal status and property, and its role in education. Hitler's Catholic upbringing had taught him the power of the Roman Catholic Church and the anti-Semitic view held by the Vatican. He thought it best to use the influence of the Vatican to his advantage.[4]

During Hitler's death and destruction campaigns upon thousands of innocent civilians, and the slaughter of six million Jews during WWII, the Vatican sat suspiciously silent throughout it all, even while Jews were rounded up a half of block from the Vatican to be transported to death camps. Following the war, the ties between the Vatican and Hitler were so strong that top Vatican officials helped top Nazi henchmen elude justice by either hiding them or helping them escape to safer havens abroad. This post-WWII movement is a well-documented fact that historians have dubbed the "Vatican Ratlines"—in which a then very young Joseph Ratzinger (later Pope Benedict XVI) was heavily involved under the Papacy of Pope Pius XII. In 2009, Pope Benedict XVI declared Pius XII as "venerable," a step toward granting Hitler's Pope the status of sainthood according to Roman Catholic doctrine.

During the surge of Jewish immigration to Palestine after Hitler's crowning, the Jewish population increased to nearly 450,000. More than any other period of immigration, this one was accompanied by extensive importation of investment capital from wealthy European Jews, which laid the foundation for economic growth and development. The peak year of immigration (1935) was followed by the most intense Arab reaction to-date (1936-39). The revolt left a strong impression on the British, who again were forced to reconsider their policy in the Holy Land. It also left a sense of urgency upon the Jews to create a centrally organized defense system.

The British reaction led to a proposal to partition Palestine that was rejected by the Arabs and which became a controversial issue among the Zionists. In response, the British abandoned the idea of partition and called for an Arab-Jewish roundtable in London for talks. After no agreement was reached, the British, in an effort to appease Arab tensions, issued what is known as the "White Paper" policy in 1939. The policy greatly restricted Jewish immigration and land purchases, and granted Palestinian Arabs independence to be implemented after an interim period; the Arabs would then remain the majority in the region. The temporary illusion of Hitler's success in Europe during WWII brought on a self-imposed suppression of resistance by the Zionists to the new policy, with the exception of illegal immigration. In 1941-42, the danger of a German invasion of the Middle East resulted in the cooperation of the Zionist leadership with the British in the war effort. Over 25,000 Jewish men and women volunteered to serve in the British army out of a then population of about 500,000.

Aspirations for Jewish independence were greatly increased when news of the Holocaust reached the settlers in Zion. In 1944, the Zionist leadership officially announced their demand for a Jewish state, enlisting the support of American Jews and American public opinion. The Zionist leadership in Palestine encouraged the settlers to hope for a change in British policy when the war was over. When the war ended, however, the new Labor government in England continued to implement the White Paper policy, which caused the Zionists to then resume their struggle in full.

The cumulative effect of Jewish resistance, American pressure, and the Jewish refugee problem in Europe, ultimately led the British to submit the Palestine resolve to the United Nations. An international commission of inquiry nominated by the UN General Assembly recommended the partition of Palestine into Jewish and Arab states. The recommendation was adopted in the resolution of November 29, 1947, being supported by more than two-thirds of the member nations. By 1948, the Jewish population in Palestine had grown to more than 700,000. The settlers had established an independent economy with private and public sectors, an education system from kindergarten to universities, a nationwide healthcare system, a tradition and institution of a parliamentary government, and a highly disciplined defense system with a good deal of allied support.[5]

On May 14, 1948, the Zionist leaders proclaimed the statehood of the nation of Israel. On the Jewish calendar the day was Iyar 5, 5707.[6] Eleven minutes after the proclamation, United States President Harry Truman extended diplomatic recognition of Israel. On May 15th, the British had to withdraw their troops. On that same day, Israel was attacked by Egyptian warplanes, which marked the beginning of Israel's "War of Independence." Later Jordan, Syria, Lebanon, Saudi Arabia, and Iraq joined Egypt in the war. Despite insuperable odds, however, Israel prevailed over their enemies and gained more territory in the process.

From the start, Zionism received opposition, such as Britain's desire for permanent dominance in Palestine, the Arab revolts, and Hitler's mad pursuit to systematically exterminate the Jews. However, the real culprit behind all these schemes was Satan, who understands all too clearly the significance of the existence of the statehood of Israel. The nation of Israel is a constant reminder to the Devil that his time is near — the time when he will be taken and cast into the bottomless pit for 1,000 years, then afterwards into the Lake of Fire. The Devil strives in vain to prevent that from occurring, or to at least slow the progress of the inevitable (Rev. 20:1-10).

■ ■ ■

Long before Zionism became practical late in the nineteenth century, the founder of the Russian Empire, Peter the Great (1682-1725), envisioned that the empire's future would never be complete until it extended to the warm shores of Palestine. Two prominent leaders in early twentieth century Russia, Lenin and Stalin (1917-53), opposed all aspects of Zionism and vehemently protested the existence of a Jewish state. Yet in 1947, the then Soviet Union supported the November 29th UN decision to partition Palestine. The decision, however, was nothing more than just a Cold War strategy by the Soviets aimed at expelling the Western imperialist British out of Palestine. Once achieved, the Soviets then retracted from their phony pro-Israel stance and openly denounced the statehood of Israel, claiming it to be a conspiracy against the Soviet Union by the West, primarily the United States.

After Stalin's death in 1953, his successors began taking interest in bringing the nations in Asia and Africa into the Soviet diplomatic arena by exploiting their anti-Western feelings. It was in this context where Moscow adopted a more serious pro-Arab position in the mounting Arab-Israeli conflict. The Soviets then began to encourage Israel's hostile neighbors by selling them arms to beef up their inferior militaries. The first ever Soviet veto was used in 1954 at the UN Security Council to prevent Western resolutions that were against the Arabs, which confirmed the more friendly Soviet/Arab relationship.[7]

Arab-Israeli tensions rose steadily during the mid-1960s due to the constant increase in Jewish casualties that were a result of Arab terrorism. The shelling of Israeli border villages by the Syrians became intense in early 1967. On April 7th, Israeli fighter jets struck at Syrian fighter planes sent to intercept them. Egypt then announced they would not tolerate any further Israeli assaults on Syria, and maneuvered tanks and troops up to Israel's border. The Soviet Union encouraged Egypt in the war preparations, giving them intelligence of Israeli troop concentration near Syria's border. Egypt's president then challenged Israel to war, boasting that his country was now better equipped to defeat them, and threatening their existence again. Leaders in other Arab nations matched Egypt's folly by making similar arrogant statements. In addition to a defense pact with Syria, Egypt also made agreements with Jordan on May 30th, and Iraq on June 4th, resulting in Israel's complete encirclement. The entire Arab coalition was heavily armed with huge supplies of Soviet-made military equipment.[8]

After gathering intelligence of the planned attack, Israel staged a preemptive attack, striking first. On June 5th, Israeli war planes set about to first destroy the coalition's air power before they could even get off the ground. During the first sixteen hours of the war, Israel eliminated 400 fighter jets belonging to Egypt, Syria, and Jordan to the loss of only 19 of their own, gaining total aerial superiority. On June 7th, Israel captured East Jerusalem and the Temple Mount from Jordan, giving them full control of the Holy City. On the Jewish calendar, the day was Iyar 28, 5726.[9] It was a day of major prophetic significance to those, such as myself, who view the world from their prophecy watchtowers, looking for the approaching signs of the end-times. According to the prophetic Scriptures, Jerusalem has to be under full control of the Jews before any other end-times prophecies can come to pass.

> *Note: This event fulfilled the prophecy foretold by Christ that Jerusalem would be under the control of the Gentiles (following the Roman's destruction of Jerusalem in 70 A.D.) until their time was fulfilled (1967) in the last-days (Luke 21:20-24). Christ also stated that when we see this come to pass, then we will know that His return is near and that the generation born when the Gentiles lose control of Jerusalem would not pass until the prophecies pertaining to the end-times up to Christ's Second Coming are fulfilled (Luke 21:28-32). According to the Bible, the average generation would live seventy to eighty years (Ps. 90:10). Seventy years from 1967 brings us to 2037. Therefore, we can look for the end-times prophecies to come to pass sometime before this time expires, or before 2047.*

When the UN Security Council called for a cease-fire, Israel was the first to draw back, followed by Jordan, then Egypt. Syria, the most militant of them all, and who considers themselves the leader against the Zionists, rejected the cease-fire and continued shelling villages inside Israel's borders from their highly strategic Golan Heights position. However, following twenty hours of relentless, uphill fighting by Israeli forces, the Golan Heights was captured, forcing the Syrians to concede. The victory gave Israel a huge military foothold in the event of any future wars with their hostile neighbor.

The war ended on June 10th and entered the history books as the Arab-Israeli "Six-Day War." During the course of the war, Israel had routed three hostile bordering nations who were heavily supported by the Soviet Union, and several Arab nations. In addition to the aircraft Israel destroyed, they also destroyed or captured over 500 tanks. Arab military loss included seventy percent of the heavy equipment of all three nations, valued well over one billion dollars. The war also left the state of Israel over three times its pre-war size.

In the following years, Israeli intelligence noted indications of Egyptian and Syrian troop buildup near their borders. The maneuvers, however, were regarded as just routine exercises, which had been taking place at frequent intervals. This assessment, along with an Israeli understanding that Egypt would not attack again without first having achieved superior air power, was misleading. On Saturday, October 6, 1973, Syria and Egypt launched an attack against Israel, catching them by surprise which they hoped would enhance their chances of success. An added ingredient to the coalition's plan was the day they chose to attack. Not only was it Saturday, the Jewish weekly Sabbath, but it was also the day known as the biblical "Day of Atonement" — the most solemn of holy days on the Jewish calendar known today as "Yom Kippur."

Thinking to catch Israel in a state of non-vigilance, the coalition forces greatly underestimated the highly trained and skilled Israeli Defense Force's ability to quickly mobilize in the event of a surprise attack. On October 12th, the Iraqi army joined Syria in the north, only to be embarrassed by Israel's more superior fighters, who inflicted heavy casualties upon them. On October

13th, Jordanian troops teamed up with the battered Iraqis, but were of little to no help. Once again, the combined forces of Syria, Egypt, Iraq, and Jordan were no match for Israel. Seeing this in advance, the Soviet Union hastily convened a UN Security Council to call for a cease-fire; had they not done so, Israel would have no doubt easily maneuvered their troops into the capitals of both Syria and Egypt, their two arch enemies.

■ ■ ■

Between 1968-78 more than 150 books were published promoting anti-Zionism in the Soviet Union alone. In 1974, the Central Committee of the Communist Party adopted a program of measures to strengthen their propaganda against the Zionists, creating a special committee to fight Zionism in all of its aspects. After a failed attempt in 1965, the Soviet Union, on November 10, 1975, finally succeeded with the UN General Assembly passing resolution 3379, which declared Zionism as racism. The resolution has since been instrumental in turning anti-Zionism into an international concept with a credible public and legal basis. This started the process that many hoped would lead to the de-legitimization of the state of Israel and its subsequent exclusion from the family of nations.[10]

In 1980, Israel proclaimed all of Jerusalem as its capital, which received a mixed international response. Due to the fact that Jerusalem is also venerated by Christians and Muslims, the move was viewed by the Vatican and the Islamic nations as offensive. In 1984, Pope John Paul II openly rejected Jewish sovereignty over Jerusalem, stating that the Holy City should be placed under international supervision. On June 15, 1994, the Vatican duped the Israeli government into signing an agreement granting the Vatican participation in any future negotiations over Jerusalem. In February of 1996, the then Secretary General of the Vatican, Serge Sebastian, announced that Rome recognized

Palestinian sovereignty over East Jerusalem, even though it was under Israeli control. On July 23, 2000, the Pope reiterated the Vatican's position on Jerusalem and attempted to gain international support to have the city placed under the auspices of the United Nations.

The Vatican's position on Jerusalem stems from its dogma that God has rejected the "Christ Killers" and that His program for the Jewish people ended with their rejection of Christ; that the Jews now need to bow the knee to the Pope if they are to be saved. The Vatican proclaims Rome to be the "New Jerusalem" and, as long as the Jews are allowed to have complete sovereignty over the Holy City, it's a complete contradiction to Roman Catholic doctrine.

Throughout the 1980s, the Vatican and the Reagan administration worked together in a covert operation to bring down the Soviet Union. On December 26, 1991, their efforts materialized when the Soviet Union collapsed, giving birth to newly independent nations in Eastern Europe that were once part of the Soviet Union, and turning Russia back into a Republic. Nevertheless, Russia continues to effectively promote anti-Zionism in a wide variety of domestic and foreign policy goals. In some form or fashion, they have successfully managed to use anti-Semitism to stir hatred upon the Jews; however, it is Satan who is the real (though invisible) culprit behind the spreading of anti-Semitism.

In one way or another, anti-Zionism can be found in virtually every nation in the world and is gaining momentum at a prophetically significant pace. Gradually, the world is being satanically influenced to hate the Jewish people more and more as the return of Jesus Christ, the most famous Jew of all, draws nigh. Televisions and newspapers worldwide report the increasing tension that is mounting against Jews, especially in Europe and the Middle East. Soon, this hatred toward the Jews is going to culminate into the time referred to by the Prophet Jeremiah as the "Time of Jacob's (Israel's) Trouble" (Jer. 30:7), which corresponds to what Jesus referred to will be the "Great Tribulation" (Matt. 24:15-21).

In referring to the precarious conditions surrounding Jerusalem in the last-days, the Lord had the Prophet Zechariah write: "Behold, I will make Jerusalem a cup of trembling unto all the people round about, when they shall be in the siege both against Judah (Israel) and against Jerusalem. And in that day will I make Jerusalem a burdensome stone for all people: all that burden themselves with it shall be cut in pieces, though all the people of the earth be gathered together against it" (Zech. 12:2-3).

On December 6, 2017, major news channels televised a live broadcast of United States President Donald Trump signing a proclamation officially recognizing Jerusalem as the capital of Israel. The proclamation paved the way for a Trump campaign promise to move the US embassy from Tel Aviv to Jerusalem. The announcement sparked immediate violent protests from the Palestinians and drew condemnation from the Vatican, Russia and the Islamic nations. The UN Security Council then quickly convened to set forth a resolution condemning the proclamation which was supported by the majority of the UN's 193 member nations. United States UN Ambassador Nikki Haley addressed the UN General Assembly stating that the US was taking names of those who side against them and will not forget. According to the above passage God is taking names too of all who are against Israel.

America has been the biggest ally of Israel since its rebirth in 1948. As such, the USA has been blessed by God to become the most powerful and wealthiest nation in the world. God told Abraham, the grandfather of Jacob (Israel), "I will bless them that bless thee (Israel), and curse him that curseth thee...." (Gen. 12:3). America was falling under this curse during the eight years of the anti-Israel Obama Administration due to Obama's anti-Zionist rhetoric and policies. Under his watch, hundreds of UN resolutions against Israel went unchallenged. Since the election of Donald Trump, however, and his Christian conservative, Christian Zionist favoring policies at home and abroad, the USA is on the rise again on all major levels. Some of Trump's foreign policies though are early precursors to Armageddon. Nevertheless, love him or hate him, Trump is God's man of the hour to favor Israel and to make America strong again on the world's stage.

Christian Zionism vs. Replacement Theology

In the United States, the majority of true born-again Christians supports the statehood of Israel from a biblically prophetic, internationally legal, and morally justified viewpoint, which is commonly known as "Christian Zionism." In contrast, the apostate liberal denominations of the National Council of Churches (NCC) oppose Christian Zionism in all aspects. All across America, pastors of these apostate churches of the NCC spew out their anti-Zionism semantics from their pulpits, newsletters, and websites. In a December 2008 news release on Christian Zionism, the NCC stated that "Christian Zionism is a dangerous movement that distorts the teaching of the church."[11]

The NCC members teach what is referred to as "Replacement Theology," which is a belief that God's purpose for Israel ended with the destruction of Jerusalem and the Temple in 70 A.D. by the Romans, and that the Church is now the sole focus in God's plan. Replacement Theology is an interpretation of New Testament claims that view God's relationship with Christians as superseding His relationship with the Jews. This teaching states that the promises, covenants, and blessings given to Israel now belong solely to the Church. The truth of the matter, however, is that God's purpose for Israel is still ongoing — separate from, but woven into, His plans for the true Church of the Lord Jesus Christ.

Replacement Theology is a satanically influenced doctrine that is also held by the Roman Catholic Church and the members of the World Council of Churches (WCC). The Vatican, the WCC, and the NCC continue to call on the United States and the world community to pressure Israel to leave what they say is "Arab land" because Jewish sovereignty in the Holy Land is a huge slap in the face to their theology.[12] These three very large organizations are gradually setting aside their differences and are on pace to merge together as one in the end-times. In all fairness, however, there are a small percentage of true churches who are currently members of either the NCC or WCC who do not hold these views. They will either succumb to them later, or separate themselves entirely from these organizations (Rev. 18:4).

Denominations and parachurch organizations who fully or have branches participating in this retreaded anti-Semitism include the United Church of Christ; Presbyterian Church (USA); the Church of England; the United Methodist Church; the Church of Scotland; the Reformed Church of America; the Methodist Church of England; the Roman Catholic Church; Bethlehem Bible College, Bethlehem, Israel; World Vision; the National Council of Churches in the USA; and the World Council of Churches. The movement's most prominent leaders over the past dozen years are: Stephen Sizer, Anglican Vicar of Christ's Church, England; Gary Burge, ordained Presbyterian minister, and professor of New Testament, Wheaton College; Donald E. Wagner, ordained Presbyterian minister, and director of the Center for Middle Eastern Studies, North Park University, Chicago, Illinois; John Stott, the late theologian and rector emeritus of All Souls Church, London; Hank Hanegraaff, author, and president of the Christian Research Institute; Tony Campolo, Baptist minister, author, and professor at Eastern University in Pennsylvania; Naim Ateek, founder of the Palestinian Ecumenical Liberation Theology Center in Jerusalem; and Mitri Raheb, pastor of the Evangelical Lutheran Christmas Church, whose website lists its address as "Bethlehem, Palestine."[13]

6

GOG AND COMPANY

"Keep not thou silence, O God: hold not thy peace, and be not still, O God. For, lo, thine enemies make a tumult: and they that hate thee have lifted up the head. They have taken crafty counsel against thy people, and consulted against thy hidden ones. They have said, Come, let us cut them off from being a nation; that the name of Israel may be no more in remembrance."
— Psalms 83:1-4

In the fall of 2005, the then newly elected president of Iran, Mahmoud Ahmadinejad, publicly stated that Israel would be "Wiped off the map." His comment sparked outrage from the international community, especially the United States, who wasted no time in condemning the madman's outburst. Russia, however, remained conspicuously quiet concerning Ahmadinejad's statement.

In early 2006, the well-known Palestinian terrorist group, Hamas, who themselves have vowed to destroy Israel, gained control of the majority of seats in the current structure of the Palestinian government. Due to Hamas' position concerning Israel, the United States withdrew their financial aid from the Palestinian Authority. As a result, Iran, who has secretly funded and trained the terrorist group for many years, publicly pledged 50 million dollars to Hamas. Shortly afterwards, the president of Russia, Vladimir Putin, campaigned for international recognition of Hamas by inviting their leaders to Moscow for talks. Russia then also pledged to financially support Hamas, after which more Islamic nations followed suit.

In the spring of 2006, Hamas, under direct orders from Iran, sent troops across Israel's southern border, killing nine Israeli soldiers and kidnapping several more. The Israeli Defense Force responded with a relentless military campaign aimed at Hamas strongholds and Palestinian livelihood in the area known as the Gaza Strip. Just weeks after Hamas' initial attack, the Lebanese-born terrorist group, Hezbollah, who themselves are funded and trained by Iran, virtually imitated Hamas' exploits by sending their militia across Israel's northern border. Israel quickly responded with massive, highly destructive air strikes upon Hezbollah strongholds in Beirut and elsewhere in Lebanon.

Up until 1935, the nation we know today as Iran was called Persia. Rooted deep in Bible history, the nation of Persia and its people, the Persians, are mentioned in the Old Testament a total of thirty-five times. Following the Muslim invasion in 637 A.D., the Shiite sect of Islam emerged as the dominant religion of Persia. Shiites believe that the 12th Imam (successor to Muhammad) has lived an invisible existence since 874 A.D., but will appear at the end-of-days as the Mahdi (Messiah figure) to usher in a kingdom under Sharia (Islamic) law over the entire world. Iran is an Islamic Theocracy under the dictatorship of Shiite cleric Ayatollah Ali Khamenei. Former Shiite President Mahmoud Ahmadinejad believes that his nation's calling is to destroy Israel and to provoke a cataclysmic upheaval against the West that will herald the appearing of the Mahdi.

Islam has two major sects, Sunni and Shiite. Sunni is the largest and is mostly found in Saudi Arabia, Turkey, Syria, Yemen, Jordan, and North Africa. Shiites are in most of these nations as the minority, but in Iran and Iraq they're the majority. The Islamic extremist agenda is to destroy the infidels, starting with the United States and Israel, to usher in the Mahdi's appearance. Also, according to their eschatology, Jesus, who Muslims revere as a Prophet, will return with the Mahdi to proclaim Islam the true religion.

Gog and Company

On December 11, 2017, Iranian Defense Minister Amir Hatami stated that United States President Donald Trump's announcement to move the US embassy in Israel to Jerusalem "will only hasten the destruction of Israel and double the unity among Muslims." That same day, Maj. Gen. Qassem Suleimani, commander of Iran's elite Quds Force, pledged "complete support for Palestinian Islamic resistance." According to Hamas's leader, Yahya Sinwar, Suleimani also said, "All of our capabilities are at your disposal in the battle for the defense of Jerusalem." According to the Prophet Ezekiel, Persia (Iran) will be involved in a plot to destroy Israel in the last-days.

In the last eleven chapters of the book of Ezekiel, we read of prophecies in regard to Israel in the "latter days" of the "latter years" in reference to the end-times, and their future in the Messianic Kingdom. The prophecy begins by revealing an all-out attempt by Israel's foes to try and "wipe them off the map," so to speak. This attempt, however, will be interrupted by God when He intervenes on behalf of Israel in biblical style and proportion as in the days-of-old. This event will then be followed by a period of seven years, just prior to the return of Jesus Christ to usher in Israel's long foretold and anticipated Messianic Kingdom Age (Ezek. 38-48).

Beginning in Ezekiel chapter thirty-eight, we read: "And the word of the Lord came unto me, saying, Son of man, set thy face against Gog, the land of Magog (Russia), the chief prince of Meshach and Tubal, and prophesy against him, And say, Thus saith the Lord God; Behold, I am against thee, O Gog...And I will turn thee back, and put hooks into thy jaws, and I will bring thee forth, and all thine army...even a great company...Persia (Iran), Ethiopia (Sudan), and Libya with them... Gomer, and all his bands; the house of Togarmah (Turkey) of the north quarters, and all his bands: and many people with thee. Be thou prepared...and all thy company that are assembled unto thee, and be thou (Russia) a guard unto them. After many days, thou shalt be visited: in the latter years thou shalt come into the land (Israel) that is brought back from the sword, and is gathered out of many people (nations), against the mountains of Israel, which have been always waste; but it (Israel) is brought forth out of the nations, and they (Jews) shall dwell safely, all of them" (Ezek. 38:1-8).

Most commentators agree that Gog, of the land of Magog, the chief prince of Meshach and Tubal, refers to the people of modern Russia. Magog, Meshach, and Tubal were Noah's grandsons by his son Japheth (Gen. 10:1-2). Their descendants migrated north beyond the Black and Caspian Seas following the Tower of Babel dispersion (Gen. 10:5). Gog, the chief prince, may have been an early leader among these people, or a leader during Ezekiel's time. Nevertheless, the prophecy is clearly directed at Russia, and the leadership of the Russian people, in the end-times. Russia is a predominantly atheistic country who harbors strong anti-Semitic feelings. And, primarily for those reasons, the Lord is "against thee, O Gog."

Currently, Russia is making a strong comeback from the humiliating breakup of their Soviet Union. As of 2017, their Gross Domestic Product (GDP) had reached 3.7 trillion, up from 250 billion in 2000. At the same time, their foreign debt has steadily declined. As a result, Russia has, in recent years, gotten more and more involved in strengthening their ties with the Islamic nations in the Middle East. In an article in the *Wall Street Journal* dated February 28, 2007, titled "Russian Deals in Middle East Snarl U.S. Strategy on Iran," the following discoveries were disclosed:

- **Iran** — bought $700M in anti-aircraft missiles; $2.1B total trade, up 4.4%; Russia building nuclear plant in Bushehr, Iran
- **Syria** — bought maintenance contracts; Russia wrote off $1B debt

- **Egypt** — bought upgrades to existing systems; $1.4B total trade, up 21%; Russia seeks nuclear plant deal
- **Libya** — bought anti-tank missiles, transport planes; Russia providing loans for arms
- **Algeria** — reached $7.5B deal for planes, tanks, missiles. Russia wrote off $4.7B debt during Putin visit; Russian gas and oil companies in cooperation deals
- **Yemen** — bought fighter jets, armored vehicles; Russia wrote off debt
- **Qatar** — Putin made first ever visit in February of 2007; discusses cooperation in global gas markets; possible arms sales
- **Saudi Arabia** — Putin made first ever visit by Russian leader in February of 2007; seeks nuclear and arms deals
- **Iraq** — bought helicopters; Russia wrote off $10B debt in 2006; Russian companies seeking oil contracts

The eighteenth century leader and founder of Russia, Peter the Great, believed that the Russian Empire would never be complete until she extends her boundaries to the warm shores of Palestine. Since then, Russia's leaders have held to that same view in hopes of one day bringing their founding forefather's dream to a reality. So, what we see going on today between Russia and the Islamic nations is what Russia hopes will be the beginning of a new union that will dominate the majority of the world's natural gas and oil supplies, which for Russia spells "superpower status" once again and elevation of their standing among the nations above the United States and Europe. With this in mind, we now can proceed to the next portion of Ezekiel's prophecy from where we left off earlier.

As Ezekiel continued with his prophecy, he wrote: "And thou (Russia) shalt say, I will go up to the land (Israel) of unwalled villages; I will go to them that are at rest, that dwell safely, all of them dwelling without walls, and having neither bars nor gates, To take spoil, and to take prey; to turn thy hand upon the desolate places that are now inhabited, and upon the people (Jews) that are gathered out of the nations, which have gotten cattle and goods (prospered), that dwell in the midst of the land" (Ezek. 38:11-12).

This particular passage is primarily directed at Russia. The reason is that the Islamic world hates Israel for religious reasons and wants the Jews out of what they believe is, and always has been, Muslim land (even though Jerusalem is not mentioned even once in the Quran, the holy book of Islam). On the other hand, Russia is power hungry and more interested in the products of the land and in building stronger alliances with the oil-rich nations of the Middle East. To achieve those goals, Russia will lead the haters of Israel into what they believe will finally be the end of Israel among the family of nations once and for all. However, God has other plans for Israel and it is His will for His elect nation that will prevail.

On February 5, 2008, it was reported on CBN that in recent months Russia had sent eighty-two tons of nuclear fuel to aid Iran in their quest for nuclear power: translation — nuclear weapons. Also reported was a statement made by then Iranian President Mahmoud Ahmadinejad that "The Zionist Endeavor was about to come to an end." This statement by Ahmadinejad is linked to his belief that his country is on the verge of producing a nuclear bomb. What Ahmadinejad doesn't know, however, is that his country's plan to destroy Israel is in conflict with God's plan to save Israel. Most likely, Israel will send their elite fighter pilots into Iran and bomb their nuclear ambitions to smithereens like they did to Iraq in 1981 and Syria in 2007. Thus far, however, Israel has been thwarting Iran's nuclear quest by using other methods of attack.

Following the overthrow of Iraq in 2003 by the United States, which began with an intense military strike upon Baghdad (code named "Shock and Awe"), President Moammar Qadhafi of Libya, fearing the same fate, volunteered to turn over their nuclear centrifuges to the West. After learning that Iran had purchased the same type of centrifuges from the same underground source as Libya, the centrifuges were later turned over to Israel for research. As a leader in cyberspace technology, Israel developed a computer virus in 2010 called "Stuxnet," which they launched into Iran's computer systems at their nuclear plants. The virus disrupted Iran's program and pushed back their ability to make a nuclear bomb until at least 2014.[1]

In November of 2011, the International Atomic Energy Agency (IAEA) issued a report that Iran is developing nuclear weapons. Five days after the IAEA report, a mysterious explosion rocked an Iranian missile base near Teheran, killing a top Iranian general and 16 elite members of Iran's Revolutionary Guard. A Western intelligence official told *Time Magazine* that the Mossad (Israeli CIA) was responsible. Shortly after the explosion, Iran disclosed that computer systems in its defense establishment had been infected with another super virus called "Duqu," that is similar to Stuxnet.[2] In January of 2012, a top Iranian nuclear scientist was killed in Teheran in a car bomb attack. He was the fourth nuclear scientist killed in the past five years. Iran blamed Israel and the United States for the attack.[3]

In 2015, the anti-Israel Obama Administration brokered a bogus international nuclear agreement with a then more moderate elected Iranian government which unfroze 150 billion in Iranian assets and lifted numerous sanctions against the terrorist regime, despite warnings from Israeli Prime Minister Benjamin Netanyahu not to. In return, Iran agreed (?) to halt their nuclear programs for 15 years. Nevertheless, future events in the Middle East will eventually mature unto this event foretold by Ezekiel.

In January 2018, retired Israeli Navy Admiral Shaul Chorev told the *Jerusalem Post* that Israel's next proxy war with Iran "could see a focus on the Mediterranean Sea." That "Iran is on the verge of establishing a presence in the Mediterranean by way of use of Syrian ports by their Navy," Chorev said, and that "Iranian ports in the eastern Mediterranean are a real risk for Israel." Also in January of 2018, Israeli ambassador to the United Nations, Danny Danon, took the extraordinary step of disclosing classified Israeli intelligence at a UN Security Council meeting revealing that Iran controls 82,000 troops in Syria and has spent $35 billion on weapons factories there. "If we turn a blind eye," Danon warned, "the Iranian threat will only grow."

In April of 2017, Syria used chemical weapons on a United States backed rebel militia who have been fighting for years against the Russian/Iranian backed Assad (Syrian president) regime, which killed innocent civilians. In response, the then new pro-Israel United States President Donald Trump ordered a strike on the airbase in Syria that launched the attack with 50 Tomahawk cruise missiles from US naval ships positioned in the Mediterranean, taking out a number of Syrian fighter jets, bunkers, and airstrips. In December 2017, Russian President Vladimir Putin submitted a proposal to the State Duma for an agreement for Moscow and Damascus (Syrian capital) to construct a full-fledged naval base in Syria's Mediterranean coastal city of Tartus. Former Russian Navy Admiral Viktor Kravchenko told Interfax that the move "will strengthen the operational capabilities of our fleet in the Mediterranean and, in general, Russia's position in the Middle East."

In April 2018, the Assad regime again used chemical weapons against the opposition fighters, which again killed innocent men, women, and children. This time Israel got in on the action and quickly responded by sending in their highly trained fighter pilots to bomb the Syrian airbase used to launch the attack, which killed 14 Iranian military personnel stationed at the base. Iran threatened to retaliate. Not long afterwards, and despite threats from Russia and Iran not to, the United States, United Kingdom (Britain), and France simultaneously launched 105 missiles upon three targets in the greater Damascus area, which the US claimed destroyed Assad's capability to make chemical weapons.

In early May of 2018, Israeli Prime Minister Benjamin Netanyahu disclosed to the world an overwhelming amount of evidence discovered by his intelligence sources that Iran was engaging in covert nuclear ambitions. On May 8, 2018, President Trump went on live television and released a condemning speech against the "Death to America" chanting regime of Iran and announced that the US was pulling out of the "horrible one-sided" 2015 Obama nuclear agreement. He also stated that he would be reinstating crippling sanctions against the "terrorist-sponsoring state" and any other state that supports Iran's nuclear efforts. That same day, Israel bombed a suspected Iranian weapons installation base in Syria, destroying missiles pointed at Israel and killing several more Iranian soldiers. These most recent events to-date in the Middle East are just more precursors to the fulfillment of Ezekiel's prophecy.

As the Prophet Ezekiel continued with his prophecy concerning Russia and Company, he was told "son of man, prophesy and say unto Gog, Thus saith the Lord God; In that day when my people of Israel dwelleth safely, shalt thou not know it? And thou shalt come from thy place out of the north parts, thou, and many people with thee...a great company, and a mighty army: And thou shalt come up against my people of Israel, as a cloud to cover the land; it shall be in the latter days, and I will bring thee against my land, that the heathen may know me, when I shall be sanctified in thee, O Gog, before their eyes. Thus saith the Lord God; Art thou he (Russia) of whom I have spoken in old time by my servants, the prophets of Israel, which prophesied in those days many years that I would bring thee against them?" (Ezek. 38:14-17).

For nearly 2,500 years now, this prophecy has for "many years" lingered toward its fulfillment. It is set to occur in the "latter days" of the "latter years" after Israel again "dwelleth safely" in their own land. God here refers to the Jews as "My people" and the land of Israel as "My land." For the Jews are a people under a special covenant with God, unlike any other nation, and in that covenant God gave them the land (Gen. 12:1-3; 15:18). The land of Israel is the land of the Bible story, the Holy Land. It is there where God, in the person of Jesus Christ, walked among men and provided a remedy for the sins of humanity.

Currently, Russia (which is located in the "north part" in relation to Israel) and its Islamic allies are being kept in check by Divine restraint. At the appointed time, however, the Lord is going to turn Israel's foes over to their hatred and lust so "that the heathen may know me (God), when I shall be sanctified in thee, O Gog, before their (the nations) eyes." In other words, the Lord is going to turn the hatred and greed of Israel's enemies around and use them to glorify His name to the world, which brings us to how the Lord plans to do this in the next phase of Ezekiel's prophecy.

As the Prophet continued, he wrote: "And it shall come to pass at the same time when Gog shall come against the land of Israel, saith the Lord God, that my fury shall come up in my face. For in my jealousy and in the fire of my wrath have I spoken, Surely in that day there shall be a great shaking in the land of Israel...and the steep places shall fall, and every wall shall fall to the ground. And I will call for a sword against him throughout all my mountains, saith the Lord God: every man's sword shall be against his brother. And I will plead against him with pestilence and with blood; and I will rain upon him, and upon his bands, and upon the many people that are with him, an overflowing rain, and great hailstones, fire, and brimstone. Thus will I magnify myself, and sanctify myself; and I will be known in the eyes of many nations, and they shall know that I am the Lord" (Ezek. 38:18-23).

When Russia and their Islamic counterparts begin to make their move and surround the tiny nation of Israel, there is first going to be a "great shaking in the land of Israel." First we must here consider what is meant by the "land of Israel." As always, we must go to the Bible for the true answer and not just speculate. When God promised the land to Abraham and his descendants, the boundaries of the land included all the land along the Mediterranean coastline "from the river (Wadi el-Arish) of Egypt unto the great river, the river Euphrates" (Gen. 15:18). So then, the above prophecy of a "great shaking in the land of Israel" concerns the biblical boundaries and not just the tiny piece of it that Israel occupies today.

The Wadi el-Arish River runs through the eastern part of Egypt and the Euphrates runs across the northern tip of Syria. In between Egypt and Syria, there is Lebanon and Israel and the two portions of land on Israel's current borders that are occupied by the Palestinians, known as the West Bank and Gaza Strip. Without a doubt, Egypt, Syria, Lebanon, and the Palestinians, who all occupy land that biblically belongs to Israel, will all be involved in the attempted invasion. As they begin to surround Israel, there is first going to be a "great shaking," or rather an earthquake that is going to cause a lot of damage in these nations. However, the land that Israel occupies today may go unharmed by the earthquake. It's also very likely that during the earthquake the earth will open up in certain areas to swallow up portions of the coalition forces.

Another shaking that will occur is that "...all the men that are upon the face of the earth, shall shake at my presence..." (Ezek. 38:20). This shaking will not be of land per se, but in the hearts of men who themselves were formed out of the "dust of the ground" (Gen. 2:7). All around the world, men's hearts will quake with fear when unholy, sinful mankind has an encounter of such magnitude with a holy and pissed-off God, who will suddenly intervene into human history as in the days-of-old to defend Israel.

Before the coalition forces of Gog and Company can set foot into the modern-day state of Israel, the Lord will first unleash an "overflowing rain" upon them that will virtually stop them in their tracks from being able to move their heavy machinery. Afterwards, "great hailstone, fire, and brimstone" will plummet their positions, killing thousands instantly. Thinking they have come under enemy fire, they will then turn their weapons on each other, killing thousands more. In the wake of all the death and blood, many more will be struck with diseases that will kill quickly, bringing the death toll to a staggering number.

In the aftermath of God's version of "Shock and Awe," the Lord will then be "known in the eyes of many nations." The entire world will come to realize that it was God who intervened on behalf of Israel "and they shall know that I am the Lord." The nations of the world will get a rude wake-up call to the fact that the God of Israel, the God of Abraham, Isaac, and Jacob (Israel), the God of the Holy Bible and the God of the true Christians, is God. The entire world, at that time, will be put on notice that Jesus Christ is Lord, the Way, the Truth, and the Life.

In all, only one-sixth of the entire combined armies of Gog and Company will survive the Divine attack (Ezek. 39:1-5). They will be spared by God for the purpose of returning to their homelands to be living eye-witnesses and reminders to their nations of the devastating defeat that came upon them by the hands of the God of Israel. All around the world, people will be talking about the God of Israel and begin to search for the truth in the Holy Bible. The truth about God will sweep through the nations like "a fire," purifying the hearts of many from the dross of their false beliefs about God (Ezek. 39:6; Jer. 23:29; Luke 24:32). Millions from around the world will give their lives to Jesus Christ after witnessing this event.

In Israel, there are Jews today who do not believe that Jesus Christ is their Messiah, nor do they even practice today's form of

Judaism, the religion of the Jews. However, when God intervenes and saves them from such destruction that will all change. For then the Lord will make His "holy name known in the midst of my people Israel; and I will not let them pollute my holy name anymore: and the heathen shall know that I am the Lord, the Holy One in Israel" (Ezek. 39:7). At this time, there is going to be an outbreak of religious fervor among the Jews in Israel and elsewhere that, from this point, will (like "a fire") spread among them. This, in turn, will prepare the Jews for other events that will soon follow that are set to occur in the final seven years before the return of the most well-known Jew of all, Jesus Christ.

As Ezekiel's prophecy continued, he wrote that "they that dwell in the cities of Israel shall go forth, and shall set on fire and burn the weapons, both the shields and the bucklers, the bows and the arrows, and the handstaves, and the spears, and they shall burn them with fire seven years: So that they shall take no wood out of the forests; for they shall burn the weapons with fire: and they shall spoil those that spoiled them, and rob those that robbed them, saith the Lord God" (Ezek. 39:9-10).

In the wake of all the devastation, an enormous supply of weapons, fuel, and other spoils will be left behind by Gog and Company. Israel will send out recovery teams to gather up whatever is salvageable. The spoil will be of such gain that Israel will convert it into resources which will last for seven years. In all, it will take Israel seven months to bury all the dead bodies of their foes (Ezek. 39:11-15).

This entire event will parallel another event in Israel's history that occurred during the reign of King Jehoshaphat, king of Judah. During his reign, an enormous combined army of several surrounding nations came against Judah, greatly outnumbering them. Nevertheless, the Lord stepped in and completely destroyed the coalition forces. Afterwards, the Jews went out to gather up all the spoil and to bury the dead. The effect of that event, we are told, upon the other nations back then was that "the fear of God was on all the kingdoms of those countries, when they heard that the Lord fought against the enemies of Israel" (2 Chron. 20:1-29). After God defends Israel from Gog and Company, it will have the same effect upon the nations of the world today, as it did back then.

As we just saw, the spoils that Israel will gather up that are left behind by Russia and Company will be able to provide Israel with resources for seven years. The mention here of a period of seven years is a well-placed prophetic piece to the end-times puzzle that is there to aid us in identifying when this event of Gog and Company is set to occur on the end-times prophetic timetable. According to end-times prophecy, there are still seven years of unfulfilled prophecy concerning the Jews, Jerusalem, and their Temple, which will be the final seven years prior to the return of Jesus Christ and His ushering in of the Messianic Kingdom Age (Dan. 9:24-27). Interestingly, the mention of a period of seven years in Ezekiel 39:9 is followed by the final nine chapters of Ezekiel (40-48), which are prophecy pertaining to the nation of Israel during the Messianic Kingdom Age. Coincidence? I think not!

The prophecy concerning the last seven years is found in Daniel 9:27, which reveals that the countdown will begin on the final seven years with a certain decree issued by the coming Antichrist. In Daniel 7:24, we see how the Antichrist will first overthrow three nations to add to his already unified seven nations under his authority, to make a total of ten. The Scriptures reveal that the three nations he will overthrow will be three nations close to Israel along the Mediterranean coastline. If ever there will be a perfect time for the Antichrist to make his move upon the Middle East, it will surely be after God virtually destroys the armies of Israel's surrounding foes.

7

THE MAN OF SIN

"And Jacob called unto his sons, and said, Gather yourselves together, that I may tell you that which shall befall you in the last days. Gather yourselves together, and hear, ye sons of Jacob; and hearken unto Israel your father....Dan shall judge his people (Jews) as one of the tribes of Israel. Dan shall be a serpent (satanic) by the way, an adder in the path, that biteth the horse heels, so that his rider shall fall backward."

— Genesis 49:1-2, 16-17

Shortly before his death, Jacob was moved by God to speak prophetically over the future of his twelve sons. The most noteworthy was what Jacob said about Judah, of whose linage Christ was to be born (Gen. 49:8-10). When considering the overall big picture of the end-times puzzle, however, what Jacob said concerning his son Dan easily finds its place of importance second behind Judah; for as the prophecy spoken over Judah referred to Christ, that which Jacob said concerning Dan alludes to the Antichrist. Along with the above passage, there are other Scriptures that verify that the Antichrist will indeed be of Jewish descent (from the tribe of Dan), whom God is going to use to judge Israel and the nations for their rejection of Jesus Christ.

Not long after the children of Israel exited Egypt under the leadership of Moses, we read that: "the son of an Israelitish woman, whose father was an Egyptian, went out among the children of Israel. And this son of an Israelitish woman and a man of Israel strove together in the camp. And the Israelitish woman's son blasphemed the name of the Lord, and cursed. And they brought him unto Moses (and his mother's name was Shelomith, the daughter of Dibri, of the tribe of Dan). And they put him in ward that the mind of the Lord might be shown them. And the Lord spoke unto Moses, saying, Bring forth him who hath cursed without the camp...and let all the congregation stone him" (Lev. 24:10-14). Here we see that it was a man of the tribe of Dan who was the first to blaspheme the name of the Lord and be put to death. In the person of the Antichrist, it will be a descendant from the tribe of Dan who will epitomize blaspheming the name of the Lord, who will then be put to death by the Lord Himself.

After the children of Israel entered the Promised Land, the twelve tribes were issued their allotted inheritance in the land of Canaan. The tribe of Dan was the last to receive their lot, which roughly consisted of a narrow strip of land west of Jerusalem that stretched toward the Mediterranean Sea coast (Josh. 19:40-48). The land, however, was unable to accommodate the growing tribe. As a result, six hundred men of war and their families ventured to the far north of Canaan where they overtook the inhabitants of the city of Laish and renamed it "Dan" after their forefather (Jud. 18:1-29). In their rebellion, they set up a graven image and continued in idol worship all the way to the Babylonian captivity (Jud. 18:30). Today, the ancient city of Dan is called "Tell el-Qadi" which means "mound of the judge." The meaning of the name can be traced back to Jacob's prophetic words concerning Dan being a "judge."

The Prophet Daniel, whose name means "God is my judge," was chosen by God to be the one to pen more prophetic Scriptures concerning the Antichrist and his end-times exploits than any other. Also, the Babylonian Empire, where Daniel was a captive, itself foreshadowed the still yet future empire of the Antichrist in the last-days.

In Daniel chapter eleven, the Prophet foretold of the events that later came to pass in the history of the Grecian Empire after the untimely death of Alexander the Great. The empire split into four smaller kingdoms after his death, which was headed up by Alexander's four generals. These four kingdoms are depicted by the four heads of the leopard in Daniel's vision (in Daniel chapter seven). The two largest of the four were known as the "Seleucid" and "Ptolemaic" kingdoms, which developed into empires of their own right. In Daniel chapter eleven, the Prophet referred to these two kingdoms as the "king of the north" and "king of the south" due to their geographical location to Israel.

The heart of the northern Seleucid Empire consisted primarily of the region of Syria. In the south, Egypt was the heart of the Ptolemaic Empire. The prophecy concerning the Seleucid dynasty came to a close in the book of Daniel with the exploits of the Grecian King Antiochus IV Epiphanes whose life and exploits against the Jews foreshadows the life and exploits of the coming Antichrist (Dan. 11:21-35). Starting in 11:36, the prophecy suddenly shifts to the Antichrist, which is a common occurrence in the complex formation of the prophetic Scriptures.

Beginning in verse 36, we read that: "And the king shall do according to his will; and he shall exalt himself, and magnify himself above every god, and shall speak marvelous things against the God of gods (by claiming to be the Jews' Messiah), and shall prosper till the indignation be accomplished: for that that is determined (by God) shall be done. Neither shall he regard the God of his fathers (Jews), nor the desire of women (Jewish women), nor any god: for he shall magnify himself above all" (Dan. 11:36-37). Okay, did you catch that? The phrase "God of his fathers" was used seventeen times by the Prophet Daniel in reference to the God of his fathers Abraham, Isaac, and Jacob. It is an expression used hundreds of times throughout the Old Testament in reference to the same. Therefore, the capital "G" in verse 37 was no mistake by the translators of the King James Version of the Bible as some ignorantly claim (*Strong's Concordance,* 433). It is a major piece of Scripture that reveals to us that the Antichrist will be of Jewish ancestry.

The Prophet Ezekiel, who was Daniel's contemporary in the Babylonian captivity, in reference to the Antichrist wrote: "And thou, profane wicked prince (Antichrist) of Israel, whose day is come, when iniquity shall have an end (end-times). Thus saith the Lord God; Remove the diadem, and take off the crown: this shall not be the same: exalt him (Christ) that is low, and abase him (Antichrist) that is high (exalts himself). I (God) will overturn, overturn, overturn, it (Antichrist's impostership): and it (Antichrist's rule) shall be no more, until he (Christ) come whose right it is; and I (God) will give it (Kingdom) him" (Ezek. 21:25-27). The Apostle Paul referred to him as the coming "Man of Sin" (2 Thes. 2:3).

> *Note: In 1942, the madman of WWII, Adolf Hitler, ordered a covert investigation in response to a blackmailing letter he received hinting at dark family secrets. The investigation was conducted by a lawyer named Hans Frank. After Hitler committed suicide, Frank later testified at the Nuremberg trials that Hitler's grandfather was an Austrian Jew named Frankenberger, which was not known to Hitler.[1] The point is that Hitler, I believe, was a twentieth century type of the coming twenty-first century Antichrist. Hitler's life and rise to power somewhat foreshadows the life and rise to power of the Antichrist. All the prophetic clues that we've reviewed in this book reveal that the Antichrist, like Hitler, will, too, be of European/Jewish descent.*

In Daniel 11:38, we are told that "in his estate shall he honor the God of forces." The "God of forces" is again a reference to God who is the "Lord of hosts," or rather the Lord of armies (*Strong's Concordance,* 4581, 6635). For we read: "...that the most High (God) ruleth in the kingdom of men, and giveth it to whomsoever he will" (Dan. 4:25). The position that the Antichrist (let's call him Dan) will have will give him power over the militaries of a combined league of nations in the last-days. In his seat of authority, Dan will unwittingly bring honor to God as he fulfills God's will during the course of his exploits. In Revelation 17:17, we read that: "For God hath put in their (ten kings') hearts to fulfill his will, and to agree, and give their kingdom unto the beast (Dan), until the words of God shall be fulfilled." In Exodus 14:4, we read of another example of this where God explained to Moses saying, "And I will harden Pharaoh's heart, that he shall follow after them (children of Israel); and I will be honored upon Pharaoh, and upon his host (by drowning Pharaoh and his army in the Red Sea): that the Egyptians may know that I am the Lord."

As Daniel continued he wrote: "and a god (Satan) whom his fathers knew not shall he honor (the Antichrist will honor Satan, too, with his exploits) with gold, and silver, and with precious stones, and pleasant things. Thus shall he do in the most strong holds (strongest nations) with a strange god (Satan) whom he shall acknowledge (dupe the world into worshipping Satan) and increase with glory: and he shall cause them (his god and his kings) to rule over many, and shall divide the land (of Israel) for gain" (Dan. 11:38-39).

In Daniel chapter seven, we saw where the lion, bear, leopard, and undescribed beast all represented the empires of Babylon, Medo-Persia, Grecia and the end-times empire of the Antichrist. The undescribed beast has ten horns, which represent ten nations that will be under the control of the Antichrist. In Daniel's vision, the Antichrist is referred to as a "little horn" who "plucks up," or rather overthrows, three horns (nations) of the ten, which tells us that Dan will take three of the ten nations by force (Dan. 7:1-24). Over the years, there has been much speculation and debate over the formation of these ten nations and just how it may all unfold. So, if you will, please allow me to add my two cents worth into the kitty concerning the matter.

Following WWII, the North Atlantic Treaty Organization

(NATO) was established in 1949 out of Western fears of further Soviet advances in Europe. Originating with the United States, Canada, and ten western European nations, today the roll call includes Turkey and sixteen more European countries. Their motto is "an attack on one is considered an attack on all." Headquarters for NATO is currently located in Brussels, Belgium from where the chairman presides over NATO interests. In the process of researching NATO information for this book, the then chairman of NATO was General Harold Kujat of Germany.

Currently, most of the European member nations of NATO are also members of the European Union (EU), whose headquarters is also in Brussels. The EU is on a steady pace to becoming the "United States of Europe" in the not-so-distant future. The forerunner for a constitution for the USE, known as the "Lisbon Treaty," was implemented by the EU in 2008. In response to the 2011 EU financial crisis, former German Chancellor Gerhard Schroeder called for the creation of a "United States of Europe...to avoid any future economic crises."[2] At a conference in Paris, officials of the European Central Bank stated that the only way to resolve the EU financial crisis would be to create a "federal government with a federal finance minister."[3] The New York based Citigroup, the world's largest financial group, says that only a "United States of Europe" will solve the EU financial problem.[4] In his September 12, 2012 state of the union speech, European Commission President Jose Manuel Barroso called for the federation of the EU.

The future USE will be structured perhaps similar to the USA. When this does occur, the roll call at NATO will drastically shrink and the USE will be counted as "one" member as the USA. Therefore, following an official inauguration of the USE, the roll call at NATO would shrink from its current twenty-nine-member head count to eight, which would look something like the following: USA, UK, USE, Canada, Iceland, Norway, Albania, and Turkey.

The Man of Sin

Although the United Kingdom (Great Britain) is a member of NATO and the EU, it's very likely that the UK will not join the mainland states in any future USE. The British Empire dominated the world for centuries and is still somewhat of an empire that sways power and influence over their many commonwealth territories throughout the world. When the EU implemented the euro dollar for its family of nations in 1999, the UK opted to not partake of the new monetary system. In response to the 2011 EU financial meltdown, twenty-six of the then twenty-seven-member EU nations agreed on a "Fiscal Pact" to rescue the euro from collapse. The UK was the sole holdout, refusing to sign the pact. These things, along with continuing strained relations between the UK and EU, spell ongoing sovereignty outside of any future USE for the United Kingdom. As a matter of fact, the Lisbon Treaty paved the way for this under its "Final Provisions," Title VI, Article 50 which states: "Any member state may decide to withdraw from the Union in accordance with its own constitutional requirements."

On October 15, 2012, British Home Secretary Theresa May announced that their government plans to opt out of more than 130 EU laws. The declaration was heralded by the *Daily Express* as "Britain's First Step to EU Exit." On October 23, 2012, Foreign Minister William Hague all but handed in Britain's exit notice to the EU when he publicly expressed his concern that eventually he sees the EU sucking up the decision making from national parliaments to the EU level. The *Telegraph* reported that Hague's declaration was "preparing the ground for Britain's withdrawal."[5]

> *Note: Several years after this writing (in the manuscript), on June 23, 2016 the British people voted in a referendum to leave the EU, referred to by the media as Brexit. Britain's official exit from the EU is set for March 2019.*

Turkey is an Islamic nation with a Western friendly government. They applied for membership in the EU, but were denied by the predominately Roman Catholic run parliament of the union. In recent years, their ties to the West have become strained, in part, due to the mounting tension between Islam and the West. They've become more outspoken and hostile against Israel, and have built an alliance with their bordering neighbor, Iran. After Israel bombed Iranian military installations in Syria in April and May of 2018, CBN reported that Turkey's President Recep Tayyip Erdogan expelled the Israeli ambassador and called for "all" Muslim nations to unify against Israel. According to Ezekiel 38:6, Turkey will be involved in Gog and Company's attempt to destroy Israel. Therefore, watch for Turkey to continue with a pseudo friendship with the West, while simultaneously building stronger alliances with their Islamic "Death to Israel" chanting counterparts.

Another thing to watch for is the possibility of Albania joining the EU and thus becoming one with the USE. If this were to occur, which it probably will, then that would put the NATO membership at seven. The hypotheses are many due to the inevitable changes that are ahead for both the EU and NATO. Watch for the continued development of the USE, and for the future roll call at NATO to lock in at seven.

As we've already seen, the Prophet Daniel referred to the Antichrist as a "little horn" who rises to power over seven nations and overthrows three nations to make a total of ten (Dan. 7:8, 20, 24). It could very well be that the Antichrist is alive today and is on pace to rise to power in Germany, the emerging leader of the EU, and one day gain control over NATO affairs in the Middle East.[6] At the February of 2010 Munich Security Conference, Germany's Defense Minister Karl-Theodor zu Guttenberg called for a long-overdue revamping of the NATO charter. In February 2018, NATO and German Defense Ministers created a new rapid troop command center in Germany. Clearly, German military elites have their eyes set on integrating German imperial goals with NATO objectives.

Under the Obama Administration, America unwisely dissed Israel in favor of the Palestinian/Islamic agenda. Occurring simultaneously, Germany has been quietly and steadily positioning itself to play a decisive role in the Israeli-Palestinian conflict. On November 19, 2012, Germany's Foreign Minister Guido Westerwelle traveled to Israel to meet with both Israeli Prime Minister Benjamin Netanyahu and the Palestinian President Mahmoud Abbas. After the meeting, Netanyahu publicly stated: "I believe that Germany can have a constructive role in seeking an end to this conflict and a long-term arrangement." In December of 2012, Netanyahu traveled to Germany who, according to Reuters, is Israel's closest ally in Europe.[7]

Note: President Obama left behind a shameful record against Israel. In June 2009, he condemned Israeli settlements in the West Bank during a speech in Cairo, Egypt. In March 2012, he leaked Israel's secret ties to Azerbaijan where Israeli planes could refuel for a strike against Iranian nuclear facilities. In March 2013, he visited Israel but refused an invitation to speak before the Knesset. In March 2015, he attempted to oust Israeli Prime Minister Benjamin Netanyahu from power by funding a political opposition party (In 2016, Obama reaped what he sowed when the Russians meddled in the US presidential election aiding a Trump victory over Hillary Clinton). In January 2016, he lifts sanctions against Iran paving the way for an Iranian nuclear bomb. In January 2017, he gave $221 million to the Palestinian Authority in his final hours in office.

On April 30, 2013, Israeli President Shimon Peres traveled to Europe to meet with Pope Francis concerning peace negotiations with the Palestinians, and the status of church properties in the Holy Land. Also on April 30th, Palestinian leader, Mahmoud Abbas, met with Austrian President Heinz Fischer in Vienna to discuss peace talks between Israel and the Palestinians. These overtures from both Israelis and Palestinians indicate that both sides believe that involving the EU and the Vatican now appears to be the best solution to the Middle East peace process.[8]

After 9-11, the US led an attack on the Taliban and al Qaeda in Afghanistan. In 2003, NATO officially entered the war; however, Turkey refused to fight against their Muslim brothers. As of August 2009, NATO had a total of 300,000 troops in Afghanistan. On 9-27-09, US Senator Lindsay Graham (R South Carolina) stated on the CBS program "Face the Nation" that: "The fight against the Taliban in Afghanistan is a NATO, not US, problem." Interestingly, just days before Graham's interview, and for the first time in NATO's 60-year history, a non-American general was appointed to one of NATO's two strategic commands. On September 9, 2009, General Stephane Abrial of France became Supreme Allied Commander Transformation. The point is that, the stage is being set for a future Germany-led USE/NATO to one day make a bold, calculated move into the Arab-Israeli conflict of the Middle East.

On the CNN 10 p.m. news report on June 15, 2003, it was stated in a discussion over the Arab-Israeli conflict that NATO should intervene with a resolve in the future if necessary. On September 17, 2004, the Bible prophecy telecast of Jack Van Impe showed a newspaper clip with the heading "E.U. Insists on Having Role in Middle East Peace Process." Once Dan is firmly established in his position, he will then have his eyes fixed on the Middle East, waiting for an opportunity to gain a foothold in the region. That chance will come following the attempted invasion of Israel by Gog and Company and their subsequent defeat by God, which we reviewed in the last chapter. More than likely, it will be due to Dan's infringement upon Middle Eastern politics, just prior to the final seven years, that will trigger Gog and Company's move upon Israel.

In light of all of this, we can now move on to the next phase of Daniel's prophecy concerning the Antichrist and his many foretold exploits. Beginning with Daniel 11:40, we read: "And at the time of the end shall the king of the south (Egypt) push at him (Dan): and the king of the north (Syria) shall come against him like a whirlwind, with chariots, and with horsemen, and with many ships; and he (Dan) shall enter also into the countries (After God whips Gog and Company), and shall overflow and pass over. He shall enter also into the glorious land (Israel), and many countries shall be overthrown: but these shall escape out of his hand, even Edom, and Moab, and the chief of the children of Ammon. He shall stretch forth his hand also upon the countries: and the land of Egypt shall not escape...and the Libyans and Ethiopians shall be at his steps (borders)" (Dan. 11:40-43).

The "time of the end" will begin when Gog and Company make their move on Israel, which will be viewed by Dan as a strategic military maneuver against the West. Following God's version of "Shock and Awe" upon Gog and Company, Dan will make his move on the Middle East virtually uncontested. He will then "pluck up," or overthrow, the nations of Syria, Lebanon, and Egypt. These three nations are not only enemies of Israel who border the tiny nation, but they are all accessible by ship from the Mediterranean Sea. All three of these nations (plus Iran, Turkey, etc.) will send "many ships" unto the Mediterranean side of Israel in the attempted invasion, only to be destroyed by God's fiery judgment. With their navies virtually wiped out, Dan will move the majority of his NATO forces into the nations of Syria, Lebanon, and Egypt by sea. He will also enter "into the glorious land (Israel)" where "he shall plant the tabernacles of his palace between seas in the glorious holy mountain..." (Dan. 11:45). At the same time Dan sends his troops into Syria, Lebanon, and Egypt, he will also enter into the land of Israel to set up a Middle Eastern Headquarters in Jerusalem, "the glorious holy mountain," which is located between the Mediterranean and Dead Seas.

Note: It is here where I must inform the reader that Bible prophecy, such as in Daniel and Revelation, is not written in an exact chronological order. For the most part it is, but not in an event-by-event perfect sequence. For example, you may have noticed I skipped over verse 44 and the last part of verse 45. The reason for such is that they allude to events to occur in the latter part of the final seven years, whereas for now, we are at the forefront of the seven years. Nearing the end of the seven years "tidings out of the east (China) and out of the north (Russia) shall trouble him (Dan): therefore he shall go forth with great fury to destroy...yet he shall come to his end, and none shall help him" (Dan. 11:44-45). We'll review these events later.

The current boundaries of the nations of Syria, Lebanon, and Egypt were all at one time under the domains of the ancient empires of Babylon, Medo-Persia, and Grecia. In Daniel chapter seven, the Prophet recorded a vision he was given wherein these empires were portrayed as a lion, a bear, and a leopard respectively (Dan. 7:1-6). Nearly seven hundred years later, the Lord gave the Apostle John a vision of Dan's empire, which was described as a beast which "was like unto a leopard, and his feet were as the feet of a bear, and his mouth as the mouth of a lion" (Rev. 13:2). What these details of Dan's empire reveal to us is that parts of the ancient boundaries of these empires past will also be included in the boundaries of Dan's empire. The entire region from Syria down to Egypt was not only part of these past empires, but also the most part of it rightfully belongs to Israel. As part of God's judgment upon Syria, Lebanon, and Egypt, these nations will lose their sovereignty over the land that God promised to Israel. Also, the characteristics of the kings of these past empires were such that some were worshipped as gods, others were great military leaders, some were friendly to Israel, yet others severely persecuted the Jews. All of these characteristics will be embodied in the person and empire of the Antichrist.

The ancient biblical boundaries of Edom, Moab, and Ammon are today located within the borders of the nation of Jordan, whose capital city is Amman. In 1994, Israel and Jordan signed a peace agreement, which put an end to years of fighting between the two nations. In 1999, the Jordanian King Hussein died and was succeeded by his son, Abdullah II, who was raised and educated in the United States. As a result of the peace accord, Jordan has completely withdrawn from the Arab-Israeli conflict, which in turn has caused a strain in their relations with their Arab neighbors. In April of 2004, Abdullah's Queen Rania led the nation in an anti-terrorism rally. In that same year, Iraqi born al Qaeda members were arrested just days before a terrorist plot was carried out against the Jordanian government. It was later discovered that Syria was in on the plot. The West is very aware of these pro-West, pro-Israel standings of Jordan. Therefore, when Dan makes his move on the Middle East, he will not view Jordan as a threat and they "shall escape out of his hand" (Dan. 11:41).

Once Egypt is overthrown and added as an extension to Dan's empire, then "the Libyans and the Ethiopians shall be at his steps (borders)" (Dan. 11:43). Today, Libya is the nation that border's Egypt in the west. To the south of Egypt lies Sudan, then Ethiopia, who both correspond as one. Therefore, this does not pose any contradiction of the prophecy concerning the Ethiopians bordering the empire of Dan when he overthrows Egypt, because both Sudan and Ethiopia combined were the boundaries of Ethiopia in biblical times.

Once the dust settles from Dan's overthrow of Syria, Lebanon, and Egypt, he will then "confirm the covenant with many for one week (seven years)" (Dan. 9:27). As you may recall from chapter one of this book, we reviewed the prophecy given to Daniel concerning his people the Jews, their beloved city Jerusalem, and the Temple. The prophecy stipulated a period of 490 years, which began ticking with the decree issued by the Persian King Artaxerxes for Nehemiah the Jew to return to Jerusalem to rebuild the wall around the city, which at the time still lay in ruins from the Babylonian invasion (Neh. 2). Between the time the decree was issued by the Persian King Artaxerxes to the death of Christ, a period of 483 years elapsed, leaving seven years of the prophecy unfulfilled. This last seven years, which also pertains to the Jews, Jerusalem, and the Temple, is foretold to be fulfilled in the last-days during the reign of the Antichrist. Some refer to this time period as the "seventieth week of Daniel" and others the "seven-year tribulation."

In Daniel 9:27, which solely relates to the last seven years, the phrase "the covenant" is a reference to "the covenant" that Daniel and his contemporaries understood to mean "the covenant" God made with their forefathers Abraham, Moses, and David. In "the covenant," Abraham built an altar upon the mount, which today is the Temple Mount in Jerusalem. Later, Moses was ordered to build a Tabernacle as part of an elaboration of "the covenant." And last, David wanted to build a more eloquent Temple to replace the portable Tabernacle. As a result, the Lord influenced David to have the Temple built upon the same mount that Abraham had built an altar (2 Chron. 3:2). Therefore, when Dan confirms "the covenant" he will approve for the Jews to build the third Temple on Temple Mount in Jerusalem. His decree will begin the countdown of the final seven years, as the decree ordered by the Persian King Artaxerxes began the countdown on the previous 483 years.

The Antichrist will not stipulate a seven-year trial or peace agreement, as some prophecy scholars ignorantly teach. It just so happens that the clock will begin to tick on the seven years when Dan decrees for the Jews to build the third Temple, which is an essential part of "the covenant." Some Bible translations have incorrectly translated the passage of Daniel 9:27 as "*a* covenant" instead of "*the* covenant." This, I believe, has occurred as a result of the translators including their private interpretations to the passage, who believe the Antichrist is going to primarily come up with a clever peace agreement for Israel and their foes. He will stipulate peace (Dan. 8:25) in the agreement to Israel's enemies, who will still be in a state of shock following Gog and Company's defeat, but a seven-year trial period will not be mentioned. The prophecy in Daniel 9:27 clearly is about "*the* covenant" and not "*a* covenant" and the building of the third Temple. The timeframe of seven years is God's prophecy, not a time period that will be brought up by the Antichrist. It's just that the countdown will begin with his decree.

There is strong Scriptural evidence that reveals that Dan may issue the decree in the seventh month, on Tishri 14th, a day before the Jews begin celebrating the Feast of Tabernacles. If this is correct, then the biblical prophetic seven years of eighty-four months, of thirty days each, will also expire on Tishri 14th seven years later. The Scriptural evidence is overwhelming, which will be disclosed in the following chapters. For now, what I would like to point out is that when the Jews of the Babylonian captivity returned to Jerusalem, by the decree of the Persian King Cyrus, to rebuild the second Temple, they first kept the Feast of Tabernacles. From that point on, we are told, they began making preparations to build the Temple, which they began to do in the second month (Ezra 3:1-8). When Dan gives his decree, the Jews may then go on to keep the Feast of Tabernacles, then begin preparations to build the third Temple.

Currently, the most prominent group among Orthodox Jews campaigning for the rebuilding of the Temple upon Temple Mount is the organization known as the Temple Mount Faithful. The TMF has held demonstrations since 1970 insisting upon their right to rebuild the Temple and to worship on Temple Mount. Presently, the Israeli government permits the mount to be in the control of the Muslims due to the Dome of the Rock, and other Islamic holy sites on the mount. The TMF has appealed the matter to Israel's High Court, who rejected their claim due to the established law for the protection of holy sites. The court then ordered for the Israeli police to take measures to prevent provocative actions by the TMF due to the religious sensitivities between Jews and Muslims. In 1988, however, despite the ruling, the TMF proceeded with plans to lay the cornerstone for the Temple on Temple Mount. After learning of their plans, Muslim worshippers on Temple Mount began throwing rocks at Jews worshipping below at the Western Wall (Wailing Wall) in the fall of 1990. Taken by surprise, the Israeli police overreacted, killing seventeen Arab Muslims and wounding another fifty.[9]

Other groups actively involved in campaigning for the rebuilding of the Temple include the group El Har Hashem, which means "To the Lord's Mount"; the Temple Mount Institute, which maintains an exhibit of Temple appurtenances; and the Movement for the Establishment of the Temple, which oversees a fund that grows annually to be used for the construction of the Temple when the time comes for it to be built (which they believe will be soon, and they are right). Once they build the Temple, they will have to have members from the tribe of Levi to oversee the daily Temple oblations and sacrifices. Therefore, today, in Israel, there are Jews who are proven descendants of Levi who are in a perpetual state of training and preparation to operate the daily operations of the Temple once it is built.

When King Solomon had the first Temple built, they began by laying the foundation in the second month of the sacred order of the Jewish calendar (2 Chron. 3:2). When the Jews of the Babylonian captivity returned to build the second Temple, to replace the first which had been destroyed by the Babylonians, they, too, laid the foundation for the second Temple in the second month (Ezra 3:8). God never outright instructed them to begin constructing these two Temples in the second month, nor is there any mention anywhere in the Bible that they were even remotely aware of the second month connection. However, when they build the third Temple, I am convinced that they, too, will begin construction in the second month. There appears to be a Divinely inspired pattern concerning the second month in which other profound biblical, and even recent, events have occurred.

We will be looking at those later.

The ancient biblical name of the second month is Zif (1 Kings 6:1). Today, it's known as Iyar, but it counts on the modern Jewish calendar as the eighth month. I'll explain. The Jews of today use a civil order of their calendar to begin their new year instead of the biblical sacred order. The sacred order begins with the first month of Nisan and ends with the twelfth month of Adar (Esther 3:7). The civil order begins with the biblical seventh month of Ethanim, but is known today as Tishri (1 Kings 8:2). When it comes to matters concerning Bible prophecy, however, the sacred order is to be used.

In the book of Revelation, chapter eleven, the Apostle John was handed a measuring rod in his vision of the future conditions for the end-times Temple and told to "Rise and measure the temple of God, and the altar, and them that worship therein. But the court which is without the temple leave out, and measure it not; for it is given unto the Gentiles (non-Jews): and the holy city (Jerusalem) shall they (Gentiles) tread under foot (occupy) forty and two months (3½ years)" (Rev. 11:1-2).

The area around the Temple included inner and outer courts. The inner courts consisted of the Court of the Priests that surrounded the Temple proper, and the Court of Israel for Jewish males. The outer courts were that of the Court of the Women for Jewish women, and the Court of the Gentiles. For many years it was held that the Dome of the Rock had been built upon the very site where the Temple twice stood. However, recent archaeological estimations have revealed that the Temple proper actually stood about 250 feet north of the Dome.[10] It is this writer's belief that the Temple will be built alongside the Dome of the Rock, but without the outer Court of the Gentiles. Also, being that the Antichrist will have no regard for the "desire of women" (Dan. 11:37; Jewish Women) [11] this writer believes that the Court of the Women will be left out as well.

The prophecy reference to the "Holy City" being under Gentile occupation for a period of three and a half years refers to the last half of the final seven years. In the first half, the Jews will continue to control Jerusalem, as they do today, and flourish under the auspices of the Antichrist's temporary false peace. During that first three and half years, the Jews will begin construction on the third Temple in the second month of Iyar, not long after Dan issues the decree that will begin the countdown on the final seven years to Armageddon and the return of Jesus Christ. Within that seven-year period, many events are set to unfold, especially beginning at the midpoint.

> *Note: In recent years, a number of books have been published proclaiming that the Antichrist will be a Muslim who emerges from a Middle Eastern Islamic background. They say his empire will consist roughly of the Islamic nations in the Middle East, and that Saudi Arabia is "Mystery Babylon," the "great whore" of Revelation 17. These theories are in total disharmony with the prophetic Scriptures for reasons already revealed in this book, and yet to be disclosed hereafter. Plus, the Islamic world does not possess the military might, nor the technology, conducive for the Antichrist's empire. The biggest role Islam will play in the end-times will be what we reviewed in chapter six of this book, and whatever role they will play seven years later in the Battle of Armageddon.*

8

DOWN TO EARTH

"And I will give power unto my two witnesses, and they shall prophesy a thousand two hundred and threescore days...."
— Revelation 11:3

Immediately following John's instruction to "measure the temple of God" (Rev. 11:1-2), the Lord then announced the coming of His Two Witnesses, who will be sent to the lost sheep of Israel to preach Jesus Christ to them for a period of three and a half years. It's no coincidence that the building of the Temple and the coming of these Two Witnesses are mentioned here so close together; as on the very day that Dan issues the decree for the Jews to build the Temple, the countdown will begin on the final seven years and the Two Witnesses will suddenly appear in Israel to begin their ministry, which will last through the first half of the seven years.

Many have speculated over the identity of the Two Witnesses. Most agree that the Prophet Elijah, who was taken up alive into Heaven (2 Kings 2:11), will be one of them. The Old Testament came to a close with the promise from God to send back "Elijah the prophet before the coming of the great and dreadful day of the Lord" (Mal. 4:5). The Jews of today are very aware of this prophecy concerning Elijah. Each year during Passover, many Jewish families leave an empty chair at the dining table, or one hanging on the wall in the dining room, symbolizing their expectation of Elijah's coming. They believe he is to appear "in the end of days to announce the arrival of the Messiah...the resurrection of the dead...and the establishment of the Divine

Kingdom upon the earth."[1]

There is some disagreement, however, concerning the identity of the other Witness. Most believe it will be Enoch. Like Elijah, Enoch was taken up alive into Heaven without tasting of death (Gen. 5:24). Others believe it may be Moses, due to the descriptions of the exploits that the Two Witnesses will perform during their ministry, which parallel some of the things Moses did during his time upon earth (Rev. 11:6). They also believe it may be Moses because he appeared with Elijah upon the Mount of Transfiguration (Matt. 17:3). The problems with this theory are; first, it was God who did the miracles through Moses; second, in the transfiguration Moses represented the law, and Elijah the Prophets; and last, Moses, unlike Elijah and Enoch, lived a full life, which ended with his death (Deut. 34:5). Actually, it's quite simple if you think about it. Everyone, or just about everyone I suppose, believes that Elijah will be one of the Two Witnesses. Well, there was only one other person in the Bible who, like Elijah, was taken alive up into Heaven. Therefore, I believe it will be Elijah and Enoch based upon these Scriptural facts.

The duo is poised to fulfill their mission "before the coming of the great and dreadful day of the Lord." The "Day of the Lord" is a repeated theme throughout the prophetic Scriptures, which alludes to the last three and half years of the final seven before the return of Christ (Zeph. 1:14-18; 1 Thes. 5:1-9). It's also known as the "Great Tribulation" (Matt. 24:21), and the "Time of Jacob's Trouble" (Jer. 30:7). This period is going to be the darkest hour of human history, wherein the judgments described by the unleashing of the seven-trumpet judgments and the seven-vial judgments in the book of Revelation will be unleashed (Rev. 8-16). The Prophet Isaiah was referring to this time when he wrote: "Behold, the day of the Lord cometh, cruel both with wrath and fierce anger, to lay the land (earth) desolate: and he (God) shall destroy the sinners thereof out of it....And I will punish the world for their evil..." (Isa. 13:9,11).

To give Israel and the nations ample space to repent, the Lord is going to have Elijah and Enoch perform their calling in the first half of the final seven years. To authenticate their message, the pair will be given supernatural powers over nature to plague the earth as often as they will (Rev. 11:6). As a result, many Jews who today do not believe that Jesus is their Messiah, will turn to Christ for salvation. On the other hand, many will continue in their disbelief. This, in turn, is going to cause a strain and division in Jewish homes, as in the days when Jesus walked the dusty roads of Judea (Matt. 10:5-21).

In Revelation 12:1, the Apostle John was shown a vision of "a woman clothed with the sun, and the moon under her feet, and upon her head a crown of twelve stars." The interpretation to the identity of the woman is found in Joseph's dream in Genesis 37. Joseph (one of Jacob's twelve sons) had a dream of the sun, moon, and eleven stars that represented his mother, father, and eleven brothers. Therefore, the woman is the nation of Israel. As John's vision continued, Revelation 12:2,5 gives further details which identifies the woman as being Israel. We also see at that same time how Satan was introduced as the "great red dragon whose tail drew the third part of the stars (angels) of heaven, and did cast them to the earth," in reference to his initial fall from Heaven (Rev. 12:3-4). The primary purpose of Revelation 12:1-5 is to introduce both Israel and Satan by using symbolic language that depicts past historical events concerning them.

Now, beginning in Revelation 12:6, the scene abruptly shifts to the end-times, which reads: "And the woman (Israel) fled into the wilderness, where she hath a place prepared of God, that they should feed her there a thousand two hundred and threescore (1,260) days." It is believed by most prophecy scholars that the "place prepared of God" is a reference to the natural rock fortress of Petra, located in the wilderness south of the Dead Sea. Petra is one of the most inaccessible places on earth. The only entrance is a narrow, mile-long gorge between towering red granite and sandstone cliffs. In some places, the gorge is only about 12-feet wide, but it eventually opens up into an enormous valley surrounded by the towering rock cliffs.

Notice in the above passage of Scripture that it reads: *"they should feed her (Israel) there."* The *"they"* is a reference to the Two Witnesses. To come to this understanding, we do so by observing how the book of Revelation only uses the numerical 1,260 days twice, both of which allude to the first three and a half years of the final seven. The first one, as we've seen, is Revelation 11:3, where we saw how the ministry of the Two Witnesses is going to last for 1,260 days. The second is Revelation 12:6, which corresponds to the same time period of the ministry of the Two Witnesses. The remaining six Scriptures that refer to a period of three and a half years in the books of Daniel and Revelation are all phrased differently and allude to the last half of the final seven years. We'll review these shortly.

The Two Witnesses are going to lead the new converts to Christ from among the Jews in Israel to Petra and "feed them there" the spiritual food of the Word of God, as well as take care of their natural needs. After these newly born babes in Christ are saved, and even perhaps baptized in the Jordan River, they may not be able to return to their homes and might have to go elsewhere. The reason for such may be that their strict Jewish families will view them as apostates and a disgrace to the family, and/or they will be inspired by God to flee to Petra.

Among this group of new converts, there will be included 144,000 young Jewish males who will be elected by God for a special purpose, perhaps to aide Elijah and Enoch in evangelizing Israel. The Lord is going to "seal," or rather save, 12,000 each from twelve tribes of Israel (Rev. 7:1-8). The "seal" is none other than the seal of the Holy Spirit upon a redeemed soul (Eph. 1:13). Interestingly, the tribe of Dan is not included in the sealing of the 144,000. The reason is that, the rebellious history of the tribe of Dan is going to culminate in the person of the Antichrist (Lev. 24:10-11; Jud. 18:30). During the end-times, the tribe of Dan will be represented by the Antichrist as he performs his role as he who is going to "judge his people as one of the tribes of Israel" (Gen. 49:16-17). To fill the void of Dan's absence, the tribe of Manasseh, who was Joseph's firstborn, and whom Jacob (Israel) adopted as his own son, receives the honor. This move also keeps in line with the promise to Joseph to receive a double portion of inheritance (Ezek. 47:13-14).

When John the Baptist fulfilled his calling in "the spirit and power of Elijah" (Luke 1:17), he baptized many Jews to prepare them to meet the Lord. Among these were the twelve who were later chosen by Christ to be His twelve Apostles, who then followed Christ (the Lamb) across Zion (Israel) during the course of Jesus' ministry. When Elijah himself returns, he is going to baptize many Jews over a period of three and a half years to prepare them to "meet the Lord in the air" at the Rapture (1 Thes. 4:17). Among them will be the 12x12,000 (144,000) who are, after the Rapture, depicted in the book of Revelation as being in Heaven following "the Lamb whithersoever he goeth" over the terrain of Heaven's Mount Zion above, while Christ executes His judgments of the seven-trumpet judgments and the seven-vial judgments during the Great Tribulation (Rev. 7:9; 14:1-4; Heb. 12:22). We'll review these events later.

Out of the original twelve Apostles, one of them, Judas Iscariot, betrayed Jesus and was later replaced by Matthias, after Judas hung himself (Matt. 27:1-10). Jesus later referred to Judas as the "son of perdition" (John 17:12). Likewise, Dan, for his betrayal, will be replaced by Manasseh in the sealing of the 144,000. And like Judas, Dan is also referred to in the Scriptures as that other "son of perdition" by the Apostle Paul (2 Thes. 2:3). And, it is my guess that Judas Iscariot was of the tribe of Dan, even though the Scriptures do not state this (but in a sense they do).

Elijah and Enoch will use Petra as a place of refuge for the

144,000 and other Jewish converts during the course of their three-and-a-half-year ministry. During that time, the nation of Israel will continue to prosper under the mask of the false peace provided by Dan. On the other hand, parts of the world in general will be enduring a time of "tribulation" (not Great Tribulation) that is depicted by the opening of the first four of seven seals mentioned in Revelation 6:1-8. The opening of the first seal releases an angelic rider upon a white horse, which depicts when the Antichrist is granted power to conquer the Middle East. The second seal unleashes a rider upon a red horse, who takes peace from a fourth part of the earth. The opening of the third seal reveals a rider on a black horse with a set of scales in his hand, depicting economic suffering and famine over a fourth of the earth. The fourth seal shows a rider on a pale horse whose name is "Death, and Hell followed with him. And power was given unto them (four horsemen) over the fourth part of the earth, to kill with sword, and with hunger, and with death, and with the beasts of the earth" (Rev. 6:8). This does not imply that a fourth of the world's population will be killed, as many renowned scholars teach, but only that these conditions will affect a "fourth part of the earth." The areas that will be mostly affected by these conditions during the first three and a half years will probably consist of parts of Asia, Africa, and the Middle East.

■ ■ ■

In his first Epistle to the Thessalonians, the Apostle Paul warned that a false cry of "peace and safety" would precede the "Day of the Lord," which will suddenly come upon Israel and the world as a "thief in the night" (1 Thes. 5:1-3). The Apostle explained that Christians would not be caught off guard by these events, who he commanded to "watch" for the signs of its approach (1 Thes. 5:4-6). He then went on to say that the believers would be spared from going through the "Day of the Lord," or

Down to Earth

rather the "Great Tribulation," and be kept from it, for God "hath not appointed us to (His) wrath" (1 Thes. 5:7-9). Paul said these things immediately following his most profound exposition on the Rapture, which is set to occur just prior to the wrath of the Great Tribulation (1 Thes. 4:13-18).

After receiving Paul's first Epistle, the Thessalonians became somewhat anxious, thinking that the Lord was about to return at any moment to take them to Heaven. In response to their uneasiness, Paul wrote them a second Epistle to calm them by giving them more details of things that must first take place before the Rapture. Beginning in chapter two of Second Thessalonians, we read: "Now I beseech you, brethren, by the coming of our Lord Jesus Christ, and by our gathering together (raptured) unto him. That ye be not soon shaken in mind, or be troubled, neither by spirit, nor by word, nor by letter as from us, as that the day of Christ (Day of the Lord) is at hand. Let no man deceive you by any means: for that day (Rapture/Day of the Lord) shall not come, except there come a falling away (apostasy; *Strong's Concordance*, 646) first, and that man of sin (Dan) be revealed, the son of perdition; Who opposeth and exalteth himself above all that is called God, or that is worshipped; so that he as God sitteth in the temple of God, shewing himself that he is God" (2 Thes. 2:1-4). In other words, the Rapture/Day of the Lord will not occur until after there develops a widespread apostasy within Christendom, and after Dan goes into the still yet unbuilt third Jewish Temple and makes his claim to be the Jews' Messiah-God. When Paul wrote Second Thessalonians, the second Jewish Temple was still standing, because it had not yet been destroyed by the Romans, which occurred after Paul's death. Paul wrote what he wrote in Second Thessalonians chapter two based upon his knowledge of the prophecies in the book of Daniel that refer to the coming man of sin, as the Holy Spirit gave him the understanding.

The Prophet Daniel, in reference to what Paul stated above,

wrote of Dan when he said, "And he shall confirm the covenant with many for one week (seven years): and in the midst of the week, he shall cause the sacrifice and the oblation to cease, and for the overspreading of abominations he shall make it (Temple) desolate, even until the consummation (end), and that determined (by God) shall be poured (wrath) upon the desolate (lifeless/unsaved)" (Dan. 9:27). In the midst of the final seven years, or rather somewhere in the middle, Dan is going to put a stop to the daily sacrifice that will be conducted after the third Temple is built. Coupled with his claim to be the Jews' Messiah, his abominable actions will bring about a lifeless gloom to the newly resurrected Temple activities. Following this, the judgments predetermined by God, which are recorded in the book of Revelation, chapters eight through sixteen, will be unleashed (poured) upon the wicked who, in the eyes of God, are already dead in their sins.

When Jesus was questioned by His disciples concerning the "sign of thy coming, and of the end of the world" (Matt. 24:3), He referred to this same event, saying, "When ye therefore shall see the abomination of desolation, spoken of by Daniel the prophet, stand in the holy place (Temple)...For then there shall be great tribulation, such as was not since the beginning of the world to this time, no, nor ever shall be...Then if any man shall say unto you, Lo, here is Christ, or there; believe it not. For there shall arise false Christs, and false prophets, and shall shew great signs and wonders; in so much that if it were possible, they shall deceive the very elect" (Matt. 24:15-24). What Jesus is saying here is that when Dan defiles the Temple (referred to as the "holy place") it will be a "sign of thy coming" and will precede the Great Tribulation. He goes on to warn of the rise of false Christs and prophets who will perform "great signs and wonders" to the extent that "if it were possible" (but it's not) even His elected believers in Him (who will be around to witness when Dan defiles the Temple) would be deceived. The emphasis here is on

Down to Earth

the "False Christ" (Dan), and the "False Prophet" of Revelation. The reason for the plural "Christs" and "prophets" being here used is because since the time of Christ, many false Christs and false prophets have come and gone, which will all come to a head in the "False Christ" and the "False Prophet" of Revelation.

■ ■ ■

In all, there are eight Scriptures that specifically mention a time period of three and a half years. Two of them, Revelation 11:3 and 12:6, refer to the first half of the last seven years, as we've already reviewed. The other six, Daniel 7:25; 12:7 and 12:11, and Revelation 11:2; 12:14 and 13:5 all refer to the bottom half of the final seven years. Three of them, Daniel 7:25; 12:7 and Revelation 12:14 refer to this three and a half years as a "time (one year), and times (two years), and half a time (half a year)." Two of the six, Revelation 11:2 and 13:5 refer to it as "forty and two months." Out of the six, however, there is one that is unique from the others, for it reveals when the Antichrist is going to stop the daily sacrifice.

The Scripture in question is Daniel 12:11, which states: "And from the time that the daily sacrifice shall be taken away, and the abomination that maketh desolate set up, there shall be a thousand two hundred and ninety (1,290) days." When Dan stops the daily sacrifice, it will occur exactly 30 days before the official prophetic clock begins to tick on the Great Tribulation period, which is set to last "forty and two months" (Rev. 11:2) of thirty days each (1,260 days).

In the Old Testament, there's a story that just may contain a clue that reveals the exact day of the Jewish calendar that Dan will stop the daily sacrifice. As you may recall from chapter two of this book, we saw how a Persian prime minister named Haman plotted to kill all the Jews throughout the empire. To decide on the day in which his evil scheme was to be carried out, Haman cast the "Pur," or rolled the dice, on Nisan 13th. The dice landed on the number twelve, so he decreed that everyone in his empire were to rise up against and kill all the Jews on Adar 13th, the twelfth month of the biblical calendar (Esther 3).

As the story goes, Haman's plot backfired and he and his ten sons were hanged. The Jews were granted power by the Persian king over their enemies and killed all those who sided with Haman on the 13th of Adar. On the 14th, the Jews throughout the Persian Empire celebrated their victory over their enemies with feasting, great joy, and giving gifts one to another. It was then decreed among them that they were to celebrate each year on Adar 14th to commemorate their victory over Haman. They named the holiday "Purim," which is still observed by Jews today and is one of the most joyous and festive celebrations on the Jewish calendar (Esther 9).

Midway into the seven-year countdown, Israel will be riding "high on their horse," so to speak, in peace and prosperity under the deceptive auspices of Dan. As the Jews prepare to celebrate Purim, Dan may stop the daily sacrifice on Adar 13th and set up the abomination of desolation, thereby defiling the Temple. It will be at this time that the Antichrist will begin to fulfill the prophecy spoken by Jacob that his son Dan shall "judge his people (Jews), as one of the tribes of Israel…Dan shall be a serpent (satanic)…that biteth the horse heels, so that his rider (Israel) shall fall backward" (Gen. 49:16-17).

Some events in the Old Testament era foreshadow a much greater event to be played out in the New Testament era — which era, by the way, will continue unto the Second Coming of Christ. The events that led to the establishment of the Jewish holiday of Purim is one of them. Haman, his ten sons, and his attempt to exterminate the Jews, all foreshadow the Antichrist, his ten kings, and what will be his attempt to destroy the Jews. Adar 13th, the day Haman had determined to kill all the Jews, will be the ideal time for Satan to have Dan begin his plot to destroy the Jews — and, in a sense, attempt to finish what he failed to complete through Haman. This would hit the Jews hard at one of their highest points of the year, as they are preparing to celebrate Purim on Adar 14th. Also, Purim is celebrated exactly 30 days before the Feast of Passover (the preparations for the Passover feast begin on Nisan 14th).

It was during the Feast of Passover, another foreshadowing Old Testament event, that Christ was put to death. Just prior to His death, Christ had gone into the outer court of the Temple area to cleanse it from the thieves and moneychangers (Matt. 21:12). Afterwards, the Jews plotted to have him put to death (Matt. 26:3-4). After Dan forces the Jews to stop the daily sacrifice, and defiles the Temple by entering forbidden space, the Jews will then plot to kill him. Jesus was marked for death after he entered the Temple area to cleanse it. On the other hand, Dan will be marked for death after he defiles it. Are these things just a coincidence? I believe not! And, as did Christ, Dan, too, will make his claim to be the Jews' Messiah.

Jesus referred to Judas Iscariot, who betrayed Christ, as the "son of perdition" (John 17:12). The Scriptures tell us that Satan entered Judas two days before the Passover (Matt. 26:1-16; Luke 22:1-6). The Passover feast is prepared in the daylight hours of the 14th of Nisan, but the feast does not officially begin until after sundown, which marks the beginning of the 15th because the Jewish day begins after sunset. Therefore, two days before Passover would be the 13th. It was on this day also that Satan entered, so to speak, Haman and had him toss the dice to set the date to kill all the Jews. It is my best guess that Satan is also going to enter, or rather possess, the Antichrist (that other "son of perdition; 2 Thes. 2:3) on the 13th of Nisan, after he is killed, to take over his body for the course of the Great Tribulation.

More than likely, Dan is going to find himself the recipient of an assassin's bullet, perhaps several days or so before Nisan 13th. The assassin will most likely be a young Orthodox Jew who is zealous for the law of God and the Temple. On November 4, 1995, a young Orthodox Jew by the name of Yigal Amir shot and killed Israel's Prime Minister Yitzhak Rabin following a peace rally in Tel Aviv. Amir later confessed that he shot Rabin because he was outraged over the peace accords Rabin had signed with Jordan and the Palestinian Liberation Organization (PLO). After Dan claims to be the Messiah and defiles the Temple, which the Jews have waited almost 2,000 years to rebuild, I can only imagine that there will be many like Amir, who will gladly volunteer to kill the blasphemer, which under the Old Testament law is punishable by death. It was this same law that was used against Christ to have Him put to death (Mark 14:61-64).

■ ■ ■

In Revelation chapter thirteen, the Apostle John wrote that he "saw a beast...having seven heads and ten horns...And the beast which I saw was like unto a leopard, and his feet were as the feet of a bear, and his mouth as the mouth of a lion: and the dragon (Satan) gave him (Dan) his power, and his seat, and great authority. And I saw one of his heads as it were wounded to death; and his deadly wound was healed" (Rev. 13:1-3). Later, John was told by an angel that "The beast that thou sawest was, and is not; and shall ascend out of the bottomless pit (Hell), and go into perdition: and they that dwell upon the earth shall wonder...when they behold the beast that was (alive), and is not (killed), and yet is (alive again). And here is the mind which hath wisdom. The seven heads are seven mountains (kingdoms)...And there are seven kings; five are fallen (past empires), and one is (currently in power in John's time), and the other is not yet come (future); and when he cometh, he must continue a short space. And the beast that was and is not, even he is the eighth, and is of the seven and goeth into perdition" (Rev. 17:8-

11). Okay, did you figure all that out yet?

Remember how, in Daniel chapter seven, we saw his vision of a lion, a bear, and a four-headed leopard, which depicted the Babylonian, Medo-Persian, and Grecian Empires? As you may also recall, the four heads of the leopard represented the four kingdoms of the massive Grecian Empire after it was divided following Alexander the Great's untimely death. Likewise, the seven heads of the beast John saw also represent seven kingdoms. The angel told John that the "seven heads are seven mountains." In the Bible, the word *"mountain"* is used sometimes in reference to an empire, such as Babylon in Jeremiah 51:25. Also, the word *"kings"* is sometimes used in reference to "kingdoms," as in Daniel 7:17. Therefore, the correct interpretation of the "seven mountains/seven kings" is as follows:

1. **Babylon — Lion**
2. **Media** ⎫
3. **Persia** ⎬ ➢ **Bear**
4. **Seleucid** ⎫
5. **Ptolemaic** ⎬ ➢ **Leopard**
6. **Rome — John's time**
7. **Antichrist's — Future**

The five fallen kings, or rather kingdoms, mentioned in the above passage refer to the first five listed above. Each of these five kingdoms had dominion over the land of Israel during the course of their reign. In Daniel's vision, they were depicted as a lion, a bear, and a leopard respectively. In John's vision, the description of the beast alludes to these past empires in the "looking back" reverse order of leopard, bear, and lion. When John wrote the book of Revelation, the Roman Empire was in power (referred to in the above Scripture as the "one is") and it, too, controlled the Holy Land. The other kingdom (mentioned as the one who had "not yet come") refers to the future empire of Dan, which is depicted by the seventh head. The death of the Antichrist is depicted by the seventh head that was "wounded to death," and after a brief stay in Hell, Dan will "ascend out of the bottomless pit." In explaining this event, the angel referred to Dan as "the beast that was (alive) and is not (dead) and yet is (alive again)." After Dan arises from the dead, he will then resume his authority and "continue a short space (3 ½ years)." And finally, the angel told John that "the beast that was, and is not, even he is the eighth, and is of the seven...." Before Dan is killed, he represents the seventh head. After his death and resurrection, he becomes "the eighth and is of the seven" in his new beginning with satanic powers. A similar expression was used by Jesus in reference to Himself being alive, then dead, then alive again in Revelation 1:18. Also, Jesus descended briefly into Hell following His death (Acts 2:27; Eph. 4:9; 1 Peter 3:18-20).

■ ■ ■

In expounding on the Antichrist in his second Epistle to the Thessalonians, the Apostle Paul wrote: "And now you know what withholdeth that he (Dan) might be revealed in his time. For the mystery of iniquity doth already work: only he (Holy Spirit/God) who now letteth (restrains; *Strong's Concordance*, 2722) will let, until he be taken (restraint lifted) out of the way. And then shall that Wicked (Dan's satanic nature) be revealed, whom the Lord shall consume with the spirit of his mouth, and shall destroy with the brightness of his coming: Even him (Dan), whose coming is after the working of Satan with all power and signs and lying wonders, And with all deceivableness of unrighteousness in them that perish; because they received not the love of the truth (Jesus), that they might be saved. And for this cause, God shall send them strong delusion (Dan's resurrection), that they should believe a lie. That they all might be damned who believed not the truth, but had pleasure in unrighteousness" (2

Thes. 2:6-12).

In the Gospel of John, Jesus referred to the Holy Spirit as "He" on numerous occasions (John 14; 16). Therefore, it is God/Holy Spirit who is currently keeping Satan in check. Otherwise, all Hell would have broken loose on earth already. At the appointed time, though, God is going to remove His restraint from the Devil and permit him to go virtually unchecked during the Great Tribulation. This God will do as part of His judgment upon Israel and the nations for their rejection of the "Truth," Jesus Christ. Satan will be permitted to perform "lying wonders" through Dan, which will begin with the "strong delusion" of his resurrection. Through the Prophet Isaiah, the Lord said, "I also will choose their delusions, and will bring their fears upon them; because when I called, none did answer; when I spake, they did not hear: but they did evil before mine eyes..." (Isa. 66:4).

The Prophet Daniel was referring to this same time when he wrote: "And in the latter time of their (Gentiles') kingdom, when the transgressors are come to the full (end-times), a king (Dan) of fierce countenance, and understanding dark sentences, shall stand up. And his power shall be mighty, but not by his own power (Satan's power): and he shall destroy wonderfully, and shall prosper, and practice, and shall destroy the mighty (kings) and the holy people (Jews/saints). And through his policy also he shall cause craft (deceit/craftiness) to prosper in his hand; and he shall magnify himself in his heart, and by peace (false peace) shall destroy many: he shall also stand up against the Prince (Jesus) of princes; but he shall be broken without hand (by Christ)" (Dan. 8:23-25).

■ ■ ■

Currently, Satan and his army of devils are, in part, kept in check by God's Heavenly body of holy angels, who are under the leadership of the archangel Michael. At the present time, Satan is permitted access to God, who he often visits to bring his accusations against the brethren, as in the case involving Job (Job 1:6-7). Also, the heavenly realm between earth and God's Throne is often the scene where battles are fought between good and bad angels over the destinies of people and nations (Dan. 10:1-21). At the midpoint of the final seven years, however, this will all abruptly change, leaving Satan and his angels totally confined to earth.

To review this, we must now return to Revelation chapter twelve, where we left off at verse 6, which refers to how Elijah and Enoch are going to care for the new Jewish converts at Petra for 1,260 days, which we saw alludes to the first half of the seven years. Then, beginning in verse 7, it states: "And there was war in heaven: Michael and his angels fought against the dragon; and the dragon fought and his angels, and prevailed not; neither was their place found any more in heaven. And the great dragon was cast out, that old serpent, called the Devil, and Satan, which deceiveth the whole world: he was cast out into the earth, and his angels were cast out with him. And I heard a loud voice saying in heaven, Now is come salvation, and strength, and the kingdom of our God, and the power of his Christ: for the accuser of our brethren is cast down, which accused them before our God day and night...Therefore rejoice, ye heavens, and ye that dwell in them. Woe to the inhabiters of the earth and of the sea! For the devil is come down unto you, having great wrath, because he knoweth that he hath but a short time. And when the dragon saw that he was cast unto the earth, he persecuted the woman (Israel)... And to the woman was given two wings of a great eagle, that she might fly into the wilderness, into her place, where she is nourished for a time (one year), and times (two years), and half a time (half a year) from the face of the serpent" (Rev. 12:7-

14).

Notice how this future demise of Satan being totally thrust from the heavenly realm is mentioned in the prophetic Scriptures between verse 6, which refers to the first half of the final seven years, and verse 14, which alludes to the last half. This event is set to occur in the middle at around the same time Dan is killed. Knowing he "hath but a short time" left (3 ½ years), before he is taken and cast into the bottomless pit (Rev. 20:1-2) for a thousand years, Satan will, at this point, possess the body of Dan and first go after the Jews. This, in turn, is going to cause many more Jews to flee to Petra than before, under the guidance and protection of God. We will be looking further into this in a later chapter.

The Prophet Daniel referred to this same event when he wrote: "And at that time (end-times) shall Michael stand up, the great prince which standeth for the children of thy people (Jews): and there shall be a time of trouble (Great Tribulation), such as never was since there was a nation even to that same time: and at that time thy people shall be delivered, every one that shall be found written in the book" (Dan. 12:1). Jesus referred to this time as well, when He said, "When ye therefore shall see the abomination of desolation, spoken of by Daniel the prophet stand in the holy place (Temple)...For then shall be great tribulation, such as was not since the beginning of the world to this time, no, nor ever shall be. And except those days should be shortened, there should no flesh be saved: but for the elect's sake those days shall be shortened" (Matt. 24:15-22).

> *Note: Michael is not Jesus Christ, as the false Christian groups (Jehovah Witnesses and Mormons) ignorantly teach; nor is "Michael" just another name, or title, for Jesus as is taught by the Seventh-Day Adventist. See Hebrews 1:1-14. Michael is the leading archangel over God's holy angels. He also personally oversees the affairs of the nation of Israel (Dan. 10:12, 21).*

In writing about Dan's resurrection, and some of his exploits that will follow, the Apostle John wrote: "...and his deadly wound was healed: and all the world wondered after the beast. And they worshipped the dragon which gave power unto the beast. And they worshipped the beast saying, Who is like unto the beast? Who is able to make war with him? And there was given unto him a mouth speaking great things and blasphemies; and power was given unto him to continue forty and two months (3 ½ years). And he opened his mouth in blasphemy against God, to blaspheme his name, and his tabernacle, and them that dwell in heaven. And it was given unto him to make war with the saints, and to overcome them: and power was given him over all kindreds, and tongues, and nations. And all that dwell upon the earth shall worship him, whose names are not written in the book of life of the Lamb (Jesus) slain from the foundation of the world" (Rev. 13:3-8).

The world will be in awe and deceived by Dan's return to life. Anyone not nailed down by the Spirit of God will be in danger of being carried away by the wind of this great "lying wonder" (Matt. 24:24). The deceived will begin to worship "the Beast" (Dan) as "the Christ" and thereby worship "the Dragon" (Satan), which will be the peak of the Devil's folly. By his claim to be the Christ, Dan will blaspheme the name of God, and everything and everyone affiliated with the Truth, Jesus Christ. Also, it will be around this time that Satan's seat will move for the final time upon earth from Rome to Jerusalem. From Eden to Babylon to Pergamum to Rome, the Devil's desire to be worshipped as God will culminate in Jerusalem, the city of our God and King, Jesus Christ.

Dan's quest to rule the world and be worshipped will begin in Jerusalem, starting with the Jews. It will be the beginning of the time period foretold by the Prophet Jeremiah as the "Time of Jacob's (Israel's) Trouble" (Jer. 30:7). His first victims will be Elijah and Enoch, after they "...have finished their testimony, the beast that ascended out of the bottomless pit (Dan's brief stay in Hell) shall make war against them, and shall overcome them, and kill them. And their dead bodies shall lie in the street in the great city (Jerusalem), which spiritually is called Sodom and Egypt, where also our Lord (Jesus) was crucified. And they of the people and kindreds and tongues and nations shall see (by television, computers, cell phones, etc.) their dead bodies three days and a half, and shall not suffer their dead bodies to be put in graves. And they that dwell upon the earth shall rejoice over them, and make merry, and shall send gifts one to another; because these two prophets tormented them that dwelt on the earth. And after three days and an half, the Spirit of life from God entered into them, and they stood upon their feet; and great fear fell upon them which saw them. And they heard a great voice from heaven saying unto them, Come up hither. And they ascended up to heaven in a cloud; and their enemies beheld them" (Rev. 11:7-12).

Dan/Satan will be permitted by God to kill Elijah and Enoch for a very noble cause. Their dead bodies will lie in the street in Jerusalem for three and a half days so that all the world will get to see that they are very much dead. This God will allow so that the length of time of their deaths equals or supersedes the amount of time that Dan will lie dead before his rising. The resurrection of the duo will counter Dan's resurrection in order to give people an option to believe the true or the false. Following the duo's departure, we read that there will be a "great earthquake, and the tenth part of the city fell, and in the earthquake were slain of men seven thousand; and the remnant were affrighted, and gave glory to the God of heaven" (Rev. 11:13). After the rising of Elijah and Enoch, and the earthquake, these events will be as God's signature upon their entire ministry, causing many, perhaps, to seek salvation in Jesus Christ.

> *Note: Many scholars say that the ministry of the Two Witnesses will occur in the last half of the final seven years, but this cannot be true for many reasons. The Great Tribulation will be the most horrific time period in the history of mankind. By the end of that time, the earth will have been thrust into total chaos and destruction; Armageddon will have reached its peak; the sun, moon, and stars will all have been darkened, and the return of Jesus Christ to earth will commence (Matt. 24; Rev. 16; 19). So how then does the killing of the Two Witnesses; their dead bodies lying in the street for three and a half days, and the whole world seeing them and making merry, sending gifts one to another, fit in during all the above mentioned? They don't. All the Scriptural evidence points to the ministry of the Two Witnesses being carried out in the first half of the final seven years.*

As a result of all the events that will occur in the first three and a half years, Christendom will have been shaken to the core because most Christians have been taught to believe that these events will occur after the Rapture. Beginning with Dan's takeover in the Middle East, and the Jews' rebuilding of the Temple, many pastors, televangelists, and authors of numerous books, all who teach the pre-seven-year Rapture theory, will be left scrambling to explain to their followers why the Rapture had not occurred by then, forcing them to seek a clearer understanding. On the other hand, many Christians will not be surprised at all by the events of the first half and will earnestly warn the masses to repent and comfort the saints to prepare to meet the Lord.

Word to the Wise

"Now learn a parable of the fig tree; when his branch is yet tender, and putteth forth leaves, ye know that summer is nigh: so likewise ye, when ye shall see all of these things (Matt. 24:15-24), know that it (Jesus' coming for His saints) is near, even at the doors...But of that day and hour knoweth no man, no, not the angels of heaven, but my Father only. But as the days of Noah were, so shall also the coming of the Son of man be. For as in

the days that were before the flood, they were eating and drinking, marrying and giving in marriage, until the day that Noah entered into the ark, And knew not until the flood came, and took them all away; so shall also the coming of the Son of man be. Then shall two be in the field; the one shall be taken, and the other left. Two women shall be grinding at the mill; the one shall be taken, and the other left. Watch (for the signs) therefore, for ye know not what hour your Lord doth come" (Matt. 24:32-42).

9

THE FIRST RESURRECTION

"Blessed and holy is he that hath part in the first resurrection."
— Revelation 20:6

You won't find the word *"Rapture"* in the Bible. It's a word used among evangelical Christians in reference to the joyous occasion when Christ comes to resurrect the bodies of His saints who have passed, and to remove the ones alive from the earth out of the Great Tribulation. The Apostle Paul wrote of this event when he stated: "But I would not have you to be ignorant, brethren, concerning them which are asleep (dead bodies of saints), that ye sorrow not, even as others (unbelievers), which have no hope. For if we believe that Jesus died and rose gain, even so them also which sleep (have died) in Jesus will God bring (their souls) with him...For the Lord himself shall descend (come) from heaven with a shout, with the voice of the archangel and with the trump of God: and the dead in Christ shall rise first: Then we which are alive and remain shall be caught up together with them in the clouds to meet the Lord in the air: and so shall we ever be with the Lord. Wherefore comfort one another with these words" (1 Thes. 4:13-18).

There are four different views held among Christians concerning when the Rapture will occur. As with any Bible topic, however, the truth about the Rapture can only be obtained by "rightly dividing the word of truth" (2 Tim. 2:15). When this fundamental Bible principle is ignored, it results in a private interpretation of a topic that turns out to be either totally untrue or partially true. Add a few renowned televangelists and authors to the list of supporters of the private interpretation, and millions will just blindly jump on board. This is how we have come to see the different views on the Rapture, even though the Bible only gives us one view.

The most popularly held view is what's known as the "imminent" coming of Christ any day now, which will then be followed by a seven-year tribulation period for those left behind. Millions of Christians wake up each day thinking that Christ could come today. Sadly, there is absolutely no Scriptural support for this view. This theory is commonly referred to as the Pre-Tribulation Rapture.

The second most commonly held view of the Rapture is that it will occur somewhere in the middle of the final seven years, before the commencement of the horrors of the "Great Tribulation" (Matt. 24:15-24). Although this belief has Scriptural support, it's only a *part* of what the Bible refers to as the "First Resurrection" (Rev. 20:6). This view is known as the Mid-Tribulation Rapture.

Next, there is what's known as the Pre-Wrath Rapture of the Church theory, which was argued by renowned author Marvin Rosenthal. This view states that the Rapture will occur well into the Great Tribulation, just prior to the unleashing of God's judgment of the seven vials (Rev. 14:12-16:21). Although this theory has Scriptural foundation, it, too, is only a *part* of the First Resurrection.

The fourth view is known as the Post-Tribulation Rapture, which has Christ resurrecting and rapturing all the saints at the end of the Great Tribulation. This theory derived from Mark 13:27, where Jesus said He will then gather together His elect "...from the uttermost part of the earth to the uttermost part of heaven." Even though Christ will indeed do here as He said, it just won't unfold in the way that is taught by the Post-Tribulation view-holders.

The First Resurrection began nearly 2,000 years ago with the

The First Resurrection

resurrection of Jesus Christ. It will end with the resurrection of the saints who get saved during the Great Tribulation, but are killed by Dan (Antichrist). The Apostle John wrote: "...and I saw the souls of them that were beheaded for the witness of Jesus, and for the word of God, and which had not worshipped the beast (Dan), neither his image, neither had received his mark upon their foreheads, or in their hands; and they lived (resurrected) and reigned with Christ a thousand years. But the rest of the dead (unsaved) lived not again until the thousand years were finished. This is the first resurrection. Blessed and holy is he that **hath part** in the first resurrection: on such the second death hath no power, but they shall be priests of God and of Christ, and shall reign with him a thousand years" (Rev. 20:4-6).

The phrase "First Resurrection" does not suggest to us that all the saints will be resurrected and raptured just prior to the inauguration of the thousand-year Kingdom of Christ. If so, then it would appear to suggest that many other Scriptures are untrue. Therefore, the correct interpretation of the phrase "First Resurrection" is that the resurrection of the saints who die during the Great Tribulation completes the First Resurrection. To paraphrase, it could easily be written "this is the completion of the First Resurrection."

In expounding on the order of the First Resurrection, the Apostle Paul wrote: "But now is Christ risen from the dead, and become the firstfruits of them that slept...But every man in his own order: Christ the firstfruits; afterwards they that are Christ's at his coming" (1 Cor. 15:20-23). First of all, one must keep in mind that the "*coming*" of Christ will officially begin when He "*comes*" for His saints at the beginning of the Great Tribulation, after the resurrections of Elijah and Enoch (1 Thes. 4:13-5:10; Rev. 3:10; 7:9-14). After this, the Great Tribulation saints (the ones who get saved after the Rapture) who remain alive up to the point where God is about to unleash his final and most devastating wrath of the seven vials (Rev. 14:12-16:21), will have to be removed off the earth. At this time, however, there will only be a rapturing of those alive and not a resurrecting of any dead. The dead Great Tribulation saints will get resurrected after the Great Tribulation, as we just saw (Rev. 14:12-15:2; 20:4). So, within the timeframe of these events, all the saints will be either resurrected or raptured in "his own order."

∎ ∎ ∎

Those who teach that the Rapture could occur any moment now use Revelation 4:1-2 as their primary Scripture reference. The passage describes the Apostle John being caught up in the spirit to God's Throne, where he is given a vision of the end-times. Around the Throne he sees twenty-four seats with twenty-four elders and four odd-looking beasts who appear to be similar to the same four cherubims of Ezekiel chapters one and ten (Rev. 4:4-11). In front of the Throne, there appears to be what looks like a "sea of glass," which depicts a vast, empty space as one would see when looking across the calm waters of a great sea (Rev. 4:6). The imminent theory teaches that John's experience of being caught up in the spirit to God's Throne symbolizes the Rapture.

First, I'd like to point out that the Prophet Ezekiel had virtually the same, identical experience as John over 600 years prior. Compare Ezekiel 1:1-10 with Revelation 4:1-7. Also, John was later told to eat a book that tasted like honey (Rev. 10:9-10). So, too, was Ezekiel (Ezek. 3:1-3). Therefore, neither Ezekiel's nor John's experiences contain any deep revelation concerning the Rapture. Second, the imminent theory holds that the twenty-four elders consists of twelve patriarchs from the twelve tribes of Israel and the twelve Apostles of Christ, but this is not true. Jesus told His twelve Apostles that they would sit on twelve thrones "judging the twelve tribes of Israel" but only during the Messianic Kingdom Age (Matt. 19:28). The twenty-four elders appear to be of the angelic priestly order who tend to the holy offices in Heaven pertaining to the worship of God and the Temple in Heaven. See Leviticus 8:1-13; 1 Chronicles 24; Hebrews 8:1-5, and Revelation 11:16-19 and 15:5-8.

In the vision, John sees that the twenty-four elders are wearing gold crowns, which the Revelation 4 Rapture theorists claim is the "crown of life" reward promised to the saints (Rev. 2:10). The problem with that theory is that once the raptured saints are revealed, none are depicted wearing a crown (Rev. 7:9). Another problem with this theory is that once John's vision gets deep into the Great Tribulation, the twenty-four elders are heard announcing that the time had come for God to "give reward unto thy servants the prophets, and to the saints" (Rev. 11:16-18).

Those who promote the imminent view also teach that the Church is not depicted on earth throughout the book of Revelation after Revelation 4:1-2. They base this claim by pointing out that the word "church" is used in chapters one through three, but not afterwards until 22:16. The reason for this is simple. Jesus was addressing the seven churches of Asia Minor, which were seven well-established churches of which John served as bishop. Therefore, to address them as "church" and "churches" was the appropriate wording to use in this context. After chapter four of Revelation, the Church in general are referred to as "saints," "souls," "great multitude," those who have "the faith of Jesus," "them that had gotten the victory over the beast," "much people in heaven," and "the bride, the Lamb's wife" (Rev. 5:8; 6:9; 7:9; 14:12; 15:2; 19:1; 21:9).

In Revelation chapter five, John sees a vision of Christ being proclaimed the "Lion of the tribe of Judah" who alone is worthy to open a book sealed with seven seals (Rev. 5:1-7). In Revelation 5:8, John again sees the four beasts and twenty-four elders who hang out around God's Throne. These four beasts and twenty-four elders are depicted together throughout the book of Revelation leading in the perpetual worship of God as a distinct entity separate from the saints (Rev. 4:4-11; 5:14; 7:11; 14:3; 19:4). In Revelation 5:8, John sees the four beasts and twenty-four elders with "every one of them harps, and golden vials full of odours, which are the prayers of saints." The sweet fragrance of the "odours" symbolizes the prayers of the saints on earth, as did the altar of incense in the Temple in Old Testament times (Luke 1:5-10). The rising of the fragrance denotes the prayers being lifted up to God and the pleasure He receives from hearing from His saints (Ps. 141:2). Those who teach the Revelation 4 Rapture theory will say these are the prayers of the seven-year tribulation saints who get saved after the Rapture, but this is not the case, as we shall see after we review all the evidence.

As the Apostle John continued he wrote: "And they (beasts and elders) sung a new song, saying, Thou (Jesus) art worthy to take the book, and to open the seals thereof: for thou wast slain, and hast redeemed us (all redeemable creation in heaven and earth; Col. 1:20; Rev. 5:13) to God by thy blood out of every kindred, and tongue, and people, and nation; And hast made us unto our God kings and priests: and we shall reign on the earth" (Rev. 5:9-10). Some scholars, such as John Walvoord and Roy Zuck in *The Bible Knowledge Commentary,* say that this Scripture validates the elders are part of the Church because they use the words "us" and "we."[1] The problem with this theory is that the beasts are singing the song too. In *The New Scofield Reference Bible* it states that most early manuscripts omit "us" and "we" and reads "them" and "they."[2] Either way you look at it (from all three of the above points of view), the above passage does not prove that the elders represent a raptured Church.

■ ■ ■

Throughout the book of Revelation (chapters six through sixteen), we see what will be the opening of the book with seven seals, which will be followed by the blowing of the seven trum-

The First Resurrection

pets, and the outpouring of the seven vials. The opening of six of the seven seals pertains to events set to unfold during the first three and a half years of the final seven. The opening of the seventh seal kicks off the second half, wherein will be released the supernatural judgments of God with the blowing of the seven trumpets then the outpouring of the seven vials. It is this time, as we have seen, that has been dubbed the "Great Tribulation," and it is this which the Lord has promised to spare His faithful believers from having to endure, the ones who are saved before the Rapture, that is (Matt. 24:15-21; 1 Thes. 4:13-5:10; Rev. 3:10).

Revelation chapter six begins with the opening of the first four of seven seals, which unleashes four angelic beings depicted riding upon four different colored horses, who are granted power over a combined total of one-fourth of the earth (Rev. 6:1-8). Compare with Zechariah 6:1-5 for this interpretation. The first horseman symbolizes the exploits of the Antichrist when he is granted power to conquer the Middle East. The other three horsemen also depict judgments to be unleashed, of the natural sort, that will involve taking peace from the earth and many deaths by various causes; including, but not limited to, wars, murders, hunger, and the wild beasts of the earth. A fourth part of the world in general during this time will be experiencing a time of tribulation. However, Israel will go virtually unscathed during this time, as they enjoy a false sense of "peace and safety" under the auspices of Dan. The Apostle Paul referred to this false peace in 1 Thessalonians 5:3 that is to precede the Rapture (1 Thes. 4:17), and the "Day of the Lord" which would suddenly come upon Israel and the world as a "thief in the night" (1 Thes. 5:2). Paul states that Christians will not be caught off guard by these events and are warned to "watch" for them to unfold prior to being raptured to Heaven (1 Thes. 4:13-5:9).

With the opening of the fifth seal, John said he "saw under the altar the souls of them that were slain for the word of God...And they cried with a loud voice, saying, How long O

Lord, holy and true, doest thou not judge and avenge our blood on them that dwell on the earth? And white robes were given unto every one of them; and it was said unto them, that they should rest yet for a little season, until their fellow servants also and their brethren, that should be killed as they were, should be fulfilled" (Rev. 6:9-11). Here John is shown the martyrs of the Church Age who were killed because they were Christians. It appears that God has a special place and purpose for those who lost their lives solely because they were His servants. Their souls cried out, "how long" implying that they have been in that state a long time.

Those who teach the Revelation 4:1-2 Rapture theory say these are the souls of the saints killed in the seven-year tribulation *after* the Rapture because they are calling for vengeance upon those on earth who killed them. No, no, no, my friend! Cast off that private interpretation. The Bible doesn't need our help with the interpretation; *we* need *its* help. Now, while it is true that there will be saints who will be killed for their faith during the first half of the seven years, their souls will join those in Heaven who have been killed over the centuries. Even today, Christians are being murdered in some parts of the world simply because they are Christians. As time goes on, this will only grow increasingly worse and will reach its peak with the Great Tribulation saints, who will be killed during that time. See Matthew 23:31-36 for the correct interpretation of Revelation 6:9-11. In Matthew 23:31-36, Jesus told the unbelieving Jews that they were going to suffer the wrath of God's vengeance for His martyred servants long dead, even as far back to "righteous Abel." And they did in 66-70 A.D. during the war between the Jews and Romans, wherein hundreds of thousands were slaughtered and the Temple destroyed.

In John's vision of the martyred souls, he sees how each of them were issued "white robes," then told they were to "rest yet for a little season" longer in their current state. Let us here con-

The First Resurrection

sider that this is the opening of the fifth seal, with only two to go before the commencement of the Great Tribulation. These precious souls of the saints are here assigned white robes to prepare them for what is about to take place shortly from this point; for it will not be long before they will be summoned from under the altar of the Temple in Heaven to take their journey with Christ down to earth to be reunited to their bodies — their new, resurrected, glorified bodies (1 Thes. 4:13-14). We will look more into this shortly.

With the opening of the sixth seal, John saw that "there was a great earthquake; and the sun became black as sackcloth of hair, and the moon became as blood; and the stars of heaven fell unto the earth, even as a fig tree casteth her untimely figs, when she is shaken of a mighty wind. And the heaven departed as a scroll when it is rolled together; and every mountain and island were moved out of their places. And the kings of the earth, and the great men, and the rich men, and the chief captains, and the mighty men, and every bondman, and every free man, hid themselves in the dens and in the rocks of the mountains; And said to the mountains and rocks, Fall on us, and hide us from the face of him that sitteth on the throne, and from the wrath of the Lamb: For the great day of his wrath is come; and who shall be able to stand?" (Rev. 6:12-17).

As a final warning to Israel and the nations before the "Great Day of His Wrath," or rather the "Day of the Lord," God is going to shake the earth and darken the sun and turn the moon blood red temporarily at the midpoint of the seven years. The Prophet Joel referred to this same event when he wrote: "the sun shall be turned into darkness, and the moon into blood, before the great and terrible day of the Lord come" (Joel 2:31). This event is not to be mistaken for when the Scriptures reveal that the sun, moon, and stars will all be darkened during the literal Second Coming of Christ to earth (Matt. 24:29-30). Joel covered that, too, and as in Matthew, it is here said that the moon will be darkened, not turned to blood red (Joel 3:14-16). Therefore, both Joel 2:31 and Revelation 6:12 refer to the midpoint of the seven years, and Joel 3:14-16 and Matthew 24:29-30 the end of the seven years.

In Revelation 6:13, we read how the "stars of heaven" will all fall "unto the earth" at around the midpoint of the seven years. Now, let us consider this for a moment. If the stars of heaven literally fell to the earth, then the earth, no doubt, would be completely destroyed. Therefore, the mention here of the stars falling to earth must be viewed symbolically and not literally. One thing about the book of Revelation is that we must—with God's help—learn how to differentiate between symbolic and literal lingo. The "stars," for example, refer to Satan and his angels, who will be thrust out completely from the heavenly realm at the midpoint of the seven years and be totally confined to earth, which we reviewed in the last chapter (Rev. 12:4, 7-12). We also reviewed how this event will occur at about the same time the Antichrist is assassinated and lay dead for several days or so.

On the day that Christ was crucified, the Scriptures state that "from the sixth hour (12 noon) there was darkness over all the land unto the ninth hour (3:00 p.m.)" (Matt. 27:45). When Christ was killed, the sun was darkened for three hours, but this was not the fulfillment of Joel 2:31. As we have already seen, the Antichrist is going to be killed near the time of Passover, when Christ was crucified. In part, the events that will surround the death of the Antichrist are going to be strikingly similar to the events that surrounded the death of Christ. Knowing the prophetic Scriptures himself, Satan will orchestrate Dan's exploits around them to give the utmost impact to his impostership. This God will permit Satan to do, as part of His judgment upon Israel and the nations for their disbelief in the True Christ.

■ ■ ■

The First Resurrection

Before the opening of the seventh seal, John is shown the vision of the saving (sealing Eph. 1:13) of the 144,000 Jews that will occur in the first half of the seven years, which we also reviewed in the last chapter (Rev. 7:1-8). Immediately following this, John wrote: "After this I beheld, and lo, a great multitude, which no man could number, of all nations, and kindreds, and people, and tongues, stood before the throne, and before the Lamb, clothed with white robes, and palms in their hands; And cried with a loud voice, saying, Salvation to our God which sitteth upon the throne, and unto the Lamb. And all the angels stood around the throne, and about the elders and the four beasts, and fell before the throne on their faces, and worshipped God, Saying, Amen: Blessing, and glory, and wisdom, and thanksgiving, and honor, and power, and might, be unto our God for ever and ever. Amen. And one of the elders answered, saying unto me, What are these which are arrayed in white robes? And whence came they? And I said unto him, Sir, thou knowest. And he said to me, These are they which came out of great tribulation, and have washed their robes, and made them white in the blood of the Lamb. Therefore are they before the throne..." (Rev. 7:9-15).

In John's previous vision of God's Throne, he described the vast, empty space as a "sea of glass" (Rev. 4:6). Now all of a sudden, he sees a "great multitude" standing before the Throne dressed in white robes. Among them will be the 144,000; for the next time John saw the 144,000 after chapter seven they are in Heaven being referred to as those who sang a "new song before the throne...which were redeemed from the earth...being the firstfruits unto God and to the Lamb," or rather being among the firstfruits of those "redeemed from among men" (Rev. 14:1-4). Also among the "great multitude" will be the martyred saints we saw earlier who were issued "white robes" and told to wait "yet for a little season." And last, we are told that these are "they which came out of Great Tribulation."

As we already know, the Great Tribulation is set to last for three and a half years. It will commence with the rising of Dan from the dead, where he will then continue in his new resurrected satanic state for "forty and two months." Shortly after he rises from the dead, his first victims will be Elijah and Enoch, whose ministry of 1,260 days will expire with Dan's rising. As we saw, Dan will then kill the duo, and they will rise from the dead three and a half days later. This may all take place in the first month of Nisan, as we have already reviewed.

Now, sometime after Elijah and Enoch are raised from the dead, the dead in Christ will be raised from the dead when Jesus comes from Heaven with their souls with Him. Then, the saints who are alive at the time, and who are walking faithfully with the Lord, shall be changed, in the twinkling of an eye, into their new glorified bodies (Luke 21:34-36; 1 Cor. 15:51-52; Rev. 3:10). This will all take place just inside the official beginning of the Great Tribulation. That's why it states that these are "they which came out of Great Tribulation." In other words, they will "come out of" the Great Tribulation at the early stages of it. The primary purpose for the resurrecting/rapturing of the saints at this point will be to rescue the faithful *out of* the designated Great Tribulation period. The Prophet Zephaniah foretold of this very moment when he wrote: "Seek ye the Lord, all ye meek of the earth, which have wrought his judgments, seek righteousness, seek meekness: it may be ye shall be hid (raptured out) in the day of the Lord's anger (Great Tribulation)" (Zeph. 2:3). No one will know neither the *"day"* nor the *"hour"* of the Rapture, but will know that it is *"near, even at the doors"* by all the signs that will precede it.

> *Note: When Jesus died on the cross, the Scripture states that the "...earth did quake, and the rocks rent; And the graves were opened; and many bodies of the saints which slept arose, And came out of their graves after his resurrection, and went into the holy city, and appeared unto many" (Matt. 27:51-53).*

> *These saints who rose from the dead "after" the resurrection of Christ were raised back into their natural bodies, not eternal bodies. Their resurrections were the same as when Jesus raised Lazarus from the dead, who eventually died again (John 11:1-46). The resurrections of those who were raised following Jesus' resurrection were probably saints who had recently died. After they were raised, they went into the city of Jerusalem and "appeared unto many." This was done by God as a sign to the house of Israel that Jesus was their Messiah, and the constant presence of the dead that were raised served as a constant reminder. These all would eventually die again as well, and today await their eternal resurrections.*

The reason I just took you through all that is because, when the Antichrist rises from the dead, his resurrection will be a "lying wonder," or rather only a natural one. The saints who will rise from the dead after him, such as Elijah and Enoch, and those who will be raised at the Rapture, will all be eternal resurrections. The resurrection of Jesus Christ was eternal. Those who were raised from the dead just shortly afterwards were of the natural sort. Dan's resurrection will be a natural one. The saints who will rise from the dead shortly after will be eternally glorified resurrections. Are all of these observations just a mere coincidence? Absolutely not!

■ ■ ■

In the Old Testament law of God, all Jewish males were commanded to appear before God at the Temple three times a year during the feasts of Passover, Pentecost, and Tabernacles (Ex. 23:14-17). The feasts were held in the first, third, and seventh months of the sacred order of the biblical Jewish calendar, and coincided with the beginning and the end of their harvest season. In his Epistle to the Hebrews, the Apostle Paul stated that the law is a "shadow of good things to come," which foreshadow future, greater events (Heb. 10:1). Jesus stated that he had come to "fulfill the law," which would be accomplished in

His life, death, resurrection, and the events which will surround His Second Coming and beyond (Matt. 5:17-18).

For example, for centuries before Christ was born, the Passover lamb symbolized Jesus Christ, the "Lamb of God which taketh away the sin of the world," before its fulfillment in Christ (Ex. 12; John 1:29). The Passover feast lasted for a total of seven days. During that time, the law commanded they begin their harvest season by reaping the firstfruits of the barley on the day after the weekly Sabbath, which was Sunday morning. The high priest was to then take the firstfruits and offer them up to God at the Temple (Lev. 23:5-11). At around the same time they did this, as Christ lay dead in the tomb, the Lord suddenly came to life in fulfillment of this law to become the firstfruits of those begotten from the dead (1 Cor. 15:20). Hours later, as the high priest was in the Temple presenting the firstfruits of harvest season unto God, Jesus ascended briefly into Heaven to present Himself before God's Throne as the firstfruits of those redeemed from the grave. For shortly after Jesus rose from the dead, He said to Mary Magdalene, "Touch me not; for I am not yet ascended to my Father" (John 20:17). After He returned, His disciples were then allowed to touch Him (John 20:19-27).

When John the Baptist preached, a repeated theme in his message was that the One (Jesus) who was to come after him was going to "...gather his wheat into his garner; but the chaff he will burn with fire unquenchable" (Luke 3:17). Years later, Jesus told His disciples the parable of the wheat and the tares (Matt. 13:24-30). Afterwards, the disciples "...came unto him saying, Declare unto us the parable." Jesus explained to them that "the field is the world, the good seed (wheat) are the children of the kingdom; but the tares are the children of the wicked one; The enemy that sowed them is the devil; the harvest is the end of the world; and the reapers are the angels" (Matt. 13:36-39).

The Jewish harvest season begins with the reaping of the barley during Passover in the first month of Nisan. Afterwards, the wheat harvest begins sometime late in the second month of Iyar, but no specific day was commanded in the law to begin reaping.³ Exactly forty days after Jesus rose from the dead on Nisan 17th, He ascended into Heaven on Iyar 27th, from atop the Mount of Olives. As His disciples stood there gazing up to Heaven, Jesus disappeared into the clouds, then two angels suddenly appeared saying, "Why stand ye gazing up into heaven? This same Jesus, which is taken up from among you into heaven, shall come in like manner as ye have seen him go into heaven" (Acts 1:11). How will the Lord return? In like manner as He left, in the second month of Iyar to first "gather his wheat (saints) into his garner (Heaven)" (1 Thes. 4:16; John 14:3). No one will be able to know the *"day"* nor the *"hour"* of this aspect of the Lord's *"coming,"* but we will know that it's *"near, even at the doors"* (Matt. 24:32-42). And not only will the Lord first come to get His saints in the second month of Iyar, the same month in which He departed, but after the Great Tribulation, at His literal Second Coming to earth, His feet will touch down upon the Mount of Olives in the exact spot, perhaps, from which He ascended (Zech. 14:4). We'll look further into this later.

Under the law, all males were commanded to appear before God at the Temple during the Feast of Pentecost, first known as the "feast of weeks, of the firstfruits of wheat harvest" (Ex. 34:22). The feast was observed exactly seven weeks plus one day (50 days) after the reaping of the firstfruits of barley on Sunday during Passover when Christ rose from the dead. The Feast of Pentecost would then also fall on a Sunday sometime in the first week of the third month of Sivan. During the feast, the high priest was commanded by the law of God to wave a bread offering unto God of bread that had been baked with the firstfruits of the wheat harvest. And, in contrast to the unleavened bread used during Passover, which symbolized the sinless body of Christ, leavening was to be used in the bread made from the firstfruits of the wheat harvest (Lev. 23:15-17). The reason, perhaps, for such was that the leavened bread symbolized the sinful body of believers who had been redeemed by the sinless body of Jesus Christ. The Apostle Paul wrote that "we (believers) being many are one bread, and one body" (1 Cor. 10:17). The Scriptures state that Jesus is our "great high priest that is passed into the heavens" (Heb. 4:14). Therefore, Jesus, our Great High Priest, will present the firstfruits of those redeemed from among men to God in fulfillment of the law of Pentecost in the early part of the third month, after the Rapture occurs in the latter part of the second month during wheat harvest.

After Moses led the children of Israel out of Egypt in the first month of Nisan, they arrived at Mount Sinai in the third month (Ex. 19:1). God instructed Moses to have the people wash their clothes (a shadow of those who have "washed their robes, and made them white in the blood of the Lamb; Rev. 7:14) to be ready in three days (sanctification period) to meet with God (Ex. 19:9-11). "And it came to pass on the third day in the morning, that there were thunders and lightnings, and a thick cloud upon the mount, and the voice of the trumpet (an angel's trumpet) exceedingly loud; so that all the people that was in the camp trembled. And Moses brought forth the people out of the camp to meet with God..." (Ex. 19:16-17). Likewise, Jesus (in fulfillment of the above type and shadow) will bring forth the people to *meet with God* in the third month, following a brief waiting period after the Rapture occurs in the latter part of the second month.

■ ■ ■

When Jesus was questioned by His disciples concerning the "sign of thy coming, and of the end of the world," He used Noah's life and time as an example (Matt. 24:3); for Jesus said, "But as the days of Noah were, so shall also the coming of the Son of man be" (Matt. 24:37). In the story of Noah and the Ark in the book of Genesis, we learn how Noah and his family entered the safety of the Ark in the second month of Noah's six hundredth year (Gen. 7:11). When they did this, to escape God's wrath, it was a foreshadowing of the Rapture. Even though the emphasis of Jesus' comment on Noah's time primarily concerned the wicked condition of mankind, Noah's faithful walk with God and entering of the Ark in the second month of his six hundredth year are both very important pieces to the puzzle as well (Gen. 6:9). Being that Noah's life was before God instituted the biblical calendar, He used the months of Noah's six hundredth and six hundred-and-first year for a guideline of events during the year-long flood experience (Gen. 7:11-8:16). As far as we know, Noah's life may have been Divinely influenced to coincide with the future biblical calendar. Either way, the fact that they entered the Ark in the second month of Noah's six hundredth year was Divinely influenced and recorded to begin a pattern of significantly profound second-month events.

When God led the children of Israel out of Egypt, He used a cloud to guide them to Mount Sinai (Ex. 12-19). There, God gave them His Commandments and had Moses build the Tabernacle (Ex. 20-31). The Tabernacle was completed and ceremoniously dedicated to the Lord about a year after they departed Egypt on the first day of the first month. At the dedication ceremony, the cloud came down and covered the Tabernacle, signifying God's approval (Ex. 40). Shortly after this, the Lord told Moses to "Make thee two trumpets of silver...that thou mayest use them for the calling of the assembly, and for the journeying of the camps" (Num. 10:2). Not long after this "...it came to pass on the twentieth day of the second month, in the second year, that the cloud was taken up from off the tabernacle of the testimony. And the children of Israel took their journeys out of the wilderness of Sinai...In the first (front) place went the standard of the camp of the children of Judah according to their armies"(Num. 10:11-14).

Here we see that trumpets were blown to signal the Israelites to break camp and move out in the second month. The tribe of Judah, whose "standard" was the emblem of a lion because of Jacob's testimony of Judah (Gen. 49:9), was positioned in the front to lead the way. And where were they headed? To the Promised Land (Num. 13). Likewise, the Lord Jesus Christ, who is the Lion of the tribe of Judah (Rev. 5:5), is going to descend from Heaven in a cloud in the second month and "...with the trump of God...the dead in Christ shall rise first: then we which are alive and remain shall be caught up together with them in the clouds, to meet the Lord in the air..." (1 Thes. 4:16-17). And where will we be headed? To the Promised Land of Heaven, of course. The saints alive at the time of the Rapture just won't know the "*day*" of it nor the "*hour*," but will know that it's "*near, even at the doors*" (Matt. 24:32-42).

According to *Strong's Concordance* the word "hour" (5610) in the New Testament was mainly used to refer to a literal hour of the day. In some cases it was used figuratively in reference to a particular period or season of time. The same also applies to the usage of the word "day" (2250). They are only used together several times, all with regard to the coming of Christ for His saints. Two of them, Matthew 24:36 and Mark 13:32, state only the Father (God) knows the *day* and *hour* implying the literal interpretation. Jesus pretty much made it plain when He said, "Watch ye, therefore; for ye know not when the master (Jesus) of the house cometh, at evening, or at midnight, or at cockcrow, or in the morning" (Mark 13:35). The primary warning is we are to be *ready* and to *watch* for the signs that Christ's coming is *near, even at the doors*. Only the Father knows the exact *day* and *hour* of this event, but by deciphering the end-times puzzle can we know the *month* and even the *year* once we reach that point?

Notable Second-Month Events
- Noah and family entered the safety of the Ark in Noah's second month of his six hundredth year (Gen. 7:11)
- Israelites departed from Mount Sinai headed for the Promised Land, with the tribe of Judah leading the way (Num. 10:11-14)
- Construction began on first Temple (2 Chron. 3:2)
- Construction began on second Temple (Ezra 3:8)
- Jesus ascended into Heaven forty days after His resurrection on or about Iyar 27th
- Israel declared independence on May 14, 1948 — Iyar 5, 5707
- Jews gained full control of Jerusalem on June 7, 1967 — Iyar 28, 5726
- United States President Donald Trump moved the US embassy in Israel from Tel Aviv to Jerusalem on May 14, 2018 — Iyar 29, 5778

Future Second-Month Events
- Construction to begin on third Temple
- Rapture — the second *part* of the First Resurrection (Jesus' resurrection was the first *part*)

Other Rapture Types and Clues
The Parable of the Ten Virgins

In Jesus' parable of the ten virgins we read: "Then shall the kingdom of heaven be likened unto ten virgins (the Church), which took their lamps, and went forth to meet the bridegroom (Jesus). And five of them were wise (true saints), and five were foolish (hypocrites). They that were foolish took their lamps, and took no oil with them: But the wise took oil in their vessels with their lamps. While the bridegroom tarried (2,000 years), they all slumbered and slept. And at midnight (darkest hour of human history) there was a cry made (signs immediately prior to Rapture), Behold, the bridegroom cometh; go ye out to meet him. Then all those virgins arose, and trimmed their lamps. And the foolish said unto the wise, Give us of your oil; for our lamps are gone out. But the wise answered, saying, Not so; lest there be not enough for us and you: but go ye rather to them that sell, and buy for yourselves. And while they went to buy, the bridegroom came; and they that were ready went in (to Heaven) with him to the marriage: and the door was shut. Afterward came also the other virgins, saying, Lord, Lord, open to us (hypocrites pray after the Rapture). But he answered and said, Verily I say unto you, I know ye not. Watch (for signs and stay ready) therefore, for ye know neither the day nor the hour wherein the Son of man cometh" (Matt. 25:1-13). I believe you get the picture. Jesus is poised to come in the darkest hour of human history (beginning of Great Tribulation) for His Bride (true saints). All the signs beforehand will be clamoring loud and clear "Behold the bridegroom cometh; go ye out to meet him" so that none in the Church are without excuse of not having ample warning.

The Deliverance of Lot

In the book of Genesis we read of the rescue of Lot and his family out of the homosexually infested city of Sodom just moments before God rained down fire and brimstone upon the wicked city (Gen. 18-19). As with Noah and the flood, Jesus also used this event as a foreshadowing of the Rapture (Luke 17:28-36). In each instance, Noah and Lot were delivered out of harm's way just before God's judgment began to fall. In the final seven-year countdown, the severe judgments of God do not begin until the midpoint beginning with the Antichrist's reign of terror. There is absolutely no reason for the Rapture to occur at the forefront of the seven years, nor is there any solid Scriptural backing for this theory. Actually, the term "seven-year tribulation" is in complete contradiction with Scripture. And, even the term "mid-tribulation" in reference to the Rapture is as well, because there is only going to be a three-and-a-half-year Great Tribulation that will affect the entire world after the Rapture.

Some scholars say that when Jesus used the events of Noah and Lot as foreshadowing types, He was referring to His Second Coming to earth at the end of the seven years. The problem with this theory is that, in both instances Jesus stated that most people on earth would be having parties, planting crops, planning building projects, having weddings, etc....and be totally oblivious to any pending danger during this aspect of His coming (Luke 17:26-28). The Great Tribulation will be the most horrific time period in the history of mankind (Matt. 24:21). No one will be carrying on with life as usual by the end of this period (Rev. 16:1-21).

Another thing that I'd like to point out here is that, in Luke 17:34 Jesus emphasized how that half of the world will be in bed asleep at the time of the Rapture. Most likely, it will be the western hemisphere, which includes America that will be in its late night hours at the time of the Rapture. The reasons for such are obvious once all the facts are considered. First, God is a merciful God, not willing that any should perish, but that all would come to repentance (2 Peter 3:9). Second, the majority of true Christians live in the western hemisphere. Third, the western nations are the most industrialized when it comes to planes, trains, automobiles, subways, ships, etc. To minimize incidental accidents, catastrophes, and deaths, the Rapture will probably occur when the western nations are in their late night/early morning hours, and the eastern nations their early evening hours.

The Rapture of Elijah

In 2 Kings 2:1-11, we saw the story of when the Prophet Elijah was taken alive up to Heaven and the events that preceded it. Elijah knew he was scheduled to catch the chariot of fire up the whirlwind expressway, and also knew the exact day and time of his departure. And not only did he know, but his understudy Elisha knew as well. The fact that these two great men of God in the Old Testament knew of this really doesn't seem to be such a big deal when considering who they were. What is a big deal though is that, the local Prophets of the towns of Bethel and Jericho, and their sons, knew of the day of Elijah's departure too. When Elijah and Elisha passed through the towns of Bethel and Jericho on their way to Elijah's going away party, the sons of the Prophets there asked Elisha, "Knowest thou that the Lord will take away thy master from thy head today? And he said, Yea, I know it." Afterwards, Elijah and Elisha headed toward the Jordan River and were followed by fifty sons of the Prophets. When they reached the river, Elijah parted the waters and he and Elisha crossed over, but the sons of the Prophets stayed put and "stood to view afar off " Elijah's departure into Heaven.

In applying all of this to the end-times Rapture, the Lord is revealing to His modern-day Prophets a more accurate understanding of the Rapture. They, in turn, are passing that information on to the next generation, and so on. And, as we draw nigh unto the end-times, God is unsealing more and more of the prophetic Word to His saints, resulting in a clearer understanding of how the end-times will unfold (Dan. 12:9). And, like the fifty sons of the Prophets, the saints living in the last-days, who have been given a clear understanding of the Rapture, will watch with eager anticipation for the Rapture after Elijah and Enoch come passing through our midst in the first three and a half years.

Prophecy of Christ's First Coming

Another thing we need to consider is the detailed prophecies in the Old Testament that specifically pointed out the exact timing of Christ's First Coming. As you may recall, the prophecy in Daniel 9:24-26 foretold that the Messiah would be "put to death" 483 years after the decree was issued to rebuild the wall of Jerusalem. The decree was later issued by the Persian King Artaxerxes exactly 483 years before Christ was crucified (Neh. 2:1-17). Many of the good Jews who were alive during the time of Christ knew of the prophecy and were anticipating the Messiah's soon arrival. In fact, the Scriptures tell us that there was an old "man in Jerusalem, whose name was Simeon; and the same man was just and devout, waiting for the consolation of Israel: and the Holy Ghost was upon him. And it was revealed unto him by the Holy Ghost, that he should not see death before he had seen the Lord's Christ" (Luke 2:25-26).

Likewise, the saints who will be alive in the last-days will know that the coming of Christ is near due to the prophecies as they watch them unfold before their eyes. And, as with Simeon, the Holy Spirit is going to reveal to the hearts of many saints that they will not taste of death as they see those signs signaling Christ's Second Coming. The Apostle Paul wrote: "Behold, I shew you a mystery; We shall not all sleep (die), but we shall be changed, in a moment, in the twinkling of an eye, at the last trump; for the trumpet shall sound, and the dead shall be raised incorruptible, and we shall be changed" (1 Cor. 15:51-52).

Prophecy Emphasizes Three and a Half Years, Not Seven

There is only one Scripture (Dan. 9:27) that directly alludes to the final seven years, which are the last seven years of Daniel's 490-year prophecy concerning the Jews, Jerusalem, and the Temple (Dan. 9:24-27) — and even that one emphasizes the latter half. It states: "And he (Antichrist) shall confirm the covenant with many for one week (seven years): and in the midst of the week (midpoint of seven years) he shall cause the sacrifice and oblation to cease, and for the overspreading of abominations he shall make it (third Temple) desolate even until the consummation (the end), and that determined (by God) shall be poured (wrath) upon the desolate (wicked)."

As we've already reviewed in the last chapter, there are a total of eight Scriptures that refer to a period of three and a half years. Two of them allude to Elijah and Enoch's ministry timeframe in the first half of the seven years (Rev. 11:3; 12:6). The other six, Daniel 7:25; 12:7 and 12:11, and Revelation 11:2; 12:14 and 13:5 all refer to the last three and a half years. In all, including Daniel 9:27, there are seven Scriptures that specifically emphasize a three-and-a-half-year Great Tribulation period. Do you think that God just may be trying to give us a clue here? The Bible does not promote a "seven-year tribulation" of horror as many preachers and numerous authors just blindly proclaim without giving any solid Scriptural support.

> *Note: When I began taking down notes for the rough draft of the manuscript for this book in 1999, I had been an avid believer in the pre-seven-year Rapture/seven-year tribulation theory for 21 years. Like many others, perhaps even yourself, I just presumed these things to be true, trusting that the teachers and writers I confided in were correct. However, as I embarked upon a more in-depth study and research necessary for writing a book of this nature, I began to notice how the Scriptures unequivocally refute this school of thought. With that said, I'm confident that what you have thus far read in this book, and what you will read hereafter, contains one of the most biblically sound accounts of the rapturing, resurrecting, and gathering of the elect in the last-days that is in print to-date.*

The first *part* of the First Resurrection was the resurrection of Jesus Christ, in fulfillment of the law and the reaping of the firstfruits of harvest season, which foreshadows how God will reap His field, the earth. Elijah and Enoch's resurrections are just as much shrouded in mystery as the characters themselves. As already mentioned, the primary purpose, timing, and whereabouts of their resurrections will be to counter the phony resurrection of Dan to give people an option to believe the true or the false.

The second *part* to the First Resurrection will be the Rapture that the Apostle Paul wrote of in 1 Thessalonians 4:13-18. This will occur, I believe, in the second month of Iyar at about the time wheat harvest begins in Israel late in that month. We just won't know the ***day*** nor the ***hour***, but will know the Rapture is ***near, even at the doors*** following the resurrections of Dan, Elijah, and Enoch. At the time of the Rapture, however, the earth (God's field) will not be fully ripe for its complete harvest. Late into the Great Tribulation, however, it will be, and thereby be reaped in accordance to the pattern of the law and the biblical Jewish harvest season. We will be looking into these events later.

Word to the Wise

Luke 21:34-36: *"And take heed to yourselves, lest at any time your hearts be overcharged with surfeiting, and drunkenness, and cares of this life, and so that day come upon you unawares. For as a snare shall it come on all them that dwell on the face of the whole earth. Watch (for the signs) ye therefore, and pray always, that ye may be accounted worthy to escape (Rapture) all these things that shall come to pass (Great Tribulation), and to stand before the Son of man (following Rapture; Rev. 7:9)."*

10

BABYLON THE GREAT

In Revelation chapter thirteen, we saw a beast with seven heads and ten horns that depicts six satanically controlled past empires and the future empire of the Antichrist. Following John's vision of this beast, he then saw a vision of a second beast. And as all the details of the first beast allude to the identity of seven empires, so, too, do the details of the second beast allude to its identity as well; for John wrote: "And I beheld another beast coming up out of the earth; and he had two horns like a lamb, and he spake as a dragon" (Rev. 13:11). Before we proceed any further, I would like to point out here that after Revelation chapter thirteen, the first beast continues to be referred to as a "beast" (Rev. 14:9; 15:2; 16:13; 17:3; 19:20). The second beast, however, is afterwards referred to as the "false prophet," revealing to us that he will be some type of a religious figure (Rev. 16:13; 19:20; 20:10).

We have already seen that the horns of beasts in prophetic visions depict seats of authority occupied by kings or rulers. For example, in chapter three of this book, we saw how the goat with the "great horn" depicts Alexander the Great, who was a strong military leader of the powerful Grecian Empire (Dan. 8:8). The second beast, we are told, has "two horns like a lamb." A lamb is less than one year of age. Its horns will not be fully developed in the lamb stage of its life. What this description of the second beast signifies is that his (False Prophet's) seat of authority will not be as powerful militarily as the fully mature horns that depict the ten nations under the control of the first Beast (Antichrist). And being that there are "two horns" upon the second beast, then there must be two seats of authority; for we also saw in chapter three of this book how the ram with "two horns" depicts the combined kingdoms of the Medes and the Persians (Dan. 8:20).

In *The World Almanac and Book of Facts* in the "nations of the world" section, you will find listed the nation of "Vatican City." The Almanac states that "the recent sovereign (king) of the state of Vatican City is the supreme pontiff (Pope)." In the "religion" section of the Almanac, we find listed that "the head of the Roman Catholic Church is the supreme pontiff." So, what we have found here is that there are two seats of authority that are occupied by one man — the Pope. And being that both Vatican City and the Roman Catholic Church are not as powerful militarily as the ten nations of the first Beast, the two horns are said to be "like a lamb."

Sometimes prophetic Scriptures can serve dual purposes, which may be the case with the expression "like a lamb." The Scriptures refer to Jesus Christ as the "Lamb of God" (John 1:29). The phrase "like a lamb" may also allude to the Pope's self-proclaimed headship of the Church of Jesus Christ. The Pope's pretentious claim of infallibility sets himself up to be equal to God. These credentials and honors belong to one man and to one man only, who is Jesus Christ the God-Man (1 Tim. 3:16). Therefore, the Pope, as we've already seen in a previous chapter, sits in a blasphemous seat (or rather seats) of lies, which ushers us to review the next description of the second beast. John wrote, that he "spake as a dragon." The word "Dragon" we know refers to Satan, whom Jesus said is the "father of lies" (Rev. 12:9; John 8:44). Therefore, if the Pope speaks "as a Dragon," then he, too, is telling lies. He is a deceiver and a liar, just like the Devil. Not that the Pope is intentionally and knowingly deceiving folks, for he truly believes everything about his position; it's just that he's been deceived himself.

The Apostle Paul warned that "...if he that cometh preacheth another Jesus, whom we have not preached, or if ye receive another spirit, which ye have not received, or another gospel, which ye have not accepted, ye might well bear with him....For such are false apostles, deceitful workers, transforming themselves into the apostles of Christ. And no marvel; for Satan himself is transformed into an angel of light. Therefore, it is no great thing if his ministers also be transformed as the ministers of righteousness..." (2 Cor. 11:4, 13-15). As we have already exhaustively reviewed in a previous chapter, the Roman Catholic Church, despite her angel of light appearance, has a satanic origin that mysteriously conceals the religion of ancient Babylon under a cloak of false Christianity.

Continuing now with John's vision of the second beast, we read that "and he (Pope) exerciseth all the power (satanic power) of the first beast before him, and causeth the earth and them that dwell therein to worship the first beast, whose deadly wound was healed" (Rev. 13:12). It will be at this point when the title "Pontifix Maximus (high priest, king, and god)" will be transferred from the Pope to Dan, who will be the Devil incarnate. He will be the ultimate fraud of Jesus Christ, who is our Great High Priest (Heb. 4:14), King (Rev. 19:16), and God (1 Tim. 3:16). The Pope will at this time use his power and influence to promote the False Christ to his own followers and to the world. The Vatican will jump aboard and ride upon the back of Dan to what they believe will be total world supremacy.

The Roman Catholic Church is a false church that does not possess the indwelling of the Holy Spirit, and thereby is incapable of knowing or understanding the truth. They do not, therefore, share the same end-times views as the true born-again, Spirit-filled and led saints of God. The Roman clergy and the people under their care are just as much deceived by Satan, or perhaps even more so, than those who do not even believe the truth (1 Tim. 4:1-3). And, I might here add, the name "Babylon" means "confusion and opposition to God" and there is plenty of that going on within the Devil's workshop.

On 5-13-05, the Jack Van Impe (JVI) Bible prophecy-centered telecast reported that some Catholic bishops are now saying that they do not believe Jesus Christ was the Son of God. As we draw closer and closer to the end-times, this belief within the Roman Catholic Church will gradually gain significant adherents, even including the apostate Protestant groups. Even today, this teaching is showing up within the increasingly growing apostate Protestant churches. The Apostle Peter warned the Church that as "...there were false prophets also among the people (Old Testament saints), even as there shall be false teachers among you, who privily shall bring in damnable heresies, even denying the Lord that bought them, and bring upon themselves swift destruction" (2 Peter 2:1). The Apostle John wrote: "For many deceivers are entered into the world, who confess not that Jesus Christ is come (First Coming) in the flesh. This is a deceiver and an antichrist" (2 John 7). The Devil, of course, is the perpetrator behind the promotion of this damnable heresy of Christ not being the Son of God. The reason for such is that Satan is preparing the false Christian churches to receive the Antichrist as the true Christ more readily when he appears.

As I just mentioned, the Catholics do not share the true Protestant's view on the end-times for reasons already stated. On 2-28-03, it was reported on the JVI telecast that Catholic theologians do not believe in a Rapture of the Church in any form. In his book *The Rapture Trap*, author Paul Thigpen (a Catholic) bashes the Protestant's belief in a Rapture, calling it a "poisonous teaching." Also, certain apostate Protestant groups are now following suit as well. On 5-20-05, the JVI program reported that some Protestant ministers are preaching that the Rapture and the return of Jesus Christ are a sham calling the teachings "religious terrorism."

The marriage union of the False Christ to his bride, the false church, is set to occur at the midpoint of the seven years just shortly after the Rapture. The Rapture will be the marriage union of the True Christ to His Bride, the True Church, when He comes to get her to take her home to the place He has gone to prepare for her (John 14:1-3). With the disappearance of hundreds of millions of true Christians at the Rapture, the entire world will be thrust into instant chaos and fear. Following Satan's revealing of the False Christ to the world, the Rapture will counter that by revealing "The Word of God" (Jesus; Rev. 19:13) is the Way, the Truth, and the Life (John 14:4-6) and has come for His Bride. The world will begin to wonder and question the disappearance of so many at once.

On 4-4-13, Sid Roth's "It's Supernatural" program, which airs on TBN, reported on the Vatican's strong belief in, and the investigation of, UFO's and aliens. The report disclosed that the Vatican owns the Mount Graham Observatory in Arizona, which has the most powerful telescope in the world, and an infrared camera named "Project Lucifer." According to a Vatican spokesman, they believe that there is an alien presence on earth. So much so that the Vatican has assigned Corrado Balducci to investigate and monitor alien activity. Being that one out of two Americans alone believe in aliens, the Vatican may try to explain away the Rapture as a mass alien abduction.

Satan is also at work among the New Agers and other channelers who are receiving, and recording in writing, messages from demonic spirits of a future mass evacuation of "improperly aligned souls." They talk of this mass disappearance of the "unenlightened" as a "cleansing" that could occur in the "twinkling of an eye" (their terminology) at a moment's notice. Satan knows all too well what lies ahead for him and his demons; "the devils also believe, and tremble" (James 2:19). He knows about the Rapture and that it will coincide with his final ousting from the heavenly realm (Rev. 12:7-12), and his unbridled takeover of the earth in the person of the Antichrist, and, as it were, in the seat of God (2 Thes. 2:3-4).[1]

Following the union between the Antichrist and the false church, the Pope will have some type of an image made of Dan

(Rev. 13:14). For those of you familiar with the Roman Catholic Church, you are then aware of the emphasis the church places on the veneration of images. All over Europe and elsewhere, the Babylonian Church has images depicting Mary or Catholics long dead, who the Roman Church has declared has met their qualifications to become saints and who allegedly have the power to answer prayers of all sorts. On July 5, 2013, Pope Francis declared that the deceased Popes John XXIII and John Paul II have met the Roman Catholic Church's qualifications to be declared saints.

> *Note: All true born-again of the Spirit Christians are saints (1 Cor. 6:11; Eph. 5:3). A saint is one who has been sanctified, or set apart unto God as sacred, by faith in the shed blood of Jesus Christ and rebirth by the Spirit.*

Images are clearly forbidden in the second of God's Ten Commandments (Ex. 20:4). The Babylonian Church's solution to that was to omit the second commandment from their catechism (Catholic commentary), and to slice the tenth commandment in two, keeping the total commandments at ten. This can clearly be seen in the Roman Catholic doctrine wherever they print out the Ten Commandments, such as on their "confessional card."

Somehow or other, the image that will be made of the Antichrist will be able to speak. With the way things are advancing in technology, we can easily see how this could occur in the future, or even today perhaps. Regardless, when it does occur, all will be compelled to either worship the Antichrist or be killed. This will be reminiscent of the Babylonian and Roman Empires, where like decrees were enforced. It will also be a reemergence, of sorts, of the Holy Roman Empire when the Popes and German kings ruled side by side, killing all that refused to worship the Pope. In the newly improved version of Babylon headed by Dan and the Pope, all will also be forced to receive some sort of a mark on their right hand or forehead in order to be able to buy or sell. The mark will also, perhaps, serve as an identifier, where the mark can be scanned and everything about the person will pop up on the screen of a hand held digital device, such as a cell phone. Again, with the recent advances in technology, we can clearly see how this prophecy could be fulfilled. And, somehow or other, the number 666 is going to identify with the name of the Antichrist (Rev. 13:15-18).

One possibility for this number could be that, as God's perfect number is seven, then a step below that, of course, would be six. When Jesus commissioned His disciples to go into all the world and preach the Gospel to all nations, He ordered them to baptize the new converts in the "...name of the Father, and of the Son, and of the Holy Ghost" (Matt. 28:19). As a result of their faith in Christ, a newly born-again saint is "sealed with that Holy Spirit of promise" (Eph. 1:13). Likewise, those who choose to believe in the Antichrist will be initiated into the Devil's family and sealed by the mark and be identified with his "name." In contrast to the "name" of the Father, Son, and Holy Ghost (777), the number 666 is identified with the "name" of the Dragon, Beast, and False Prophet. In Revelation 16:13, John wrote of the unholy trio when he stated, "...and I saw three unclean spirits, like frogs, come out of the mouth of the dragon, and out of the mouth of the beast, and out of the mouth of the false prophet. For they are the spirits of devils, working miracles..." (Rev. 16:13-14).

Over the years, the Vatican has reported on alleged miracles occurring by people who had prayed to Mary or some other patron saint. In March of 2007, all major news networks reported on a story about a nun who said she was healed from Parkinson's disease by praying to the deceased Pope John Paul II. As time goes on, these "lying wonders" will increase and come to their peak with the resurrection of Dan, and the Pope being granted power by Satan to make "...fire come down from heaven on the earth in the sight of men" (Rev. 13:13). In the book of Job, we see where Satan was permitted by God to cause fire to fall "from heaven" to consume Job's sheep and servants (Job 1:16).

At around the same time Dan begins to force people to receive his mark or be killed, he will also "...think to change times and laws..." (Dan. 7:25). The year 2018 is The Year of Our Lord Jesus Christ, which dates back to around the time of His birth. If Dan is going to claim to be the Messiah (which he will), he will have to do something about the calendar. He may declare the day of his resurrection as day one of year one. He may also proclaim his kingdom to be the thousand-year reign of Christ on earth. He will also have to ban the celebration of Christmas and Easter, or turn them into special days meant to worship him. Already today, the "spirit of antichrist" is at work trying to remove the name of Jesus Christ from the Christmas season and elsewhere (1 John 4:3).

In case you are not yet convinced that the second beast is the Pope (the head of the Roman Catholic Church and Vatican City), there is even more Scriptural evidence that will leave you with no doubt. As we saw in Revelation chapter thirteen, there will be a union struck between the Antichrist and the False Prophet who, no doubt, is a high-ranking religious figure — a fact, I believe, we can all agree on. After Revelation chapter thirteen, the next time John sees the beast with seven heads and ten horns is in chapter seventeen. This time, however, there is a woman riding on the back of the beast, which is referred to as being a "great whore."

Beginning in Revelation chapter seventeen, we read of the following description and details of the woman that was shown to John by an angel, who said to him "Come hither; I will shew unto thee the judgment of the great whore that sitteth upon many waters: With whom the kings of the earth have committed fornication (political alliance), and the inhabitants of the earth have been made drunk with the wine (intoxicating deception) of her fornication. So he carried me away in the spirit into the wilderness: and I saw a woman sit upon a scarlet colored beast, full of names of blasphemy, having seven heads and ten horns. And the woman was arrayed in purple (royalty; Jud. 8:26), and scarlet (sins; Isa. 1:18), and decked with gold and precious stones and pearls (great riches), having a golden cup in her hand full of abominations (loathsome acts) and filthiness of her fornication (all above mentioned): And upon her forehead was a name written, MYSTERY, BABYLON THE GREAT, THE MOTHER OF HARLOTS AND ABOMINATIONS OF THE EARTH. And I saw the woman drunken with the blood of the saints, and with the blood of the martyrs of Jesus: and when I saw her, I wondered with great admiration. And the angel said unto me, Wherefore didst thou marvel? I will tell thee the mystery of the woman, and of the beast that carrieth her, which hath the seven heads and ten horns. The beast that thou sawest was, and is not; and shall ascend out of the bottomless pit, and go into perdition (reviewed in chapter eight): and they that dwell on the earth shall wonder whose names were not written in the book of life from the foundation of the world, when they behold the beast that was, and is not, and yet is. And here is the mind which hath wisdom. The seven heads are seven mountains (seven kingdoms; reviewed in chapter eight), on which the woman sitteth (her roots are embedded in the seven kingdoms). And there are seven kings: five are fallen (Babylon, Media, Persia, Seleucid, Ptolemaic), and one is (Roman Empire was in power when John wrote Revelation), and the other is not yet come (Antichrist's kingdom); and when he cometh, he must continue a short space (3 ½ years). And the beast that was (head of seventh kingdom), and is not (killed), even he is the eighth (Dan's resurrection), and is of the seven (Dan's kingdom is the seventh head, then he becomes the eighth in his new resurrected satanic nature), and goeth into perdition (Lake of Fire awaits him). And the ten horns which thou sawest are ten kings, which have received no kingdom as yet; but receive power as kings one hour (Great Tribulation) with the beast. These have one mind, and shall give their power and strength unto the beast. These shall make war with the Lamb (Jesus; at Armageddon), and the Lamb shall overcome them: for he is Lord of lords, and King of kings: and they (saints) that are with him are called, and chosen, and faithful. And he (angel) saith unto me, The waters which thou sawest, where the whore sitteth, are peoples, and multitudes, and nations, and tongues (her global influence). And the ten horns which thou sawest upon the beast, these shall hate the whore, and shall make her desolate and naked, and shall eat her flesh, and burn her with fire (destroy her near the end of Great Tribulation). For God hath put in their hearts to fulfill his will, and agree, and give their kingdom unto the beast, until the words of God (prophecies) shall be fulfilled. And the woman which thou sawest is that great city (Vatican City), which reigneth over the kings of the earth" (Rev. 17:1-18).

The angel begins by referring to the "judgment of the great whore," which will occur late into the Great Tribulation, which we will review in the next chapter of this book. The reference to her being not just a "whore" but a "great whore" alludes to her unfaithfulness to the Word of God, Jesus Christ, to whom she claims to be faithful. In contrast, the True Church of Jesus Christ is referred to in the Scriptures as being a "chaste virgin" who is faithful to her Lord, as one espoused to be married to her Husband (2 Cor. 11:2).

The "many waters" upon which the whore sitteth are "peoples, and multitudes, and nations, and tongues." This signifies the Roman Catholic Church's global reach, in which her over one billion members consist of people out of nearly every nation in the world. To add to that, Vatican City is also recognized internationally as a nation of the world, listed as such in almanacs, on maps, and in encyclopedias. Its government is built upon the foundation of the senate of its forerunner, the Roman Empire, but with a religious twist. The whore exchanges ambassadors with virtually every other nation in the world, and has built her embassies in those nations just like any other nation. By this means, the whore "commits fornication with the kings of the earth" as she pursues her global interests, which currently is to bring the entire world into subjection to the Roman Pontiff. That will change, however, with the union of the whore and the Antichrist, when the Vatican will then promote the False Christ. And, it is from within this spiritual context that perhaps billions from around the globe out of "all kindreds, and tongues, and nations" (Rev. 13:7) shall worship the Beast and be under his authority.

The whore is said to be dressed in purple, which denotes her royal hierarchy of pretenders from the Pope down to the cardinals and archbishops. If you happened to see the funeral of Pope John Paul II on television in 2005, then you witnessed a funeral which rivaled the funeral of the former president of the United States, Ronald Reagan. Many dignitaries from all over the world attended the funeral of Pope John Paul II, which was a funeral fit for a Roman Caesar.

Next, we learn that the whore is dressed in a scarlet-colored fabric. The color scarlet, or red, alludes to the enormity of her many sins (Isa. 1:18). She is also decked out with gold, precious stones, and pearls, which denotes the great wealth she has accumulated over the centuries by her deception, bloodshed, and shrewd political alliances that we reviewed in chapter four of this book. In her hand, the whore is pictured holding a golden cup, "full of abominations," which symbolizes her many false doctrines and Babylonish practices that are all abominations to Jesus, who she claims to represent.

After this, John said he saw a name written on her forehead: "MYSTERY, BABYLON THE GREAT, THE MOTHER OF HARLOTS...." First of all, the whore's identity is shrouded in mystery, which links her to ancient Babylon. She is not who she pretends to be; and in fact, she is not only Babylon, but "Babylon the Great," signifying that in the last-days she will have reached her highest peak and greatest potential, just prior to her complete destruction (Rev. 17:16-17).

Second, the whore is said to be the "Mother of Harlots." When a mother gives birth to a daughter, that daughter will have many characteristics like her mother, such as her looks and mannerisms. Likewise, Mother Rome, or the "Mother Church" as she is sometimes referred to by the Vatican elite, has daughters who possess Mother's characteristics. By far, the whore's eldest daughter is the false Christian religion commonly known as Eastern Orthodoxy, out of which came forth the Greek and Russian Orthodox churches. The Orthodox Church, which is basically the same as Roman Catholic (but without a Pope or images), developed after a split in the Mother Church around the year 1054 over doctrinal disagreements. In recent times, however, Roman Popes and Orthodox Patriarchs have inched toward healing the great schism, meeting to pray and discuss reconciliation. In a speech on February 12, 2010, Pope Benedict XVI told a group of Romanian bishops that the Catholic and Orthodox churches must unite in order to defend Europe's Christian roots from the gradual influx of Islam. At the request of Pope Francis, Orthodox Church leader Bartholomew I attended Francis' installment. It was the first such occurrence since the break up. Bartholomew stated that he foresees a reunion between Orthodox and Roman churches.

Next, there is what we know today as the Anglican Church, or the Episcopal Church, that formed after England broke ties with Mother Rome during the reign of King Henry VIII. This group, even though they claim to be Protestant, still cling to many Roman Catholic beliefs and practices. On 5-21-05, it was reported on a program called "Religion and Ethics," which aired on PBS, that the Anglican Church now agrees with the Roman Church that Mary was herself born of a virgin by the Holy Spirit, just as was Jesus in her own womb. Therefore, Mary, they believe, was without sin, as was Christ, making her equal to Christ.

On 2-19-07, the *Times* of London reported that "Radical proposals to reunite Anglicans with the Roman Catholic Church under the leadership of the Pope are to be published this year. The proposals have been agreed on by senior bishops of both churches. In a 42-page statement prepared by an international commission of both churches, Anglicans and Roman Catholics are urged to explore how they might reunite under the Pope."

On 6-8-03, it was reported on the ABC Evening News that out of the 2.5 million Episcopalians in the United States, 15 percent are openly gay. On 11-2-03, an openly gay Episcopal priest by the name of Gene Robinson was consecrated as bishop. In a televised interview on 11-8-03, on the program Religion and Ethics, Robinson said that "It has always been the tradition of the Anglican Church to not take the Scriptures literally." Obviously! Like we really needed for him to tell us that (Lev. 20:13; Rev. 21:8). Robinson's election caused a rift in the Anglican Church. After years of debate, however, the Episcopal Church announced in July of 2009, that it is their belief that God has consecrated gays and lesbians to serve in all administrative offices.

> Note: Like the Anglican Church, the Evangelical Lutheran Church of America (ELCA) meets every two years to discuss church doctrines. At their 2009 session, the ordination of gays and lesbians to serve in the ministry topped the list. As with Robinson's 2003 election in the Anglican Church, the subject is stirring up controversy with the more conservative Lutherans. However, as with the Episcopal Church, the ELCA succumbed to the homosexual agenda.

The election of an openly gay bishop in the Anglican Church is a precursor to what lies ahead for the apostate Protestant churches, and eventually Rome herself. Actually, already today throughout the apostate Protestant groups, the election of gays and lesbians to the pulpits is gaining momentum. Within these groups, some gay and lesbian marriages have been conducted in the name of "another Jesus" and not the Jesus of the Holy Bible (2 Cor. 11:4).

As a kingdom of this world, the Vatican of the future will evolve, as it has over the centuries, along with the ever-changing world in which it "commits fornication" with. Just days before the 2013 election of Pope Francis, major news networks aired interviews with renowned Catholics questioning them on how they believe the new Pope will address the increasing pressure to ordain women priests, allow priests to marry, and on same-sex marriages. The church also faces the dilemma of how to address the now growing number of admittedly gay priests. On 7-29-13, CNN reported that Pope Francis was aware of the "gay lobby" within the church. Francis told reporters that "Being gay is not a crime...homosexuals are our brothers too." Jesus Christ, whom Pope Francis claims to represent, said that His true brothers are they "which hear the word of God, and do it" (Luke 8:19-21). The Word of God clearly forbids homosexuality (Lev. 18:22-30; 1 Cor. 6:9-10; Rev. 21:8).

The most alarming atrocity within the Roman Catholic Church is all the corruption and cover-up that has been exposed thus far between 2000-2018 in regard to the thousands of child sex abuse cases committed by hundreds of homosexual Catholic priests. In September 2018, Pope Francis and top archbishops and cardinals in America were under fire to resign for their alleged knowledge and cover-up of hundreds of child sex abuse cases committed in Pennsylvania and elsewhere. Germany also released a report in September of at least 3,600 child sex abuse confirmations by hundreds of priests over decades. Catholic priests are forbidden to marry, which is just one of the RCC's many demonically influenced "commandments of men" (Mark 7:7). The sin of homosexuality throughout the RCC and the world is gaining momentum at a prophetically significant pace, which is a major precursor of the last-days (Luke 17:28-30).

As of May 2015, Ireland, Denmark, France, Spain, Belgium, the Netherlands, Great Britain, Iceland, Sweden, Norway, Portugal, Canada, and in the United States: Minnesota, Maine, Massachusetts, Connecticut, Rhode Island, Vermont, New Hampshire, New Jersey, New York, Maryland, Delaware, Washington State, Iowa, and Washington, D.C. had all legalized same-sex marriages. In the future, other European countries will follow in the footsteps of their European counterparts in legalizing gay and lesbian marriages where Catholicism is the predominant religion. We will also see this gradually gain impetus in the United States as well.

> Note: On June 26, 2015, the US Supreme Court ruled 5-4 that "a constitutional right existed for same-sex couples to marry in any state." That evening President Obama lit the White House up with the LGBT colors in his support of the Gay Pride Movement. Following the June 12, 2016 murder of 49 people at the Pulse Gay Night Club in Orlando, certain nations lit up their well known landmarks with the Gay Pride colors as a show of their approval of homosexuality.

Under the auspices of the World Council of Churches, the Roman Catholic Church and her harlot daughters are gradually sweeping aside their differences and merging together as one. By the time the Antichrist is launched onto the world's stage, "Mystery, Babylon the Great" will have come to its peak and be a full-blown trash bin of abominations, even much more than she is today. Gay and lesbian ministers conducting same-sex marriages will, by then, have become the norm. The Holy Spirit must have had these people in mind when He had the Apostle Paul write: "For the time will come when they (professing Christians) will not endure sound doctrine; but after their own lusts shall they heap to themselves teachers, having itching ears (tell them what they want to hear); And they shall turn away their ears from the truth (God's Word), and shall be turned unto fables (lies)" (2 Tim. 4:3-4).

And get this! On 11-21-06, Israel's Supreme Court ordered the government to begin recognizing same-sex marriages from other countries. Lawmaker, Moshe Gafni, afterwards stated on Israel's Army Radio, saying, "We don't have a Jewish state here, we have Sodom and Gomorrah." In the spring of 2007, a conservative Jewish seminary in New York agreed to admit gays and lesbians who want to become rabbis. The seminary announced its decision three months after the Rabbinical Assembly's Committee on Jewish Law and Standards authorized the ordination of gays and lesbians.[2] In 2013, Israel held its 15th annual Gay Pride Parade that attracted a record crowd of about 100,000 to the streets of Tel Aviv. Mayor Ron Huldai told the cheering crowd that he was "...proud that Tel Aviv is the most gay-friendly city in the world."[3] In the book of Revelation, we are told that the spiritual condition of Jerusalem (Israel) in the last-days will have become as "Sodom" (Rev. 11:8).

Moving on now with the descriptions the angel gave John of the whore, he wrote that he "...saw the woman drunken with the blood of the saints, and with the blood of the martyrs of Jesus." As you may recall from chapter four of this book, we saw how the Roman Catholic Church has put to death millions of true Christians. So many, in fact, that the whore is said to be "drunken with the blood of the saints." Give the whore a breathalyzer test, which detects the innocent shed blood of the "martyrs of Jesus," and she'll score a perfect 10.0. And, despite her current deceptive "angel of light" appearance, the whore is thirsty for more. If given the opportunity, the Vatican will not hesitate to reactivate the dormant Inquisition policy to hunt down and murder any and all who oppose them. In fact, the whore will get that opportunity to drink more of the saints' blood when she rides the Beast in pursuit of the Great Tribulation saints. For now though, she is just playing the role of an innocent-appearing Sleeping Beauty while she awaits her Prince of Darkness to come kiss her and awaken her to her true satanic nature for all the world to behold one last time. The marriage union of the false church to the False Christ will be reminiscent of the Holy Roman Empire, when Popes and German kings ruled in unison as they executed brutal force upon their subjects in their quest to rule the world.

As already mentioned, some biblical prophecies can serve a dual purpose. In chapter four of this book, we saw how Satan transformed the Roman Empire (the sixth head of the seven-headed beast) into the Holy Roman Empire, both of which reigned "over the kings of the earth." Symbolically, the Holy Roman Empire could be viewed as the seventh head of the beast that received a deadly wound in 1870. Once the Pope and Antichrist (re)unite, so to speak, in the midst of the final seven years, it could be viewed as the deadly wound being healed. They will then pick up from where they left off in 1870 and go on to "continue" for a space of three and a half years as the "eighth" that is of the seventh (Rev. 17:10-11).

John's vision of the great whore concludes with her destruction by the Antichrist late into the Great Tribulation, after he's finished using her for his own pleasurable gains. We read he shall "burn her with fire," perhaps by launching a nuclear bomb upon Vatican City in fulfillment of God's Word and will (Rev. 17:16-18:8). In the midst of John's vision of Babylon's utter demise, John hears a "voice from heaven, saying, Come out of her, my people, that ye be not partakers of her sins, and that ye receive not of her plagues" (Rev. 18:4). Here God reveals that there are some, or perhaps many, in Babylon's court who have entered into true saving, life-changing faith as did the once renowned Roman Catholic, Martin Luther, in the sixteenth century. And, as did Luther and many others, these are commanded to "come out from among them, and be ye separate, saith the Lord" (2 Cor. 6:17).

11

THE HOUR OF TEMPTATION

In His address to the seven churches of Asia Minor, Jesus commended the church of Philadelphia for their faithfulness, telling them, "...behold, I have set before thee an open door, and no man can shut it: for thou has a little strength, and hast kept my word, and hast not denied my name....Because thou hast kept the word of my patience, I also will keep thee from the hour of temptation, which shall come upon all the world, to try them that dwell upon the earth" (Rev. 3:8,10).

The phrase "Hour of Temptation" here primarily refers to the Great Tribulation of which the faithful followers of Christ, who have kept His Word, will be kept from having to go through. The secondary purpose of the above passage is that it was a promise to the church of Philadelphia to be spared from an outbreak of persecution, which did occur around that time (Rev. 2:10, 13). It's not uncommon for some prophetic Scriptures to serve dual purposes, of which this one is a good example. Other than the above Scripture, the word *"hour"* is used several more times in the book of Revelation in reference to the Great Tribulation period. The second is Revelation 14:7. The Apostle John was well into his vision of the Great Tribulation when he said he saw an angel cry out with a loud voice saying, "Fear God, and give glory to him; for the *hour* of his judgment is come." The phrase *"Hour of His Judgment"* is the same as the *"Hour of Temptation."* In this particular passage, the phrase "is come" was used by the angel because the vision was deep into the Great Tribulation.

The next Scripture we will look at that contains the word *"hour,"* referring to the Great Tribulation, is Revelation 17:12. In it, we read how the ten kings, who will be under the authority of the Antichrist, "receive power as kings one *hour* with the beast." This Scripture immediately follows the passage that depicts Dan's death and resurrection, which we have already reviewed in a previous chapter (Rev. 17:11). As we saw, the Antichrist will be killed, then rise from the dead at the midpoint of the seven years. He will then proceed in his newly satanic nature for the duration of the Great Tribulation. Therefore, the emphasis of the *"one hour"* in Revelation 17:12 is on the Great Tribulation, despite the fact that some, or all, of the ten kings will also be under Dan's authority during the course of the first half of the final seven years.

In Revelation chapter six, we saw the opening of six of the seven seals that depict events that will occur during the first three and half years of the final seven. In Revelation chapter seven, we reviewed the scene of the saints in Heaven following the Rapture, which will occur just inside the beginning of the official timeframe of the Great Tribulation period (Rev. 7:9, 14). Beginning in chapter eight, the Apostle John wrote: "And when he had opened the seventh seal, there was silence in heaven about the space of half an hour. And I saw the seven angels which stood before God; and to them were given seven trumpets" (Rev. 8:1-2).

The opening of the seventh seal reveals seven angels with seven trumpets, which contain Divine judgments predetermined by God to be unleashed upon the wicked during the Great Tribulation (Rev. 8:7-9, 13). However, the mentioning of there being "silence in heaven about the space of *half an hour*" reveals that these judgments will not be executed until halfway into the Great Tribulation. The Great Tribulation is set to last for "forty and two months" (Rev. 11:2; 13:5). Therefore, for the first twenty-one months Heaven will remain silent. We know that God is longsuffering, not willing that any should perish, but that all should come to repentance (2 Peter 3:9).

Following the Rapture, many are going to "awake to righteousness" and believe in Jesus Christ to the saving of their souls, which brings us to the next phase of John's vision, following the seven angels he saw with the seven trumpets. John wrote that afterwards he saw "...another angel come and stood at the altar, having a golden censer; and there was given unto him much incense, that he should offer it with the prayers of all saints upon the golden altar, which was before the throne. And the smoke of the incense, which came with the prayers of the saints, ascended up before God, out of the angel's hand. And the angel took the censer, and filled it with fire of the altar, and cast it into the earth" (Rev. 8:3-5).

Inside the Temple, during the Old Testament era, there stood the altar of incense. The burning of the incense signified the prayers of the saints being lifted up to God, symbolized by the smoke of the incense going up (Luke 1:9-10; Ps. 141:2). Likewise, in the above passage, the meaning to what John saw is the same. In his vision, John saw the angel was given "much incense" because following the Rapture, Heaven is going to be flooded with "much" prayer by those who get saved, and the backsliders who've repented and turned back to the Lord. Following this, John saw that the angel took the censer and "filled it with fire of the altar, and cast it into the earth." This act symbolizes all the prayers being answered.

As already mentioned, there will be no Divine judgments unleashed from Heaven by the seven angels with the seven trumpets in the first twenty-one months of the Great Tribulation. However, during that time, there will be judgments unleashed from below as a result of God lifting His restraint off of Satan, as part of His judgment upon Israel and the nations for their wickedness and their refusal to receive Jesus Christ. It will be at this point that after "...the dragon (Satan) saw that he was cast unto the earth, he persecuted the woman (Israel), which brought forth the man child (Jesus). And to the woman were given two wings of a great eagle, that she might fly into the wilderness, into her place (Petra again), where she is nourished for a time, and times, and half a time (3 ½ years), from the face of the serpent. And the serpent (Satan/Dan) cast out of his mouth (commanded) water as a flood (his army) after the woman, that he might cause her to be carried away of the flood. And the earth helped the woman, and the earth opened her mouth (earthquake), and swallowed up the flood (army), which the dragon cast out of his mouth. And the dragon was wroth with the woman, and went to make war with the remnant of her seed (Gal. 3:29), which keep the commandments of God, and have the testimony of Jesus Christ (Great Tribulation saints)" (Rev. 12:13-17).

As we have already reviewed, Satan and his angels will be cast out of the heavenly realm and be totally confined to earth at the midpoint of the seven years (Rev. 12:7-12). Afterwards, Satan will first, in the person of Dan, persecute the Jews in Jerusalem and throughout Israel who refuse to worship him. By Divine unction, those who reject Dan will flee to Petra, where they will find plenty of supplies left behind by the 144,000 and others taken in the Rapture. Upon realizing this, Dan will send out an army after them, which God will feed to the depths of the earth. This event will parallel the time the Israelites fled Egypt and how God drowned the Egyptians who chased after them, in the Red Sea (Ex. 14). Coincidently, in the book of Revelation we learn that by the time of the end-times Jerusalem "spiritually is called...Egypt" in reference to the worldly condition of the people's hearts (Rev. 11:8). Also, when the Israelites fled Egypt, God told Moses to tell them to see "...how I bare you on eagles' wings, and brought you unto myself" (Ex. 19:4). Those who flee from Dan are said to be "given two wings of a great eagle" signifying that it will be God who will lead and protect them away from Dan, as He did the Israelites long ago (Isa. 59:19).

Note: Not all eight million (projected number) Jews living in

> *Israel at that time will flee into the wilderness from the Antichrist as they all did when the Israelites fled Egypt under Moses. Many will be deceived into taking the mark of the Beast, remain in Israel, and by this means be destroyed of Satan in the end (Rev. 19:20-21).*

At Petra, God will nourish and protect these Great Tribulation Jews as He did the Israelites in the wilderness for forty years. At the end of the forty years, the Lord chose Joshua to be Moses' successor to lead the children of Israel into the Promised Land. From the Greek language, Joshua's name is translated into English as Jesus (Heb. 4:8). At the end of the Great Tribulation, Jesus will lead this group into the Promised Land of the Millennium Kingdom of God on earth.

With full support of the Vatican, Dan will attempt to weed out all Jews within his empire who refuse to worship him and receive his mark. Two thirds of the Jews living in Israel will perish during the Great Tribulation, "but the third shall be left in it. And I (God) will bring the third part through the fire, and will refine them as silver is refined, and will try them as gold is tried; they shall call on my name, and I will hear them. I will say, It is my people; and they shall say, The Lord is my God" (Zech. 13:8-9).

Meanwhile, the Great Tribulation Christians will be growing in numbers by the day, which will include more Jewish converts from around the world. Once Dan is content with his efforts against the Jews, he will then "make war with the saints," who will also be greatly resisting his authority (Rev. 13:7). Many will be hunted down and captured, then killed for refusing to take the mark. It is truly going to be an "Hour of Temptation" for many.

Twenty-one months into the Great Tribulation, the seven angels John saw with the seven trumpets will begin to sound off one by one, thereby unleashing a series of Divine judgments. These judgments will, perhaps, be executed over a period of months, which will be as follows:

The Seven Trumpets

- **Revelation 8:7** — A third of earth's vegetation is burned.
- **Revelation 8:8-9** — Huge asteroid plummets into the ocean, killing a third of all sea life and destroying a third of all ships and turning a third of the sea to blood.
- **Revelation 8:10-11** — A third part of all rivers and fountains of water poisoned, killing many (no saints killed).
- **Revelation 8:12** — A third part of the sun, moon, and stars darkened.
- **Revelation 9:1-11** — A hoard of demons released from the bottomless pit to torment people with pain, similar to the sting of a scorpion, for five months. Those who have "the seal of God" (saints) are not touched.
- **Revelation 9:13-20** — Four evil angels are loosed to lead an army of 200 million demons to slay a third of mankind with plagues (no saints killed).
- **Revelation 10:7** — An angel announces to those in Heaven that when the seventh trumpet sounds "the mystery of God should be finished, as he hath declared to his servants the prophets." The conclusion to the mystery of God alludes to the rewarding of the saints in Heaven, the seven-vial judgments, Armageddon, the destruction of Babylon, the destruction of the wicked, and the Second Coming of Christ to earth (Rev. 11:15-19:21).

In the period between the sounding of the seventh trumpet and the start of the unleashing of the seven-vial judgments, John stated that he "...saw another angel fly in the midst of heaven, having the everlasting gospel to preach unto them that dwell on the earth, and to every nation, and kindred, and tongue, and people, saying with a loud voice, Fear God, and give glory to him; for the hour of his judgment is come: and worship him that made

The Hour of Temptation

heaven, and earth, and the sea, and the fountains of waters....And the third angel followed them, saying with a loud voice, If any man worship the beast and his image, and receive his mark...The same shall drink of the wine of the wrath of God, which is poured out without mixture..." (Rev. 14:6-7,9-10).

Here we see what will be a last attempt by God to save those who have not, by this stage into the Hour of Temptation, received the mark of the Beast nor accepted Christ. An angel is here depicted preaching the Gospel to all nations as a final warning not to take the mark of the Beast. If they do not heed the warning and take the mark anyway, then they will suffer the full brunt of God's wrath, which up to this point will have been diluted with His patience, but will afterwards be "poured out without mixture" when He unleashes the seven-vial judgments (Rev. 16).

After these things, John's attention was then drawn to the saints themselves, about whom he said, "Here is the patience of the saints: here are they that keep the commandments of God, and the faith of Jesus. And I heard a voice from heaven saying unto me, Write, Blessed are the dead which die in the Lord from henceforth: Yea, saith the Spirit, that they may rest from their labors, and their works do follow them" (Rev. 14:12-13). Basically, what this passage is saying is, "Hey, check this out, I've got something to tell you about the Great Tribulation saints."

First, there is an acknowledgement of those saints who will "die in the Lord" during that time. Due to the dire circumstances that the saints will be under near the latter portion of the Hour of Temptation, those who die are considered "Blessed." Before we get to what John saw and recorded concerning the saints who will not die in the Hour of Temptation, I would like to point out that the Apostle Paul even referred to the "dead in Christ" first, before the living, who will be alive at the time of the Rapture, or rather the second *part* of the First Resurrection.

As John's vision continued, he wrote: "And I looked, and

behold a white cloud, and upon the cloud one sat like unto the Son of man (Jesus; see Dan. 7:13; Rev. 1:13), having on his head a golden crown, and in his hand, a sharp sickle. And another angel came out of the temple, crying with a loud voice to him that sat on the cloud, Thrust in thy sickle, and reap: for the time is come for thee to reap; for the harvest of the earth is ripe. And he that sat on the cloud thrust in his sickle on the earth; and the earth was reaped. And another angel came out of the temple which is in heaven, he also having a sharp sickle. And another angel came out from the altar, which had power over fire; and cried with a loud cry to him that had the sharp sickle, saying, Thrust in thy sharp sickle, and gather the clusters of the vine of the earth; for her grapes are fully ripe. And the angel thrust in his sickle into the earth, and gathered the vine of the earth, and cast it into the great winepress of the wrath of God" (Rev. 14:14-19).

In the Old Testament, God had Moses institute a second Passover in the second month for those who were unable to keep the original Passover in the first month due to their being defiled or on a long journey (Num. 9:9-11). Likewise, a Second Rapture will be provided for the backsliders who were defiled by unrepentant sin at the time of the First Rapture (Rev. 2:22), but afterwards repented; and for the others who were on a far journey from God's grace to Hell, but got saved after the First Rapture. For as there were two raptures (Enoch and Elijah's) during the Old Testament era, likewise, there will be two Raptures during the New Testament era, which era will continue up until the Second Coming of Christ.

Another thing I'd like to point out before we move on is that, other than the agricultural parable of the wheat and tares that Jesus used in reference to God's field (the earth), the only other agricultural parable that He used in reference to God's field was the vineyard. In Matthew 21:33-43, for example, the Householder is God and the husbandman (vinedresser) is Israel. After Israel failed to properly care for God's vineyard, He turned it over to a new vinedresser, the Church.

Following the First Rapture, which will occur just inside the midpoint of the last seven years at about the time of wheat harvest, the earth (God's field) will not be fully ripe. Hundreds of millions, perhaps, will get saved during the Great Tribulation. Many of them will be hunted down and killed by the Antichrist; however, many others will remain alive up to even late into the Great Tribulation, at which time the earth will then be fully ripe for the harvest. Due to the severity of God's final outpouring of wrath, which will affect the entire globe, the Lord will see fit to remove the saints who remain alive up to this point, who will be raptured. This will be the third *part* of the First Resurrection. In this phase, however, none will be raised from the dead, being that the saints who die during the Hour of Temptation will be raised at the end of it (Rev. 20:4). The Lord shall remove (or reap) these saints off the earth at about the same time a Jewish farmer would be reaping his vintage in the fifth month, known as Av. Those who will have received the mark of the Beast will then be cast into the "great winepress of the wrath of God."

As John's vision continued, he said he saw, "...another sign in heaven, great and marvelous, seven angels having the seven last plagues; for in them is filled up the wrath of God. And I saw as it were a sea of glass mingled with fire: and them that had gotten the victory over the beast, and over his image, and over his mark, and over the number of his name, stand on the sea of glass, having the harps of God" (Rev. 15:1-2).

The expression "sea of glass" is how John described the vast empty space in front of God's Throne in Revelation 4:6; "And before the throne there was a sea of glass." In Revelation 7:9, John saw a vision of the raptured saints standing "before the throne" in that same vast space. Following his vision of the rapturing of the Great Tribulation saints, John describes them as those "who had gotten the victory over the beast...his image...his mark, and over the number of his name, stand on the sea of glass." And where is this "sea of glass"? In front of God's Throne in Heaven. But, you may be thinking, couldn't this be the Great Tribulation saints who died and went to Heaven? No, because those who die during the Hour of Temptation are mentioned in Revelation 20:4, where John said "...I saw the souls of them that were beheaded for the witness of Jesus...which had not worshipped the beast...and they lived (resurrected) and reigned with Christ a thousand years...This is the first resurrection (completion of the First Resurrection)" (Rev. 20:4-5).

The Great Tribulation saints, who will be raptured out before God releases the seven-vial judgments, were depicted standing upon the sea of glass in their glorified bodies just as were the raptured saints of Revelation 7:9. Before the First Rapture vision, however, John saw a vision of the martyred saints of the Church Age, which he referred to as seeing their "souls" in Revelation 6:9. John said that he saw they were all given "white robes" and told to rest a "little" longer. They were then, shortly after, "standing" before the Throne, draped in the white robes along with all the other raptured saints. Therefore, those depicted as "standing" before the Throne are those who have been either raptured or resurrected in their glorified bodies. Those who are depicted as "souls" are just "souls" who have yet to receive their new bodies.

After the Lord removes the Great Tribulation saints, those left behind, or rather them that worship the Beast, will be cast into the "great winepress of the wrath of God." For as John's vision continued, he wrote: "And I heard a great voice out of the temple saying to the seven angels, Go your ways, and pour out the vials of the wrath of God upon the earth" (Rev. 16:1).

The seven-vial judgments will be unleashed within the last few months of the Hour of Temptation, which will be as follows:

The Seven Vials

- **Revelation 16:2** — A bothersome painful sore afflicts everyone who has the mark of the Beast.
- **Revelation 16:3** — The entire ocean around the world is turned to blood, killing off all sea life.
- **Revelation 16:4-7** — All rivers, fountains, lakes, reservoirs, etc. turned to blood.
- **Revelation 16:8-9** — The heat of the sun is turned up higher than normal to scorch mankind with intense heat.
- **Revelation 16:10-11** — The "seat of the Beast, and his kingdom" covered in darkness.
- **Revelation 16:12-16** — The Euphrates River is dried up to make way for the kings of the East: China, India, Iran, etc. The Dragon, Beast and False Prophet instigate the nations to converge to a place in Israel to battle, here referred to as Armageddon. During the course of this war, the Antichrist turns on the whore and destroys Vatican City, perhaps with a nuclear bomb, in fulfillment of God's will (Rev. 17:16-18:8).
- **Revelation 16:17-21** — Worldwide earthquake crumbling every mountain, hiding every island under water, and destroying every city on earth. Italy broken into three parts with the city of Rome (Vatican City) being the epicenter. Global hailstorm of hail weighing 100 lbs each.

Nearing the end of the Great Tribulation, "tidings out of the east (China) and out of the north (Russia) shall trouble him (Dan): therefore, he shall go forth with great fury to destroy..." (Dan. 11:44). Over the past two decades, China and Russia have gradually set aside their differences to strengthen their common economic and global interests. In recent years, they also have engaged in joint military exercises, even as recent as 2018 todate. At about this point into the Great Tribulation, China and Russia will view Dan's actions as threatening and begin to prepare for war. By this time, many will have been deceived by the Antichrist and received his mark. On the other hand, many others will not, which will cause China and Russia, as well as other eastern nations, to be dragged into that widely anticipated war to end all wars, the Battle of Armageddon (Rev. 16:13-16). From this point on, the nations will gradually build up to this war, which will basically be a showdown between East and West when viewing it from a non-biblical standpoint. The biblical viewpoint is that it will be of God's doing (Zeph. 3:8).

The name "Armageddon" derived from two Hebrew words compounded into one; the first being "har," which means a range of hills or mountains; the second, "Megiddon" or "Megiddo," is the name of a town located on the southern rim of the Great Plain of Esdraelon in Israel. In the Scriptures, the Great Plain is referred to as the "Valley of Jezreel" in Joshua 17:16 and as the "Valley of Megiddon" in Zechariah 12:11. It's an enormous valley totally surrounded by hills and small mountains located between the biblical regions of Samaria and Galilee. It is there that the Lord has predetermined to "...gather the nations that I may assemble the kingdoms, to pour upon them mine indignation, even all my fierce anger..." (Zeph. 3:8). And, again, in Zechariah, the Lord said, "...I will seek to destroy all the nations that come against Jerusalem....For I will gather all nations against Jerusalem to battle..." (Zech. 12:9; 14:2).

In the book of Joel, we find where the Prophet foretold of this same event when he wrote: "For, behold, in those days, and in that time, when I shall bring again the captivity of Judah (Israel) and Jerusalem (re-gathering of Jews back to biblical Zion in 1948, and Jerusalem in 1967), I will also gather all nations, and will bring them down into the valley of Jehoshaphat (synonym for Valley of Megiddo), and will plead with them there for my people and for my heritage Israel, whom they have scattered among the nations, and parted my land....Proclaim ye this among the Gentiles; Prepare war....Assemble yourselves and come, all ye heathen ...come up to the valley of Jehoshaphat: for there will I sit to judge all the heathen round about. Put ye in the sickle, for the harvest is ripe: come, get you down; for the press is full, the vats overflow; for their wickedness is great. Multitudes, multitudes in the valley of decision: for the day of the Lord is near in the valley of decision. The sun and the moon shall be darkened, and the stars shall withdraw their shining. The Lord also shall roar out of Zion, and utter his voice from Jerusalem: and the heavens and the earth shall shake: but the Lord will be the hope of his people and the strength of the children of Israel" (Joel 3:1-3, 9, 11-16).

In Israel, there is no actual place called the "Valley of Jehoshaphat." Jehoshaphat was king of Judah at a time when Judah's enemies came together against them for war, who greatly outnumbered them. After petitioning God to deliver them, the Lord slew the entire combined forces of those nations who had encamped on the outskirts of Jerusalem (2 Chron. 20). In the final years, Satan will continue to stir up the nations to hate Israel all the way to the end. And being that it will be the Lord who is going to destroy these nations in the end (as He did in Jehoshaphat's day) the synonym "Valley of Jehoshaphat" here is used to signify that the same fate shall fall upon these nations, as it did the nations who came against Jehoshaphat. The name "Jehoshaphat" means "Jehovah is Judge."[1]

In the above passage of Joel's prophecy, we also see that he wrote: "Put ye in the sickle, for the harvest is ripe: come, get you down; for the press is full, the vats overflow; for their wickedness is great." This passage corresponds to Revelation 14:17-20, which we reviewed earlier. Let's compare it to what the Apostle John wrote: "Thrust in thy sharp sickle and gather the clusters (wicked) of the vine of the earth; for her grapes are fully ripe. And the angel thrust in his sickle into the earth, and gathered the vine of the earth, and cast it into the great winepress of the wrath of God. And the winepress was trodden without the city and blood came out of the winepress, even unto the horse bridles, by the space of a thousand and six hundred furlongs." I believe you get the picture.

Another phrase that the Prophet Joel used in the above prophecy was "Valley of Decision." Joel wrote: "Multitudes, multitudes in the valley of decision: for the day of the Lord is near in the valley of decision." The phrase "Valley of Decision" may allude to the entire stretch of the Great Tribulation period, where "multitudes" will be forced to decide to believe the true or the false, because Joel also mentioned that the "Day of the Lord is near in the Valley of Decision." We already know that the "Day of the Lord" refers to the Great Tribulation period. Another possibility is that the "Valley of Decision" corresponds to the "Valley of Jehoshaphat," where the decisions of the nations will culminate in their destruction at the conclusion of the "Day of the Lord."

The Day of the Lord will come to a close when "The sun and the moon shall be darkened, and the stars shall withdraw their shining. The Lord also shall roar out of Zion, and utter his voice from Jerusalem: and the heavens and the earth shall shake: but the Lord will be the hope of his people, and the strength of the children of Israel." Once the Day of the Lord has concluded, God is going to darken the sun, moon, and stars to direct the utmost attention of those on the earth to the glorious return of Jesus Christ, "the hope of his people" and the dread of His enemies.

12

WHEN THE LIGHTS GO OUT

Most Christians have only a vague understanding of the Second Coming of Jesus Christ. Ask a hundred of them for their view on the matter and you'll get back a wide variety of opinions. Fortunately, however, the Bible paints a very vivid picture of the event of Christ's return to earth and His exploits that will surround it. From the Major to Minor Prophets in the Old Testament, and from the Gospels to Revelation in the New Testament, the Scriptures speak more on the events of the Second Coming than any other Bible prophecy topic.

Once the Battle of Armageddon reaches its peak, "...after that tribulation, the sun shall be darkened, and the moon shall not give her light. And the stars of heaven shall fall, and the powers that are in heaven shall be shaken. And then shall they see the Son of man coming in the clouds with great glory. And then shall he send his angels, and shall gather his elect from the four winds, from the uttermost part of the earth to the uttermost part of heaven" (Mark 13:24-27). At the end of the Great Tribulation, God is going to "turn out the lights," so to speak, by darkening the sun, moon, and stars, producing a worldwide blackout. This, in turn, will give the utmost attention to the glorious return of Christ with His saints. Those on earth will be compelled to look upward at the brilliant splendor of Christ's glory. His return to earth will not be sudden, as many assume, but slow and gradual in which "every eye shall see him" as the earth continues to rotate (Rev. 1:17).

Shortly after God "turns out the lights," the Lord is going to send forth His angels to gather His elect "...from the uttermost part of the earth to the uttermost part of heaven." The "elect" here is in reference to the people on earth out of each nation whom God has chosen to spare, who did not worship the Beast, to enter the Kingdom Age in their natural bodies in order to be able to produce offspring. In the Bible, the word "elect" is used in referring to the nation of Israel, the Old Testament saints, the New Testament saints, the angels, and the people out of all nations that God will spare for His Kingdom Age on earth (Isa. 45:4; 1 Peter 1:2; 1 Tim. 5:21; Isa. 65:22; Matt. 24:22).

As we have previously reviewed, God is going to reap mankind from the earth similar to how He instructed the Israelites in the law to reap their crops during and between the feasts of Passover, Pentecost, and Tabernacles. When the Lord instructed them on how to reap their crops He specified that "...when ye reap the harvest of your land, thou shalt not make clean riddance of the corners of thy field when thou reapest, neither shalt thou gather any gleaning of thy harvest: thou shalt leave them unto the poor, and to the stranger: I am the Lord your God" (Lev. 23:22).

The Israelites were told not to reap the corners of their crops, nor pick up that which had fallen to the ground, so that the poor among them and the strangers passing by could eat. Likewise, when God reaps His field He, too, is not going to "make clean riddance of the corners" of His crop. In this case, however, it will be the poor and the strangers themselves who will not be reaped. These will be those who did not receive the mark of the Beast, nor had they gotten saved before the Second Rapture. They will be the ones Jesus was referring to when He said, "And except those days should be shortened, there should no flesh be saved: but for the elect's (those chosen to be spared; Mark 13:20) sake, those days shall be shortened" (Matt. 24:22). These will enter the Kingdom Age to have children to repopulate the earth.

In referring to the Wrath of God being unleashed upon the nations in the last-days, and the flesh that is to be spared out of those nations, the Prophet Zephaniah wrote: "Therefore wait ye upon me, saith the Lord, until the day that I rise up to the prey: for my determination is to gather the nations, that I may assemble the kingdoms, to pour upon them my indignation, even all my fierce anger: for all the earth shall be devoured with the fire of my jealousy....I will also leave in the midst of thee an afflicted and poor people, and they shall trust in the name of the Lord" (Zeph. 3:8,12). The Prophet Isaiah had this same event in mind when he wrote: "Behold, the Lord maketh the earth empty, and maketh it waste....therefore the inhabitants of the earth are burned, and few men left" (Isa. 24:1,6).

Jesus told His disciples that He had not come to destroy the law of God of the Old Testament, but to fulfill it (Matt. 5:17). This not only applies to His First Coming, but also to the events that will surround His Second Coming and beyond as well. The Feast of Tabernacles was the last of three major yearly feasts that God had commanded in His law to be kept, which, like the other things commanded in the law, were a "shadow of things to come" (Col. 2:16-17). The feast was to be observed in the seventh month of the biblical sacred calendar known as Tishri. It was observed to commemorate the Israelites' deliverance from the Egyptian bondage and to celebrate the year's harvest. The feast lasted for a total of eight days, from the 15th to the 22nd. Both of these days, being the first and last days of the feast, were designated to be holy convocations, or rather religious gatherings of the people (Lev. 23:34-43).

As we previously reviewed, the Great Tribulation could officially begin on Nisan 14th, the first month of the biblical order of the Jewish calendar. The Great Tribulation, we know, will last for forty-two months of thirty days each, which turns out to be 1,260 days. From Nisan 14th, when you count off 1,260 days, it comes to a stop on Tishri 14th. Jesus said that "Immediately" after the Great Tribulation was over, He would gather together all of His elect in Heaven and those on earth (Matt. 24:29-31). In fulfillment of the law, Jesus may gather all of these together to one enormous gathering on Tishri 15th. The Scripture that states that no one will know the "*day*" or the "*hour*" of Christ's coming only applies to the midpoint First Rapture, not His Second Coming to earth.

Another thing that we have already reviewed is that there is going to be 1,290 days from the day the Antichrist stops the daily sacrifice unto the end of the Great Tribulation (Dan. 12:11). Jesus stated that "Immediately" after the Great Tribulation, His return to earth would commence (Matt. 24:29). Therefore, in light of these things, it would be easy to determine the exact day of Jesus' return. And it is for this reason, along with all the other evidence we've reviewed, that the Post-Tribulation Rapture theory is totally untrue.

■ ■ ■

In Revelation chapter nineteen, the Apostle John recorded his vision in which he saw Christ's future gathering of His saints in Heaven to prepare them to descend with Him to earth. In the vision, John said he "...heard a great voice of much people in heaven, saying Alleluia; Salvation, and glory, and honor, and power, unto the Lord our God: For true and righteous are his judgments: for he hath judged the great whore, which did corrupt the earth with her fornication, and hath avenged the blood of his servants at her hand. And again they said, Alleluia. And her smoke rose up forever and ever. And the four and twenty elders and the four beasts fell down and worshipped God that sat on the throne, saying, Amen; Alleluia. And a voice came out of the throne, saying Praise God, all ye servants, and ye that fear him, both small and great. And I heard as it were the voice of a great multitude, and as the voice of many waters, and as the voice of mighty thundering, saying Alleluia: for the Lord God omnipotent reigneth. Let us be glad and rejoice, and give honor to him: for the marriage of the Lamb is come and his wife hath made herself ready. And to her was granted that she should be arrayed in fine linen, clean and white: for the fine linen is the righteousness of saints. And he sayeth unto me, Write, Blessed are they which are called unto the marriage supper of the Lamb. And he saith unto me, These are the true sayings of God. And I fell at his feet to worship him. And he said unto me, See thou do it not: I am thy fellowservant, and of thy brethren that have the testimony of Jesus: worship God: for the testimony of Jesus is the spirit of prophecy. And I saw heaven opened, and behold a white horse; and he that sat upon him was called Faithful and True, and in righteousness he doth judge and make war. His eyes were as a flame of fire, and on his head were many crowns; and he had a name written, that no man knew, but he himself. And he was clothed with a vesture dipped in blood: and his name is called The Word of God. And the armies which were in heaven followed him upon white horses, clothed in fine linen, white and clean. And out of his mouth, goeth a sharp sword that with it he should smite the nations: and he shall rule them with a rod of iron: and he treadeth the winepress of the fierceness and wrath of Almighty God. And he hath on his vesture and on his thigh a name written, KING OF KINGS AND LORD OF LORDS. And I saw an angel standing in the sun; and he cried with a loud voice, saying to all the fowls that fly in the midst of heaven, Come and gather yourselves together unto the supper of the great God (marriage supper of the Lamb); That ye may eat the flesh of kings, and the flesh of captains, and the flesh of mighty men, and the flesh of horses, and of them that sit on them, and the flesh of all men, both free and bond, both small and great. And I saw the beast and the kings of the earth, and their armies, gathered together to make war against him that sat on the horse, and against his army. And the beast was taken, and with him the false prophet that worked miracles before him, with which he deceived them that had received the mark of the beast, and them that worshipped his image. These both were cast alive into the lake of fire, burning with brimstone. And the remnant was slain with the sword of him that sat upon the horse" (Rev. 19:1-21).

Here we see a depiction of Christ and His saints in Heaven preparing to return to earth, riding upon white horses. These will be those who have been either previously raptured or resurrected. They are the Church, the Bride, the Lamb's Wife who, by this time, will have "made herself ready (complete)" for the "marriage of the Lamb."

> *Note: Most Christians, who are taught the pre-seven-year Rapture theory, are also taught that the "marriage supper of the Lamb" is an enormous banquet held in Heaven following the Rapture wherein billions of saints sit down to have a meal with the Lord. However, as with the pre-seven-year Rapture theory itself, this is not true, as you can clearly see by the above passage. The phrase "marriage supper of the Lamb" is a metaphorical reference to the devouring of the enemies of the Lord upon His return to earth with His Bride (the Church).*

It will be at this point when the armies of Armageddon will be satanically influenced to fight against Christ and His army of saints. In the Lord's mouth, John said he saw a "sharp sword that with it he should smite the nations." The "sword" alludes to what the Apostle Paul referred to as the "sword of the Spirit, which is the word of God" in Ephesians 6:17. What this tells us is that Jesus will be the One who will execute the judgments upon the wicked, which are already written in the Word of God. The Word of God here states that the Beast and False Prophet will, at this point, be taken and cast alive into the Lake of Fire. Just where the Lake of Fire is, is not mentioned; only that it's hot and burning with brimstone. See Daniel 7:11-14, which corresponds to this same time period.

> *Note: When the Antichrist destroys Vatican City late into the Great Tribulation, the Pope will not be there at that time. Ac-*

cording to the above passage, God is going to reserve him to be cast alive into the Lake of Fire.

Occurring about the same time Dan and the Pope will be taken up alive from the earth to be transported to their destiny, the people (flesh) that is to be spared out of all nations will be lifted up off the earth as well, to move them out of harm's way. To where these will be transported is unclear. Perhaps they will join the gathering in Heaven to await their return to the earth once Christ slays the remnant left on earth (who worshipped the Beast) with the sword in His mouth (the Word of God). So, let's take a look at what the Word of God has to say concerning how these will be slain.

To begin with, the Prophet Joel was referring to this same time period when he wrote: "Blow ye the trumpet in Zion, and sound an alarm in my holy mountain: let all the inhabitants of the land tremble: for the day of the Lord cometh, for it is at hand; A day of darkness and of gloominess, a day of clouds, and of thick darkness, as the morning spread upon the mountains: a great people and a strong; there hath not been ever the like, neither shall be anymore after it, even to the years of many generations. A fire devoureth before them; and behind them a flame burneth: the land is as the Garden of Eden before them, and behind them a desolate wilderness; yea, and nothing shall escape them. The appearance of them is as the appearance of horses; and as horsemen so shall they run....The earth shall quake before them; the heavens shall tremble: the sun and the moon shall be dark, and the stars shall withdraw their shining. And the Lord shall utter his voice before his army: for his camp is very great: for he is strong that executeth his word" (Joel 2:1-4, 10-11).

Without a doubt, as you can see, this passage refers to the Second Coming of Jesus Christ to rule the world with His army of saints. Before that occurs, however, the wicked, and the devastation of the world left behind in the wake of the Great Tribulation, will have to be dealt with. Therefore, we read that a "fire devoureth before them," which will cause the earth to become as the "Garden of Eden before them." This falls into harmony with other Scriptures that speak of a fiery judgment upon the wicked in the last-days that will be followed by a newly revamped earth for the Kingdom Age.

In the book of Zechariah, for instance, we read: "Behold, the day of the Lord cometh...For I will gather all nations against Jerusalem to battle...Then shall the Lord go forth, and fight against those nations....and the Lord my God shall come, and all the saints with thee....And this shall be the plague wherewith the Lord will smite all the people that have fought against Jerusalem; Their flesh shall consume away while they stand upon their feet, and their eyes shall consume away in their holes, and their tongue shall consume away in their mouth" (Zech. 14:1-3, 5, 12).

Some commentators say that the above passage refers to a nuclear holocaust perpetrated by man in the final days of the Battle of Armageddon. While God is known to use the armed forces of the nations to execute His judgments upon them, that will not be the case in the above Scripture. God Himself is going to send down fire from Heaven, which will consume everyone in its path. This fire will be the same type of fiery judgment that fell upon the 250 men who rose up against Moses with Korah in the wilderness. Those 250 men were all consumed in an instant by the fire that God rained down upon them (Num. 16:35). The Prophet Isaiah concluded his book with a solemn warning of a pending fiery judgment upon the wicked when he wrote: "For, behold, the Lord will come with fire, and with his chariots like a whirlwind, to render his anger with fury, and his rebuke with flames of fire. For by fire and by his sword (Word; Eph. 6:17) will the Lord plead with all flesh; and the slain of the Lord shall be many" (Isa. 66:15-16). See 2 Thessalonians 1:7-10.

Note: Between our present times to the end-times, nuclear

weapons will probably be used by terrorists and nations who have them in very limited occurrences. During the end-times, the use of nuclear weapons will increase, especially during the Battle of Armageddon. And were it not for the return of Christ, all flesh would be destroyed (Matt. 24:22). However, it will be the fire of God that will finish off the wicked after the people who will be spared are removed.

In the last book and chapter of the Old Testament, the Prophet Malachi put the icing on the cake when he wrote: "For, behold, the day cometh, that shall burn as an oven; and all the proud, yea, and all that do wickedly, shall be stubble: and the day that cometh shall burn them up, saith the Lord of hosts, that it shall leave them neither root nor branch. But unto you that fear my name shall the Sun of righteousness (Jesus) arise with healing in his wings; and ye shall go forth, and grow up as calves of the stall. And ye shall tread down the wicked; for they shall be ashes under the soles of your feet in the day that I shall do this, saith the Lord of hosts" (Mal. 4:1-3). The carcasses of the wicked, that are appointed to be destroyed in this fiery judgment at the return of Christ, will be turned to ashes to be trampled underfoot by the saints as they rule and reign with Christ during the one thousand-year Kingdom Age. The phrase "Sun of righteousness" refers to Jesus Christ, whose return to earth will be as the sunrise to the dawn of a new day and era. His return will be the beginning of a new day indeed — the seventh day, or rather the seventh thousand-year period of time since creation.

In the New Testament, the Apostle Peter had these same Old Testament Scriptures in mind when he wrote: "Knowing this first, that there shall come in the last days scoffers, walking after their own lusts, and saying, Where is the promise of his (Jesus') coming? For since the fathers fell asleep (died), all things continue as they were from the beginning of the creation. For this they willingly are ignorant of, that by the word of God...the world that then was, being overflowed with water, perished: But the heavens and the earth, which are now, by the same word are kept in store, reserved unto fire against the day of judgment and perdition of ungodly men...But the day of the Lord will come as a thief in the night; in the which the heavens shall pass away with a great noise, and the elements shall melt with fervent heat, the earth also and the works that are therein shall be burned up" (2 Peter 3:3-10).

Before the official start of the one thousand-year reign of Christ, the earth will have to go through a purification process. Not only will the wicked be burned alive, but every creature and all man-made objects and structures that God intends to destroy will be reduced to ashes as well. The Prophet Zephaniah was referring to this when he wrote: "I will utterly consume all things from off the land, saith the Lord. I will consume man and beast; I will consume the fowls of the heaven, and the fishes of the sea, and the stumbling blocks with the wicked; and I will cut off man from off the land saith the Lord....And them that worship the host of heaven (astrology) upon the housetops; and them that worship and that swear by the Lord, and that swear by Malcam (hypocrites); And them that are turned back (backsliders; *Strong's Concordance,* 5253) from the Lord; and those that have not sought the Lord, nor inquired for him....Neither their silver nor their gold shall be able to deliver them in the day of the Lord's wrath; but the whole land shall be devoured by the fire of his jealousy; for he shall make even a speedy riddance of all them that dwell in the land" (Zeph. 1:2-3, 5-6, 18).

In the wake of 6,000 years of sin, disease, and death that will culminate with the devastation of the Great Tribulation, the earth will be in dire need of an extreme makeover. Beginning with the satellites and other objects orbiting the earth, the fire that shall "devoureth before" the heavenly army of Christ and His saints will consume everything and everyone in its path that God wishes to eliminate or purify. Afterwards, the earth will be restored back to its original Garden of Eden condition that it was in before the fall of man; for after there was mention of the fire that "devoureth before them," we also read that "the land is as the Garden of Eden before them" as well (Joel 2:3). The Prophet Isaiah referred to this, too, when he wrote: "For the Lord shall comfort Zion: he will comfort all her waste places; and he will make her wilderness like Eden, and her desert like the garden of the Lord" (Isa. 51:3). And also, the Prophet Ezekiel stated that "...they shall say, This land that was desolate is become like the garden of Eden" (Ezek. 36:35).

■ ■ ■

When Jesus ascended into Heaven forty days after His resurrection, He did so from atop the Mount of Olives, which overlooks Jerusalem from the east. As His disciples stood there, looking upward as He faded away into the clouds, two angels suddenly appeared and said, "...why stand ye gazing up into heaven? This same Jesus, which is taken up from you into heaven, shall so come in like manner as ye have seen him go into heaven" (Acts 1:11-12). In referring to Christ's return, the Prophet Zechariah wrote: "And his feet shall stand in that day upon the mount of Olives, which is before Jerusalem on the east, and the mount of Olives shall cleave in the midst thereof toward the east and toward the west, and there shall be a very great valley; and half of the mountain shall remove toward the north, and half of it toward the south....And it shall come to pass in that day, that the light shall not be clear, nor dark: But it shall be one day which shall be known to the Lord, not day, nor night: but it shall come to pass that at evening time it shall be light. And it shall be in that day, that living waters shall go out from Jerusalem; half of them toward the former sea (Mediterranean), and half of them toward the hinder sea (Dead Sea): in summer and in winter shall it be. And the Lord shall be king over all the earth: in that day shall there be one Lord, and his name one" (Zech. 14:4, 6-9).

When Christ returns to earth with His saints, after the earth is restored, His feet will touch down upon the exact spot from which He ascended. The Mount of Olives will then split in half, opening up into a valley in between. Living water will then flow from Jerusalem toward the Mediterranean Sea, and toward the Dead Sea. The glory of Christ's return will be of such splendor that it will illuminate the entire earth in such a way that when the evening comes, there will still be light as if it were daytime. The Prophet Isaiah mentioned this when he said, "Then the moon shall be confounded, and the sun ashamed, when the Lord of hosts shall reign in mount Zion, and in Jerusalem, and before his ancients gloriously" (Isa. 24:23).

Going back now to the Apostle John's vision of when he saw the Beast and False Prophet taken and cast into the Lake of Fire, the Revelator then said he "...saw an angel come down from heaven, having the key of the bottomless pit, and a great chain in his hand. And he laid hold on the dragon, that old serpent, which is the Devil, and Satan, and bound him a thousand years. And cast him into the bottomless pit, and shut him up, and set a seal upon him, that he should deceive the nations no more, till the thousand years should be fulfilled: and after that he must be loosed a little season" (Rev. 20:1-3).

Sometime shortly after the Beast and False Prophet are taken and cast alive into the Lake of Fire, Satan, along with his angels, will be shut away in the bottomless pit, where they will remain for the duration of the thousand years. The Prophet Isaiah wrote of this, too, when he said, "Yet thou (Satan) shalt be brought down to hell, to the sides of the pit" (Isa. 14:15). And again, in reference to Satan, his angels, and the evil rulers of the earth, Isaiah also wrote: "And it shall come to pass in that day, that the Lord shall punish the host (Satan) of the high ones (evil angels) that are on high, and the kings of the earth upon the earth. And they shall be gathered together as prisoners are gathered in the pit, and shall be shut up in prison (Hell), and after many days

(1,000 years) shall they be visited" (Isa. 24:21-22).

Following his vision of Satan's future casting into the bottomless pit, John then said he "...saw the souls of them that were beheaded for the witness of Jesus, and for the word of God, and which had not worshipped the beast, neither his image, neither had received his mark upon their foreheads, or in their hands; and they lived (resurrected) and reigned with Christ a thousand years. But the rest of the dead (unsaved) lived not again until the thousand years were finished. This is the first resurrection (completion of First Resurrection). Blessed and holy is he that *hath part* in the first resurrection: on such the second death hath no power, but they shall be priests of God and of Christ; and shall reign with him a thousand years" (Rev. 20:4-6).

Here John sees the fourth and last *part* of the First Resurrection, which will be those who died during the Great Tribulation. They will be raised, perhaps, when Christ and the saints with Him return to earth. They will go on to reign with Christ, as kings and priests, over the nations during the thousand years in God's "holy mountain (Kingdom)" (Isa. 11:9).

The book of Daniel came to a close with the revealing prophecy that there is going to be 1,290 days from the day the Antichrist stops the daily sacrifice to the end of the Great Tribulation. However, the prophecy and the number of days do not end here. As Daniel continued, he was told by the angel to write: "Blessed is he that waiteth, and cometh to the thousand three hundred and five and thirty (1,335) days. But go thy way (Daniel) till the end be: for thou shalt rest (die) and stand in thy lot at the end of the days" (Dan. 12:12-13).

Here we see there is an added 45 days to the back end of the 1,290, to make it a total of 1,335 days. We are told that those who make it to see the end of those days is considered "Blessed." Daniel was then told to go on about his daily life and that he would die, but be resurrected to stand in his allotted inheritance in the Kingdom of God on earth at the end of the 1,335 days. Therefore, the resurrection of the deceased Great Tribulation saints could occur anytime from the end of Great Tribulation to the end of the 45 days. Another thing is that Christ and His saints could touch down upon the earth at any time during the 45 days, but only after the fiery judgment of the wicked and renovation of the earth. So, within the timeframe of the 45 days, the wicked will be burned, Satan will be bound in the bottomless pit, the earth will be revamped, Jesus will return with His saints and the people spared out of all nations, the Great Tribulation saints will be resurrected, all the saints will be assigned to their position in the Kingdom, and the nation of Israel will receive their promised allotted inheritance in the Kingdom. Once all these things are accomplished, the official countdown will begin on the one thousand-year Kingdom at the conclusion of the 45 days.

■ ■ ■

In Genesis chapters twenty-nine and thirty, we can read about the births of eleven of Jacob's twelve sons he fathered by his two wives, Leah and Rachel, and their two handmaidens. After each child was born, the mother was Divinely inspired to speak inspirationally over the circumstances surrounding the child's birth. Nothing was said, however, concerning Benjamin, whose mother, Rachel, died while giving birth (Gen. 35:18-19). Joseph, Benjamin's only brother by Rachel, had two sons, Manasseh and Ephraim, while he was in Egypt, who Jacob later adopted as his own (Gen. 48:3-5). When Manasseh and Ephraim were born Joseph, too, was Divinely influenced to speak over the circumstances of their births. When you run all the sayings together in the order of their births, there appears to be a hidden Divinely inspired message to Israel pertaining to their triumphant prevailing in the last-days, and their everlasting endurance in the Kingdom of God.

The Message

1. **Reuben (Gen. 29:32):** *"Surely the Lord hath looked upon my affliction,*

2. **Simeon (Gen. 29:33):** *Because the Lord hath heard that I was hated.*

3. **Levi (Gen. 29:34):** *Now this time will my husband (Jesus) be joined unto me,*

4. **Judah (Gen. 29:35):** *Now will I praise the Lord.*

5. **Dan (Gen. 30:6):** *God hath judged me (by the Antichrist), and hath also heard my voice (of repentance).*

6. **Naphtali (Gen. 30:8):** *With great wrestlings have I wrestled with my sister (the Church) and I have prevailed.*

7. **Gad (Gen. 30:11):** *A troop cometh (Christ and His saints at the Second Coming).*

8. **Asher (Gen. 30:13):** *Happy am I, for the daughters (churches) will call me blessed.*

9. **Issachar (Gen. 30:18):** *God hath given me my hire, because I have given my maiden (the Church) to my husband (Jesus).*

10. **Zebulun (Gen. 30:20):** *God hath endued me with a good dowry (land of Israel); now will my husband (Jesus) dwell with me.*

11. **Joseph (Gen. 30:23):** *God hath taken away my reproach.*

12. **Manasseh (Gen. 41:51):** *For God hath made me forget all my toil,*

13. **Ephraim (Gen. 41:52):** *And, hath caused me to be fruitful in the land of my affliction."*

13

THY HOLY MOUNTAIN

"And it shall come to pass in the last days, that the mountain (Kingdom of God) of the Lord's house shall be established in the top of (above) the mountains (other kingdoms), and shall be exalted above the hills; and all nations shall follow into it. And many people shall go and say, Come ye, and let us go up to the mountain of the Lord, to the house of the God of Jacob; and he will teach us of his ways, and we will walk in his paths: For out of Zion shall go forth the law, and the word of the Lord from Jerusalem. And he shall judge among the nations, and shall rebuke many people: and they shall beat their swords into plowshares, and their spears into pruning hooks: nation shall not lift up sword against nation, neither shall they learn war any more....The wolf also shall dwell with the lamb, and the leopard shall lie down with the kid; and the calf and the young lion and the fatling together; and a little child shall lead them. And the cow and the bear shall feed; their young ones shall lie down together: and the lion shall eat straw like the ox. And the suckling child shall play on the hole of the asp, and the weaned child shall put his hand on the cockatrice' den. They shall not hurt nor destroy in all my holy mountain: for the earth shall be full of the knowledge of the Lord, as the waters cover the seas."

— Isaiah 2:2-4; 11:6-9

For nearly 4,000 years since the time of Abraham, the Jews have longed for the day their Messiah would come to usher in the Kingdom of God on earth (Heb. 11:8-10). Just prior to when Jesus ascended up into Heaven from atop the

Mount of Olives, His disciples, who were then all Jewish, asked Him "Lord, wilt thou at this time restore again the kingdom of Israel?" (Acts 1:6). Their question, no doubt, was born from their understanding of the Old Testament prophecies that foretold of Israel's future hope in the Messianic Age, or rather the Kingdom Age.

The Apostle Paul (a Jew) wrote: "For I would not, brethren, that ye should be ignorant of this mystery, lest ye should be wise in your own conceits; that blindness in part is happened to Israel, until the fullness of the Gentiles be come in (saved). And so all Israel shall be saved: as it is written, There shall come out of Zion the Deliverer (Christ), and shall turn away ungodliness from Jacob (Israel)..." (Rom. 11:25-26). Here Paul refers back to his understanding of the Old Testament promises of God, made to His elect nation Israel, to quell any notion that God had forsaken the Jews, which is even taught today by the false Christian groups. Paul clearly points out that the unbelieving Jews were intentionally blinded to the truth of Jesus Christ for the purpose of offering Him up to be sacrificed to save the world from sin. Paul also wrote: "...if the casting away of them (Israel) be the reconciling of the world, what shall the receiving of them be, but life from the dead?" (Rom. 11:15). In other words, the entire house of Israel, from Abraham to the Second Coming of Jesus Christ, and even beyond, is under a special covenant with God unlike any other nation in the world (Deut. 7:6). However, just how and to what extent God plans to save "all Israel" is unclear (Rom. 11:33).

In Ezekiel chapter thirty-six, the Lord foretold of a glimpse of Israel's future in the Messianic Kingdom. Here we saw previously that, during the Kingdom Age, the land of Israel and the world will "become like the garden of Eden" (Ezek. 36:35). In that same chapter, we also find it written that "all the house of Israel, even all of it" will be there in the Kingdom (Ezek. 36:10). To what extent "all" is meant to convey here, as with Paul's "all," is still unclear. In quoting the Prophet Isaiah, Paul stated that "Though the number of the children of Israel be as the sand of the sea, a remnant shall be saved" (Rom. 9:27). It is my best guess that the "all" refers to the fact that a "remnant shall be saved" out of "all" the house of Israel.

In Ezekiel chapter thirty-seven, the Prophet was shown a vision of a valley full of dry human bones. He was instructed by God to speak life to the bones, then watched as they all came together into bodies, as if they were people being raised from the dead (Ezek. 37:1-10). The Lord then told Ezekiel that the bones represented the "whole house of Israel" (Ezek. 37:11). As the prophecy continued, the Lord elaborated on how He would bring the whole house of Israel to their land, where He would then place His Spirit in them and cause them to walk in His judgments, and that they would remain with Him forever; and that during that time "David (Jesus Christ the seed of David) my servant shall be king over them" (Isa. 9:6-7; Ezek. 37:24; Zech. 12:8).

Some commentators suggest that Ezekiel chapters thirty-six and thirty-seven allude only to the restoration of the nation of Israel in 1948. However, that, in fact, is not the case here at all. In reading these two chapters, one can clearly see that it is prophecy concerning Israel's restoration in 1948 *and* their future in the Kingdom of their Messiah. Also, some commentators suggest that the reference to "David" being king over the house of Israel is actually referring to King David himself. However, again, this is not true. It will be none other than Jesus Christ, "the root and offspring of David," who will reign and rule over Israel, and the world, during the Kingdom Age (Rev. 22:16). Furthermore, Jesus stated that it will be His twelve Apostles who will be sitting upon twelve thrones "judging the twelve tribes of Israel" (Matt. 19:28).

A remnant out of the "whole house of Israel" will probably be raised from the dead just shortly after the deceased Great

Tribulation saints are raised when Christ returns to earth. But, the Old Testament saints could all be raised at the First Rapture, or at anytime between the end of the Great Tribulation and the end of Daniel's prophetic 1,335 days. Also, the Jews who flee the Antichrist to hide out at Petra during the entire stretch of the Great Tribulation will probably end up being the people (flesh) that will be spared out of the nation of Israel. They will then enter the Kingdom Age in their natural bodies in order to be able to produce offspring. But truly, as Paul said, this is all a "mystery," of sorts, and just how and to what extent God plans to deal with Israel at this stage, and beyond, remains to be seen.

In Ezekiel chapters thirty-eight and thirty-nine, we saw how there is going to be an all-out attempt by Israel's foes to wipe them off the map in the last-days. This, as we saw, will be headed up by Russia and Iran, who will lead virtually the entire Middle East against Israel. Nevertheless, God is going to intervene and destroy all but one-sixth of the entire combined army of these coalition forces (Ezek. 39:2). In the wake of the devastation left behind, Israel will send out troops to gather up the massive amount of spoil left behind, which will provide the tiny nation with resources to last for "seven years" (Ezek. 39:9). As we have already reviewed in a previous chapter, this seven-year period corresponds to the final seven years before the Second Coming of Jesus Christ to earth. Then, starting in Ezekiel chapter forty, on through to the end of his book to chapter forty-eight, it's all about the nation of Israel in the Messianic Kingdom.

Beginning with chapter forty, Ezekiel is caught up in a vision where he sees an angel measuring the Temple area and Temple proper for the Temple Mount in Jerusalem, which continues on through chapter forty-two. This Temple has never been built by the Jews, nor will it be the Temple built during the end-times. The measurements of the Temple in Ezekiel's vision, and its courts, are much larger than the Temple built by Solomon and the one built by the exiles who returned to Jerusalem following the Babylonian captivity. Plus, Ezekiel's Temple has an outer court, whereas the Temple that will be built in the last-days will not have an outer court (Rev. 11:1-2). Also, in John's vision of the end-times Temple, it is John (a man) who is told to do the measuring, but in Ezekiel's vision it is an angel doing the measuring.

In the book of Revelation, there is reference made to a Temple in Heaven eleven times. In this Temple, there is mention made of the Ark of the Covenant in Revelation 11:19. The Ark of the Covenant was kept in the Holy of Holies in the Temple, where the high priest was only allowed to enter once a year, under very strict ordinances, to place the blood of the atoning sacrifice for Israel's sins upon the top of the Ark, known as the mercy seat (Ex. 25).

When the Babylonians invaded Judah, they destroyed the first Temple built by Solomon and took all the gold and vessels of the Temple back to Babylon (2 Chron. 36:7). After this, the Ark is not seen in the Scriptures until John sees it in the Temple in Heaven (Rev. 11:19). Both the Scriptures and history confirms that the Ark was never in the second Temple that was built by the Jews who had returned from the Babylonian captivity (Ezra 1:1-11).[1]

Over the centuries, there has been much speculation regarding the whereabouts of the "alleged" lost Ark. But was the Ark actually ever lost? Could it be possible that God had this most holy and important vessel of the Temple transported to the Temple in Heaven before the Babylonians could get their hands on it, so that Christ could there fulfill the most central and important aspect of the law? (Heb. 9:11-12, 23-34). The Temple that is now in Heaven, that was constructed by angels, may be Ezekiel's Temple that may be brought down to earth to Temple Mount for the Kingdom Age; for after the thousand-year reign of Christ on earth (Rev. 20:4), John wrote: "And I saw no temple therein" anymore in Heaven (Rev. 21:22).

Following his vision of the Millennial Temple, Ezekiel then wrote: "Afterward he (angel) brought me to the gate, even the gate that looketh toward the east: And, behold, the glory of the God of Israel came from the way of the east: and his voice was like a noise of many waters: and the earth shined with his glory....And the glory of the Lord came into the house (Temple) by the way of the gate whose prospect is toward the east. So, the spirit took me up, and brought me into the inner court; and, behold, the glory of the Lord filled the house. And I heard him (Lord) speaking unto me out of the house: and the man (angel) stood by me. And he (Lord) said unto me, Son of man, the place of my throne, and the place of the soles of my feet, where I will dwell in the midst of the children of Israel for ever..." (Ezek. 43:1-2, 4-7).

The Mount of Olives is on the east side of Temple Mount, where Christ is scheduled to touch down upon His return to earth (Zech. 14:4). In Ezekiel's vision, Jesus Christ is portrayed as the "glory of the Lord" that will enter the Temple complex from the eastern gate, as the Prophet is allowed to see into the future this glorious event. Although Ezekiel was, perhaps, not permitted to see Christ's figure, the message is clear, nevertheless; for Ezekiel wrote: "his voice was like a noise of many waters." When the Apostle John was first shown his vision of Christ, he, too, stated that "his voice as the sound of many waters" (Rev. 1:15). The mention God made to "the place of the soles of my feet" is here to be taken in the literal sense; for in the person of Jesus Christ (God with us; Matt. 1:23) shall God dwell in the "midst of the children of Israel" in Jerusalem during the Kingdom Age. Ezekiel also mentioned in the above passage that "the earth shined with his glory." This corresponds to what we reviewed in the previous chapter of this book, where we saw how both Zechariah and Isaiah mentioned that the earth is going to be brightly illuminated with the glory of God upon Christ's return (Zech. 14; Isa. 24).

During the thousand-year reign of Christ, the saints are going to rule with Him (Rev. 2:26). The twelve Apostles will sit upon twelve thrones overseeing the twelve tribes of Israel (Matt. 19:28). Levites from the descendants of Zadok, who were faithful to God when others strayed during the reign of King David, will serve as priests in the Millennial Temple (Ezek. 44:15). Animal sacrifices will be conducted to commemorate the sacrifice of Christ, without which there would not be a Millennial Age, nor would there be those redeemed therein. In the Old Testament days, the animal sacrifices pointed forward to the time Christ would come and be sacrificed for the sins of the world. During the Church Age, the only ordinances that were given were the Water Baptism and the Lord's Supper. During the Kingdom Age, all the laws of God will be completely observed in which the sacrifices will point back to the redemptive work of Christ for the sake of those who will be born during that time. Again, this is all somewhat a mystery, and it remains to be seen just how it will all be (Ezek. 44-46).

In the Millennium, the Feast of Passover will be observed to again commemorate the death of Christ, who made it possible for all to be passed over from death to eternal life (Ezek. 45:21). We must keep in mind that the Kingdom Age will be filled with people in their unregenerate, natural state. They will go on to produce offspring, which will raise the earth's population into the tens of millions in a short time. Their obedience or disobedience to the laws of God will determine their future (Zech. 14:16-19). The Prophet Isaiah wrote of these when he said, "There shall be no more thence an infant of days, nor an old man that hath not filled his days: for the child shall die an hundred years old; but the sinner being an hundred years old shall be accursed. And they shall build houses, and inhabit them; and they shall plant vineyards, and eat the fruit of them. They shall not build, and another inhabit; they shall not plant, and another eat: for as the days of a tree are the days of my people, and mine elect shall long enjoy the work of their hands. They shall not labor in vain, nor bring forth for trouble; for they are the seed of the blessed of the Lord, and their offspring with them" (Isa. 65:20-23).

Although Satan will be bound during the Millennium, the sin nature will still be in effect in the people who will be in their natural bodies. Life will be similar, perhaps, to how it was when Adam and Eve first sinned, except Satan will be bound. Adam lived to be 930 years old in the first 1,000 years of time. According to the above Scripture, the length of time people will be able to live will be "as the days of a tree." This could mean that they could live to be hundreds or even a thousand years old. However, the above passage reveals that some will die early as a result of sinful behavior, and that to die at the age of 100, one would be considered an infant.

> *Note: The Feast of Pentecost for some reason is not mentioned here. It is, however, referred to indirectly (Ezek. 46:9). The feast will be observed to commemorate the giving of the law at Mt. Sinai (Ex. 19-20), the outpouring of the Holy Spirit at Pentecost (Acts 2), the resurrecting and rapturing of the saints out of the Great Tribulation (Rev. 7:9-14), and it will be a time of thanksgiving for the wheat harvest for the people during the Kingdom Age (Lev. 23:15-21).*

During the Millennium, the Feast of Tabernacles will also be observed yearly (Ezek. 45:25). In Old Testament times, the children of Israel were commanded to keep the feast to commemorate their deliverance from Egyptian bondage and to celebrate the year's harvest (Lev. 23:39-43). Pharaoh, king of Egypt, was a type of Satan who holds people in bondage and slavery to sin. Egypt personified the world full of all manners of idolatry and vice. The Scriptures reveal that the spiritual condition of Jerusalem in the end-times will be as "Egypt" (Rev. 11:8). Actually, that's the way it is today, and the whole worldly system headed by its "god" Satan (2 Cor. 4:4). The Feast of Tabernacles will be observed during the Millennial reign of Christ, perhaps to commemorate our deliverance from the bondage of the former worldly system headed up by Satan. And, as the Israelites celebrated their yearly harvest at the end of the Feast of Tabernacles, those in the Millennium will celebrate God's harvest of mankind, which is what the feast has foreshadowed since its conception. They will also be celebrating their yearly harvest of their crops during that time.

In writing on the keeping of the Feast of Tabernacles during the Kingdom Age, the Prophet Zechariah wrote: "And it shall come to pass, that everyone that is left of all nations (flesh spared) which came against Jerusalem (Armageddon) shall even go up from year to year to worship the King (Jesus), the Lord of hosts, and to keep the feast of tabernacles. And it shall be, that whoso will not come up of all the families of the earth unto Jerusalem to worship the King, the Lord of hosts, even upon them shall be no rain...This shall be the punishment...of all nations that come not up to keep the feast of tabernacles" (Zech. 14:16-19). During the Millennium, Christ is going to "rule the nations with a rod of iron," where all the laws of God will be strictly enforced (Rev. 19:15). Violators will be sought out and punished accordingly. For example, those who fail to observe the Feast of Tabernacles will not get any rain upon their land. Being that the feast will be a time of thanksgiving for their harvest, and rain is needed for a successful harvest, their disobedience will result in no rain and a poor harvest, if any.

In Zechariah 14:8, we saw that during the Millennium "living waters shall go out from Jerusalem" toward the Mediterranean Sea to the west and toward the Dead Sea east of Jerusalem. The Prophet Ezekiel elaborated on this further, adding that this river of "living waters" will flow from the Temple to the Jordan River, then into the Dead Sea (Ezek. 47:1-2). On the banks of this river "shall grow all trees for meat (food), whose leaf shall not fade, neither shall the fruit thereof be consumed (rot): it shall bring forth new fruit according to his months, because their waters they issued out of the sanctuary (Temple): and the fruit thereof shall be for meat, and the leaf thereof for medicine" (Ezek. 47:12).

Upon the renovation process of the earth for the Kingdom Age, the geographical layout in Israel and elsewhere will be somewhat altered from what we are accustomed to today. From the Temple in Jerusalem, living waters shall go out to all the world as the waters flow into the Mediterranean Sea toward the west and into the Jordan River and Dead Sea in the east. The oceans, lakes, and rivers of the earth will all be touched, perhaps by the living waters as the waters circulate around the globe (Ezek. 47:8-9). Along this river from Jerusalem, trees growing all manner of fruits will line its banks. The fruits will contain nutrients that will promote health and longevity for those in their natural bodies. These trees will probably be located elsewhere too.

The saints, who will be in their glorified bodies, will have no need of food, but will be capable of eating if so desired. After Jesus rose from the dead, He ate and drank with the disciples (Luke 24:41-43). The disciples recognized that it was Jesus, but they could tell He was different (Luke 24:36-40). The Lord, in His resurrected body, could suddenly appear in a room without entering through the door (John 20:19). He could experience both the natural and the supernatural realms simultaneously. The Scriptures state that "...when he shall appear, we shall be like him" (1 John 3:2). Therefore, the saints, in their glorified bodies, will be able to recognize one another, they will be able to eat and drink, and they will be capable of experiencing the natural and the supernatural realms simultaneously. They will be able to travel back and forth between Heaven and earth at will (Matt. 22:23-30).

Nearly 4,000 years ago, God promised to give Abraham and his descendants all of the land that stretches along the Mediterra-

Thy Holy Mountain

nean Sea, from the Euphrates River to the Wadi el-Arish River (Gen. 15:18). Today, the Euphrates runs through the northern tip of Syria into Turkey, which is what God intended to be Israel's border in the north. The Wadi el-Arish runs through what is still today the eastern part of the nation of Egypt, which biblically is Israel's southern border. All of the land between these two points along the Mediterranean coast, to beyond the Jordan River, rightfully belongs to Israel. However, in all of the nation's history they possibly have never possessed all of that land. During the Millennial Age, however, they will just as God promised.

Following his vision of the living waters, Ezekiel was then told: "Thus saith the Lord God; This shall be the border, whereby, ye shall inherit the land according to the twelve tribes of Israel: Joseph shall have two portions. And ye shall inherit it, one as well as another. Concerning the which, I lifted up my hand to give unto your fathers: and this land shall fall unto you for inheritance" (Ezek. 47:13-14). Beginning in the far north of the biblical boundaries of the land promised to Israel, the tribe of Dan will receive their allotted inheritance. South of Dan, the tribes of Asher, Naphtali, Manasseh (Joseph), Ephraim (Joseph), Ruben, and Judah will have their lots, which will all be on the north side of Jerusalem (Ezek. 48:1-7). Around the surrounding area of Jerusalem, the tribe of Levi will dwell in their inheritance (Ezek. 48:8-22). Starting with the tribe of Benjamin, just south of Jerusalem, the tribes of Simeon, Issachar, Zebulun, and Gad will all receive their portions of land (Ezek. 48:23-29).

Around the city of Jerusalem will be a wall with three gates each on the north, south, east, and west. Each gate will have the name of one of the tribes of Israel thereon (Ezek. 48:31-34). Although not much is said concerning the city of Jerusalem, it is my guess that there will be a refurbished version for the Millennium, which will probably be built by angels. This is not to be confused with the "new Jerusalem" mentioned in Revelation 21:1-27. The "new Jerusalem" will be let down upon the "new earth," which will have no sea, or sun, nor moon, but in the Kingdom Age, those things will still be present. We will look further into the new heaven, the new earth, and the New Jerusalem in a later chapter.

The book of Ezekiel came to a close saying, "...and the name of the city from that day shall be, The Lord is there" (Ezek. 48:35). The Lord Jesus Christ, the root and offspring of David, will sit upon His earthly Throne in Jerusalem, which will be the capital of the Kingdom of God on earth during the Millennium. The saints, who will also be in their glorified bodies, will reign and rule with Christ over the nations. Those in their natural bodies will be capable of living the entire 1,000 years. Some will die prematurely as a result of sinful behavior. Sea life will be restored in new, purified waters. The land animals and fowls of the air will all be restored as well. It's going to be a very pleasant and exciting experience, to say the least. However, the best will still be yet to come for the redeemed of the Lord.

14

THE SECOND RESURRECTION

"And when the thousand years are expired, Satan shall be loosed out of his prison, and shall go out to deceive the nations, which are in the four quarters of the earth, Gog and Magog, to gather them together to battle: the number of whom is as the sand of the sea."

— Revelation 20:7-8

During the Millennial reign of Christ, the earth is going to be repopulated by the people who enter the Kingdom Age in their natural bodies. The majority of them will live out the entire 1,000 years, producing offspring, and their children will have children, and so on. This, in turn, is going to increase the earth's population into the hundreds of millions, or perhaps billions, by the end of the Millennium. Some, however, will die prematurely for failing to follow God's Word, the prescribed path to life and longevity in the Kingdom (Isa. 65:20-22). Those born during the Kingdom Age will have a free will, of course, and will be given the opportunity to express their belief, or disbelief, by either obeying or disobeying the laws of the Kingdom (Zech. 14:16-19).

At the end of the Millennium, the true believers will need to be separated from the hypocrites who could easily be influenced into an all out insurrection against Christ if given the opportunity. In order to make a speedy separation of the true believers and hypocrites, so that both can go on to their destination, Satan and his angels will be loosed from the bottomless pit for a short recess to "deceive the nations." The Devil will then influence the already disgruntled peoples of the Kingdom, the hypocrites and rebels, to rise up against Christ and His saints in a futile attempt to take over the Kingdom.

The reference to "Gog and Magog" in this text is to be taken in its symbolic, not literal, sense. In the Old Testament, the phrase was used in connection to the land of Russia and the Russian people. As you may recall, we reviewed in a previous chapter how "Gog" of the "land of Magog" is going to oversee an attempted invasion of Israel in the last-days (Ezek. 38:1-8). However, Gog and Company will, as we saw, find themselves on the receiving end of God's Wrath. In the book of Revelation, the phrase "Gog and Magog" is purely symbolic lingo to refer to the enemies of the Lord who are destined to meet a similar, but worse, defeat than "Gog and Company" will. As John's vision of the insurrection continued, he wrote: "And they went up on the breadth of the earth, and compassed the camp of the saints about, and the beloved city (Jerusalem): and fire came down from God out of heaven, and devoured them" (Rev. 20:9).

The rebels will meet the same fiery fate at the end of the Millennium, as will the wicked at the end of the Great Tribulation. After their bodies are consumed by the fire, their souls will be ushered to a brief stay in Hell. Occurring at this same time, "the devil that deceived them was cast into the lake of fire and brimstone, where the beast and false prophet are, and shall be tormented day and night for ever and ever" (Rev. 20:10). At the end of the Great Tribulation, the Antichrist and the then Pope will be taken up alive by the angels of God and thrown into the Lake of Fire. At the end of the Millennium, the Devil and his angels will all be cast into the Lake of Fire as well.

Following these events, John then said he saw "...a great white throne, and him that sat on it, from whose face the earth and the heaven fled away; and there was found no place for them. And I saw the dead, small and great stand (in resurrected bodies) before God; and the books were opened: and another book was opened, which is the book of life: and the dead were judged out of those things which were written in the books, according to their works. And the sea gave up the dead, which were in it; and death and hell delivered up the dead, which were in them: and they were judged every man according to their works. And death and hell were cast into the lake of fire. This is the second death. And whosoever was not found written in the book of life was cast into the lake of fire" (Rev. 20:11-15).

When some people imagine the "Great White Throne," they picture in their minds an enormous white marble Throne with a huge figure of a man sitting thereon, supposing it to be God the Father. The truth, however, is that it's the "...throne of God and of the Lamb (Jesus)" (Rev. 22:3). Jesus and God are One and it will be God sitting on the Throne in the person of Jesus Christ. For Christ Himself said, "For the Father judgeth no man, but hath committed all judgment unto the Son" (John 5:22). Also, it is written: "In the beginning was the Word, and the Word was with God, and the Word was God....And the Word was made flesh (Jesus), and dwelt among us" (John 1:1, 14). Jesus stated that "He that rejecteth me, and receiveth not my words, hath one that judgeth him: the word that I have spoken, the same shall judge him in the last day" (John 12:48). Therefore, it is clear that Jesus "the Word" will be the One "...who shall judge the quick (saved) and the dead (unsaved) at his appearing and his kingdom" (2 Tim. 4:1).

In Acts 24:15, the Apostle Paul said, "...there shall be a resurrection of the dead, both the just (saved) and the unjust (unsaved)." As there will be a resurrection of the saved, who will all "...appear before the judgment seat of Christ; that everyone may receive the things done in his body, according to that he hath done, whether it be good or bad" (2 Cor. 5:10), so, too, will there be a resurrection of the condemned, who will also be judged by Christ "...according to their works" (Rev. 20:12). The redeemed shall be rewarded in Heaven for their faithful service to Christ, which will determine their position in, and enjoyment of, the afterlife (1 Cor. 3:11-15). Likewise, the punishment of the condemned will be decided in accordance to "their works," which will determine the degree of their suffering in the hereafter.

Once the resurrected condemned are cast into the Lake of Fire, as Jesus warned, there will be "weeping and gnashing of teeth" (Matt. 13:42; 24:51; 25:30). Their suffering, however, will not be for all eternity as some suppose, for that would make God appear to be unjust in His ways for allowing someone to suffer more than offenses called for. The duration of the condemned in the Lake of Fire will be determined by the Judge, Jesus Christ, based upon "their works." Once their sentence is up, they will cease to exist; for Jesus said, "...fear not them which kill the body, but are not able to kill the soul: but rather fear him which is able to destroy (to destroy fully; *Strong's Concordance,* 622,) both soul and body in hell" (Matt. 10:28) in the "everlasting fire, prepared for the devil and his angels" (Matt. 25:41). And it will be in the Lake of Fire that both the soul and body of the unsaved will be destroyed, which will be the "second death." They "shall be punished with everlasting destruction" (2 Thes. 1:9). The phrase in Revelation 20:10 that states they "...shall be tormented day and night for ever and ever" only refers to Satan, his angels, the Beast, the False Prophet; and all who take the mark of the Beast (Rev. 14:9-11).

> *For as there is a second and higher life that awaits the redeemed, so there is a second and deeper death that awaits the condemned. And as there is no more death after that higher life, there is no more life after that deeper death. — Author unknown*

After the condemned are judged and cast into the Lake of Fire, we read that "death and hell" will be cast into the Lake of Fire as well. After the Great White Throne Judgment, there will be no more need for a place called Hell, which is basically just a holding pen for the souls of the unsaved as they wait to stand before the Judge to be sentenced for their offenses. Along with Hell, death will also cease to exist in any form, once the last "body and soul" is destroyed in the Lake of Fire, which, as we saw, will be the "second death." As it is written: "...he (Jesus) must reign, till he hath put all enemies under his feet. The last enemy that shall be destroyed is death" (1 Cor. 15:25-26).

Among the "books" that were mentioned to be present at the Great White Throne Judgment was the "Book of Life." This Book of Life is the "Lamb's Book of Life" (Rev. 21:27). The only way one can have their name written in this book is to believe in the Lord Jesus Christ and receive Him into their heart as Lord and Savior (Luke 10:20; Phil. 4:3). Obviously, the names of the condemned will not be listed in the Book of Life, so what will be the purpose of having this book at the Great White Throne Judgment, other than to show the condemned their names are not there?

To begin with, Jesus warned His Church in general that it is possible to have their name written in the Book of Life, but later have it blotted out (Rev. 3:5). If it were not possible, then Jesus would not have said so. It is very clear in the Holy Scriptures that there will be some who may begin well, but not finish well (Heb. 6:4-6); for only "...he that shall endure to the end, the same shall be saved" (Matt. 24:13). And again "...be thou faithful unto death, and I will give thee a crown of life...and thou shall not be hurt of the second death" (Rev. 2:10-11). And we read that Jesus is the "...author of eternal salvation unto all them that obey him" (Heb. 5:9). And last, we read: "Take heed, brethren, lest there be in any of you an evil heart of unbelief, in departing from the living God....For we are made partakers of Christ, *if* we hold the beginning of our confidence stedfast unto the end" (Heb. 3:12,14).

Just before being beheaded by Nero, the Apostle Paul wrote to Timothy, saying, "For I am now ready to be offered, and the time of my departure is at hand. I have fought a good fight, I have finished my course, I have kept the faith: Henceforth there is laid up for me a crown of righteousness, which the Lord, the righteous judge, shall give me at that day (Judgment Seat of Christ for saints; 2 Cor. 5:10): and not to me only, but unto all them also that love his appearing" (2 Tim. 4:6-8). Apostates, hypocrites, and those who backslide and die in a state of unrepented sin will not love His appearing when they stand before Jesus at the Great White Throne Judgment, ashamed and without confidence (1 John 2:28).

Therefore, those who start well, but do not "endure to the end," or rather who are not "faithful unto death," will have their names blotted out of the Book of Life. At the Great White Throne Judgment, these one-time faithful saints who either turned apostate or hypocrite, or who died in a hardened state of unrepented sin, will be shown that their names were at one time in the Book of Life, but were later blotted out based upon "their works," which will be recorded in the other "books" (Rev. 20:12; 22:19).

In His seven letters to the seven churches, Jesus began each one with "I know thy works" and ended each with a "he that overcometh." To the church at Thyatira, He said, "And he that overcometh and keepeth my works unto the end, to him will I give power over the nations" (Rev. 2-3). The works of Christ are to believe in Him and obey Him by walking in the light of His Word and using the gifts and talents He has given us to serve Him (1 John 1:6-2:6; Matt. 25:14-30). To the Laodicians, Jesus said, "To him that overcometh will I grant to sit with me on my throne, even as I overcame, and am set down with my Father on his throne" (Rev. 3:21). And how did Jesus overcome? He was "obedient unto death, even the death of the cross" (Phil. 2:8).

In Hebrews chapter six, we read: "For it is impossible for those who were once enlightened, and have tasted of the heavenly gift, and were made partakers of the Holy Ghost, And have tasted the good word of God, and the powers of the world to come, If they shall fall away (apostatize; *Strong's Concordance,* 3895), to renew them again unto repentance; seeing they crucify to themselves the Son of God afresh, and put him to an open shame...whose end is to be burned" (Heb. 6:4-8). This Scripture only applies to those who accept Christ and are "made partakers of the Holy Ghost" (Acts 2:38), but who then later renounce Him. Paul penned the above passage primarily because, most likely, some of the Jews who at first believed in Christ as their Messiah, later renounced Him and returned back to Judaism, and thereby forfeited their crown of life. Jesus warns His Church to "...hold that fast which thou hast, that no man take thy crown" (Rev. 3:11).

The belief that such a failure is not possible for a regenerate soul is a theological proposition that is not supported by the Word of God (Col. 1:23; Heb. 3:6, 14; 10:35-39). Paul knew that false doctrine could over-throw the faith of some (2 Tim. 2:17-18). The Apostle warns that those who renounce their Christian faith amounts to a public rejection of Christ. By doing this, they reaffirm the view of Jesus' enemies that He deserved to die on the cross and thereby "crucify to themselves the Son of God afresh, and put him to an open shame." Such a person, therefore, would not be won back through repentance, the consequence of this atrocious act.[1]

The above passage does not apply to those Christians who backslide into a life of practicing sin, which many have done, including this author. This is a dangerous state to be in, because even though they haven't renounced Christ from their heart with their mouth, they do deny Him by their "works," or actions (Titus 1:16). But even still, they can repent and turn back to the Lord to be restored and thereby "save a (their) soul from death" (James 5:19-20). God chastens those whom He loves so that they should "not be condemned with the world," or rather lost to the flames (1 Cor. 11:32; John 15:1-6). The Scriptures warn us, however, not to despise the chastening of the Lord lest we "fail of the grace of God" and become bitter and defiled (Heb. 12:5-15).

For the record, I believe that out of the many who are "made partakers of the Holy Ghost" only a very few will be deceived into later renouncing Christ and forfeit their crown of life (Rev. 3:11). And, out of those who backslide — as portrayed in the story of the prodigal son who, while abiding in Christ, was "alive" unto God, but in sin became "dead" unto Him, but after repenting became "alive again" (Luke 15:24, 32) — only a very small number, perhaps, will resist God's chastening and perish in a state of willful disobedience, which is another form of denying Christ (1 John 2:1-6; Jude 3-7). We read that "...if we deny him, he also will deny us" (2 Tim. 2:12). Although some disagree with this, nevertheless, the Scriptural warnings are numerous; too many, in fact, to cover here (Rom. 11:20-22).

> *Note: As with the doctrines of the Rapture and the eternal state of the unsaved, the doctrine of eternal security has also been a topic of controversy within the Church. Nevertheless, we as Christians should never allow these debates to become contentious to the point of ongoing conflict and separation (Phil. 2:14-15), but instead should be found working together to carry out the Great Commission to reach the lost for Christ and teach them His Word (Matt. 28:18-20).*

The second purpose for the Book of Life being at the final judgment of the nations will be to show those who were deceived by all the false Christian groups, and other false religions, that their names were never written there. Jesus warned that many false prophets would arise and deceive many (Matt. 24:11). He also said that "Not everyone that saith unto me, Lord, Lord, shall enter into the kingdom of heaven; but he that doeth the will of my Father which is in heaven. Many will say to me in that day, Lord, Lord, have we not prophesied in thy name? and in thy name have cast out devils? And in thy name done many wonderful works? And then will I profess unto them, I never knew you: depart from me, ye that work iniquity" (Matt. 7:21-23). These will be those professing Christians who were never born of the Spirit (John 3:3-6), but instead trusted in their own good works derived from the commandments and doctrines of men (Mark 7:7). Groups such as the ones we've already covered in this book, and the Jehovah Witnesses; Church of Jesus Christ of Latter Day Saints (Mormons); Christian Science; Scientology, and the Unification Church to name some of the more larger false Christian groups.[2] Among these, also, will be the many professing Christians in the apostate Protestant churches (and even some from within the good churches) who have "turned the grace of our God into lasciviousness" (Jude 4) and thereby worked all manner of iniquity.

Another reason for the Book of Life being present at the Great White Throne Judgment may be for the sake of the redeemed out of the Kingdom Age, for they, like everyone else, will have to stand before God to be judged and rewarded "according to their works." Although nothing is said of them being present at the Great White Throne Judgment, the wording of the text in Revelation 20:15 makes it clear that they will be there; for we read that "...whosoever was not found written in the book of life was cast into the lake of fire." The redeemed out of the Kingdom Age will be found written in the Book of Life and not be cast into the Lake of Fire. They will all be changed from mortal to immortal beings in the blink of an eye, just like the saints who will be changed likewise at the Raptures of Revelation 7:9 and 15:2.

At the start of John's vision of the Great White Throne, he said that he saw that the "...earth and the heaven fled away; and there was found no place for them" (Rev. 20:11). In reference to the same, the Apostle Peter wrote that "...the heavens shall pass away with a great noise, and the elements shall melt with a fervent heat, the earth also and the works that are therein shall be burned up. Seeing then that all these things shall be dissolved, what manner of persons ought ye to be in all holy conversation and godliness…nevertheless we, according to his promise, look for new heavens and a new earth, wherein dwelleth righteousness. Wherefore, beloved, seeing that ye look for such things, be diligent that ye may be found of him in peace, without spot, and blameless" (2 Peter 3:10-14).

15

THE NEW JERUSALEM

Following the Great White Throne Judgment, the Apostle John said that he then "...saw a new heaven and a new earth: for the first heaven and the first earth were passed away; and there was no more sea. And I, John, saw the holy city, new Jerusalem, coming down from God out of heaven, prepared as a bride adorned for her husband. And I heard a great voice out of heaven saying, Behold, the tabernacle of God is with men, and he will dwell with them, and they shall be his people, and God himself shall be with them, and be their God. And God shall wipe away all tears from their eyes; and there shall be no more death, neither shall there be any more pain: for the former things are passed away. And he that sat upon the throne said, Behold, I make all things new. And he said unto me, Write: for these words are true and faithful. And he said unto me, It is done. I am Alpha and Omega, the beginning and the end. I will give unto him that is athirst of the fountain of the water of life freely. He that overcometh shall inherit all things: and I will be his God, and he shall be my son. But the fearful, and unbelieving, and the abominable, and murderers, and whoremongers, and sorcerers, and idolaters, and all liars, shall have their part in the lake of fire and brimstone: which is the second death. And there came unto me one of the seven angels, which had the seven vials full of the seven plagues, and talked with me, saying, Come hither, I will show thee the bride, the Lamb's wife. And he carried me away in the spirit to a great and high mountain, and showed me that great city, the holy Jerusalem, descending out of heaven from God, Having the glory of God: and her light was like unto a stone most precious, even like a jasper stone, clear as crystal: And had a wall great and high, and had twelve gates, and at the gates twelve angels, and names written there on, which are the names of the twelve tribes of the children of Israel: On the east three gates; on the north three gates; on the south three gates; and on the west three gates. And the wall of the city had twelve foundations, and in them the names of the twelve apostles of the Lamb. And he that talked with me had a golden reed to measure the city, and the gates thereof, and the wall thereof. And the city lieth four square, and the length is as the breadth: and he measured the city with the reed, twelve thousand furlongs (approximately 1,500 miles). The length and the breadth and the height of it are equal. And he measured the wall thereof, and hundred and forty and four cubits (216 feet), according to the measure of a man, that is, of the angel. And the building of the wall of it was of jasper: and the city was pure gold, like unto clear glass. And the foundations of the wall of the city were garnished with all manner of precious stones. The first foundation was jasper; the second, sapphire; the third, a chalcedony; the fourth, an emerald; the fifth, sardonyx; the sixth, sardius; the seventh, chrysolyte; the eighth, beryl; the ninth, a topaz; the tenth, a chrysoprasus; the eleventh, a jacinth; the twelfth, an amethyst. And the twelve gates were twelve pearls; every several gate was of one pearl: and the street of the city was pure gold, as it was transparent glass. And I saw no temple therein: for the Lord God Almighty and the Lamb are the temple of it. And the city had no need of the sun, neither of the moon, to shine in it: for the glory of God did lighten it, and the Lamb is the light thereof. And the nations of them which are saved shall walk in the light of it: and the kings of the earth do bring their glory and honor into it. And the gates of it shall not be shut at all by day: for there shall be no night there. And they shall bring the glory and honor of the nations into it. And there shall in no wise enter into it anything that defileth, neither whatsoever worketh abomination, or maketh a lie: but they which are written in the Lamb's book of life. And he

The New Jerusalem

showed me a pure river of water of life, clear as crystal, proceeding out of the throne of God and of the Lamb. In the midst of the street of it, and on either side of the river, was there the tree of life, which bare twelve manners of fruits, and yielded her fruit every month: and the leaves of the tree were for the healing of the nations. And there shall be no more curse: but the throne of God and of the Lamb shall be in it; and his servants shall serve him: And they shall see his face; and his name shall be in their foreheads. And there shall be no night there; and they need no candle, neither light of the sun; for the Lord God giveth them light: and they shall reign forever and ever. And he said unto me, These sayings are faithful and true: and the Lord God of the holy prophets sent his angel to show unto his servants the things which must shortly be done. Behold, I come quickly: blessed is he that keepeth the sayings of the prophecy of this book. And I, John, saw these things, and heard them. And when I heard and seen, I fell down to worship before the feet of the angel which showed me these things. Then saith he unto me, See thou do it not: for I am thy fellow servant, and of thy brethren the prophets, and of them which keep the sayings of this book: worship God. And he saith unto me, Seal not the sayings of the prophecy of this book: for the time is at hand. He that is unjust, let him be unjust still: and he who is filthy, let him be filthy still: and he that is righteous, let him be righteous still: and he that is holy, let him be holy still. And, behold, I come quickly; and my reward is with me, to give every man according as his work shall be. I am Alpha and Omega, the beginning and the end, the first and the last. Blessed are they that do his commandments that they may have right to the tree of life, and may enter in through the gates into the city. For without (not there) are dogs (evil-doers), and sorcerers, and whore-mongers, and murderers, and idolaters, and whosoever loveth and maketh a lie. I, Jesus, have sent mine angel to testify unto you these things in the churches. I am the root and the offspring of David, and the bright and morning star. And the Spirit and the bride (Church) say, Come. And let him that heareth say, Come. And let him that is athirst come. And whosoever will, let him take the water of life freely. For I testify unto every man that heareth the words of the prophecy of this book. If any man shall add unto these things, God shall add unto him the plagues that are written in this book. And if any man shall take away from the words of the book of this prophecy, God shall take away his part out of the book of life, and out of the holy city, and from the things which are written in this book. He which testifieth these things saith, Surely I come quickly. Amen. Even so, come, Lord Jesus. The grace of our Lord Jesus Christ be with you all. Amen" (Rev. 21-22).

EPILOGUE

Where are we on the prophetic clock?

In response to Jesus' disciples' question concerning the signs of His coming and of the end of the age (Matt. 24:3), He told them there would first be a noticeable increase in wars, famines, pestilences (viruses ect.), and earthquakes in many places (Matt. 24:7). Jesus said these things would be just the "beginning of sorrows" (Matt. 24:8), and it is this time period that we are now smack dab in the midst of. And, as time goes on, these things will gradually worsen in intensity and in frequency, which will also include such things as: volcanic eruptions, floods, tornadoes, hurricanes, tsunamis, economic collapse and unrest, terrorism, crime, and domestic violence, just to name a few. Also, watch for the continuing increase in the persecution of Christians around the world (Matt. 24:9), and the continued increase in hostility toward Jews.

Another big sign Jesus told us to watch for is the preaching of the Gospel of Jesus Christ in all nations (Matt. 24:14). Thanks to the brave efforts of missionaries, and the inventions of the television and Internet, the Gospel is being preached in virtually every language and nation in the world. The Trinity Broadcasting Network (TBN), founded by Paul and Jan Crouch in 1973, alone reaches virtually this entire dark world with the light of the Gospel of Jesus Christ using all the latest up-to-date technology. Likewise, the Christian Broadcasting Network (CBN), founded by Pat Robertson in 1961, reaches millions daily around the globe for Jesus Christ through their various outreach programs.

What will be the next big prophetic event?

Most Christians have been taught to believe it's the Rapture, but many are now beginning to wonder about that. At the beginning of a prophecy conference held in the spring of 2010 by a former host on TBN, he began the meeting by asking his renowned prophecy guests— which included: Tim LaHaye, Hal Lindsey, and Jack Van Impe—"Why hasn't the Rapture occurred yet? Did we miss something in the Scriptures?" All three of these prophecy scholars—who I greatly admire—have been preaching and writing in their books for over 50 years that the Rapture is going to occur any day now. Not one of them, by the way, ever definitively answered the question, but instead eased their way into speaking the same old rhetoric that prompted the question to begin with.

Dear reader, yes "we" (pre-seven-year Rapture theorists) did miss, and/or ignored, some things in the Scriptures that clearly refutes their school of thought. However, what you have just read in this book answers the above question with one of the most exhaustive, biblically sound accounts of the rapturing, resurrecting, and gathering of the elect of God in the end-times that is in print to-date.

So, what's the next major event scheduled on the prophetic timetable? Without a doubt, it's the event covered in chapter six of this book involving the attempted invasion of Israel by Gog and Company, as foretold in Ezekiel 38-39. Continue to watch for the gradual build-up in alliances between Russia, Iran, Turkey, Syria, Lebanon, Palestinians, Egypt, Libya, Sudan, and other nations, and for their growing hostility toward Israel and the West. Also, watch for the progressive formation of the United States of Europe with Germany continuing to gain more and more momentum as its leader. And last, watch for the revamping of the NATO charter that will one day provide the Antichrist with a platform to control the massive superpower alliance of NATO from within the USE.

Epilogue

Timeline of the Final Seven Years

1. Gog and Company make their move upon Israel. God defends Israel putting the world on notice that He — the God of the Holy Bible — is the one and only True God.

2. The first seal is broken allowing Dan to conquer the Middle East and set up a Middle Eastern Headquarters in Jerusalem.

3. Dan confirms *the old* covenant, possibly on Tishri 14th, for the Jews to build the third Temple. Countdown begins on the final seven years. Elijah and Enoch suddenly appear in Israel.

4. The Jews begin building the Temple in the second month of Iyar. Israel under a false sense of peace and safety.

5. Seals two through five are broken in succession; a fourth part of the earth experiences a time of tribulation.

6. Dan stops the daily sacrifice at the midpoint of the seven years, possibly on Adar 13th, and claims to be the Jews' Messiah. He is assassinated in Jerusalem about a month later around the time of Passover.

7. The sixth seal is broken; the sun is darkened and the moon is turned blood red as Dan lies dead for several days. Satan and his angels are thrust from the heavenly realm to be totally confined to earth for the Great Tribulation.

8. Dan is possessed by Satan and rises from the dead, possibly on or around Nisan 14th, to begin his reign of terror beginning with the Jews, and the killing of Elijah and Enoch who rise from the dead three and a half days later.

9. The First Rapture occurs during the time of wheat harvest in the second month of Iyar at the forefront of the Great Tribulation. The dead in Christ are raised from the dead and the saints who are still alive are all transported to Heaven in their new glorified bodies.

10. The seventh seal is broken revealing the seven-trumpet judgments to be unleashed halfway into the Great Tribulation. The Beast (Antichrist) and False Prophet (Pope) unite following the First Rapture for their reign of terror during the Great Tribulation. Mark of the Beast enforced at this time.

11. The Second Rapture occurs near the end of the Great Tribulation during the time of grape harvest in the fifth month of Av. Only the Great Tribulation saints who are alive up to this point are transported to Heaven. No deceased saints resurrected at this time.

12. The seven-vial judgments are poured out upon the wicked. The Dragon, Beast, and False Prophet instigate the Battle of Armageddon. Nations of the world converge to the land of Israel for the Battle of Armageddon.

13. The sun, moon, and stars are darkened at the end of the Great Tribulation. Jesus summons His elected flesh from earth, possibly on Tishri 15th, to move them out of harm's way while the wicked are destroyed and earth revamped.

14. The wicked are burned, the Beast and False Prophet are cast into the Lake of Fire, Satan is bound in the bottomless pit, the dead Great Tribulation saints are resurrected, and the earth is revamped for the Kingdom Age.

About the Author

DAVID HEAD is a native of Newport News, Virginia. A former career criminal turned committed Christian and avid Bible scholar while in prison serving 80 years no parole under a controversial Virginia 3-Strike law. After nearly three decades in prison God miraculously stepped in to set him free. A remarkable testimony of faith and the sovereignty of God. David had been studying Bible prophecy and following Middle East developments spanning over 30 years. His exceptional insight makes him one of the leading Bible prophecy and Middle East experts of the 21st century.

ENDNOTES

Chapter 3: The Four-Headed Leopard
1. Herbert May, *The Oxford Bible Atlas,* Oxford University Press, Third Edition, 1987.
2. Alexander Hislop, *The Two Babylons.*
3. John F. Walvoord and Roy B. Zuck, *The Bible Knowledge Commentary,* Cook, 2000.
4. R.F. Youngblood, F.F. Bruce, and R.K. Harrison, *Nelson's New Illustrated Bible Dictionary,* Completely Revised and Updated Edition, Thomas Nelson Publishers, 1995.

Chapter 4: Satan's Seat
1. Alexander Hislop, *The Two Babylons.*
2. Herbert May, *The Oxford Bible Atlas,* Oxford University Press, Third Edition, 1987.
3. Alexander Hislop, *The Two Babylons.*
4. *Halley's Bible Handbook,* Zondervan.
5. Ibid.
6. *Foxe's Book of Martyrs.*
7. *Halley's Bible Handbook,* Zondervan.
8. John Hagee, *In Defense of Israel,* Frontline, 2007.
9. Dave Hunt, *A Woman Rides the Beast,* Harvest House.
10. *Halley's Bible Handbook,* Zondervan.
11. Ibid.
12. Ibid.
13. *Foxe's Book of Martyrs.*
14. *Halley's Bible Handbook,* Zondervan.
15. John Hagee, *In Defense of Israel,* Frontline, 2007.
16. *Foxe's Book of Martyrs.*
17. *Halley's Bible Handbook,* Zondervan.
18. Alexander Hislop, *The Two Babylons.*
19. *The Daily Press,* Newport News, Va., February 24, 2013.

20. "Restoring Europe's Latin Empire," www.thetrumpet.com, May/June 2013.

Chapter 5: Jerusalem Rising
1. John Hagee, *In Defense of Israel,* Frontline, 2007.
2. Bernard Reich and David H. Goldberg, *The Political Dictionary of Israel,* Scarecrow Press, 2000.
3. *Encyclopedia Britannica, Inc.*, 2010.
4. James Taylor and Warren Shaw, *Dictionary of the Third Reich,* Penguin, 1997.
5. Bernard Reich and David H. Goldberg, *The Political Dictionary of Israel,* Scarecrow Press, 2000.
6. Alfred J. Kolatch, *The Jewish Book of Why,* Jonathan David Publishers, Revised Edition, 2000.
7. Bernard Reich and David H. Goldberg, *The Political Dictionary of Israel,* Scarecrow Press, 2000.
8. *Encyclopedia Britannica, Inc.*, 2010.
9. Alfred J. Kolatch, *The Jewish Book of Why,* Jonathan David Publishers, Revised Edition, 2000.
10. Bernard Reich and David H. Goldberg, *The Political Dictionary of Israel,* Scarecrow Press, 2000.
11. *Israel My Glory,* May/June 2009.
12. *Jewish Voice Today,* March/April 2012.
13. *Israel My Glory,* "The New Anti-Semitism," January/February 2013.

Chapter 6: Gog and Company
1. TBN "The Hal Lindsey Report," January 28, 2011.
2. "Will Israel Attack Iran?," *Israel Today,* December 2011.
3. NBC "Today Show," January 11, 2012.

Chapter 7: The Man of Sin
1. James Taylor and Warren Shaw, *Dictionary of the Third Reich,* Penguin, 1997.
2. www.reuters.com, September 4, 2011.
3. www.euobserver.com, September 6, 2011.
4. Ibid., September 21, 2011.
5. "Break from Europe?," www.thetrumpet.com, December 2012.
6. "Germany Dominates Europe Again," Ibid., September 2011.
7. "Germany Is the New America," Ibid., February 2013.
8. "A New Peace Broker," Ibid., July 2013.
9. Bernard Reich and David H. Goldberg, *The Political Dictionary of Israel,* Scarecrow Press, 2000.
10. TBN "Christ In Prophecy," May 18, 2013.
11. C. I. Scofield, *The New Scofield Reference Bible,* Oxford University Press, 1967.

Chapter 8: Down to Earth
1. Rabbi Solomon Ganzfried, *The Code of Jewish Law,* Hebrew Publishing Company, 1991.

Chapter 9: The First Resurrection
1. John F. Walvoord and Roy B. Zuck, *The Bible Knowledge Commentary,* Cook, 2000.
2. C. I. Scofield, *The New Scofield Reference Bible,* Oxford University Press, 1967.
3. R.F. Youngblood, F.F. Bruce, and R.K. Harrison, *Nelson's New Illustrated Bible Dictionary,* Completely Revised and Updated Edition, Thomas Nelson Publishers, 1995.

Chapter 10: Babylon the Great
1. Dr. Cynthia D. Wallace, *Don't Miss the Rapture,* Creation House, 2011.

2. *Sword of the Lord,* May 2007.
3. "The Gay Politics of Israel," *Israel Today,* July 2013.

Chapter 11: The Hour of Temptation
1. Merrill C. Tenney and J.D. Douglas, *The New International Bible Dictionary,* Zondervan, 1987.

Chapter 13: Thy Holy Mountain
1. R.F. Youngblood, F.F. Bruce, and R.K. Harrison, *Nelson's New Illustrated Bible Dictionary,* Completely Revised and Updated Edition, Thomas Nelson Publishers, 1995.

Chapter 14: The Second Resurrection
1. John F. Walvoord and Roy B. Zuck, *The Bible Knowledge Commentary,* Cook, 2000.
2. Walter Martin, *The Kingdom of the Cults,* Revised, Updated, and Expanded Edition, Bethany House Publishers, 2003.

www.ingramcontent.com/pod-product-compliance
Lightning Source LLC
LaVergne TN
LVHW041540070426
835507LV00011B/851